IMAGES
of America

BELLEVUE

I0807677

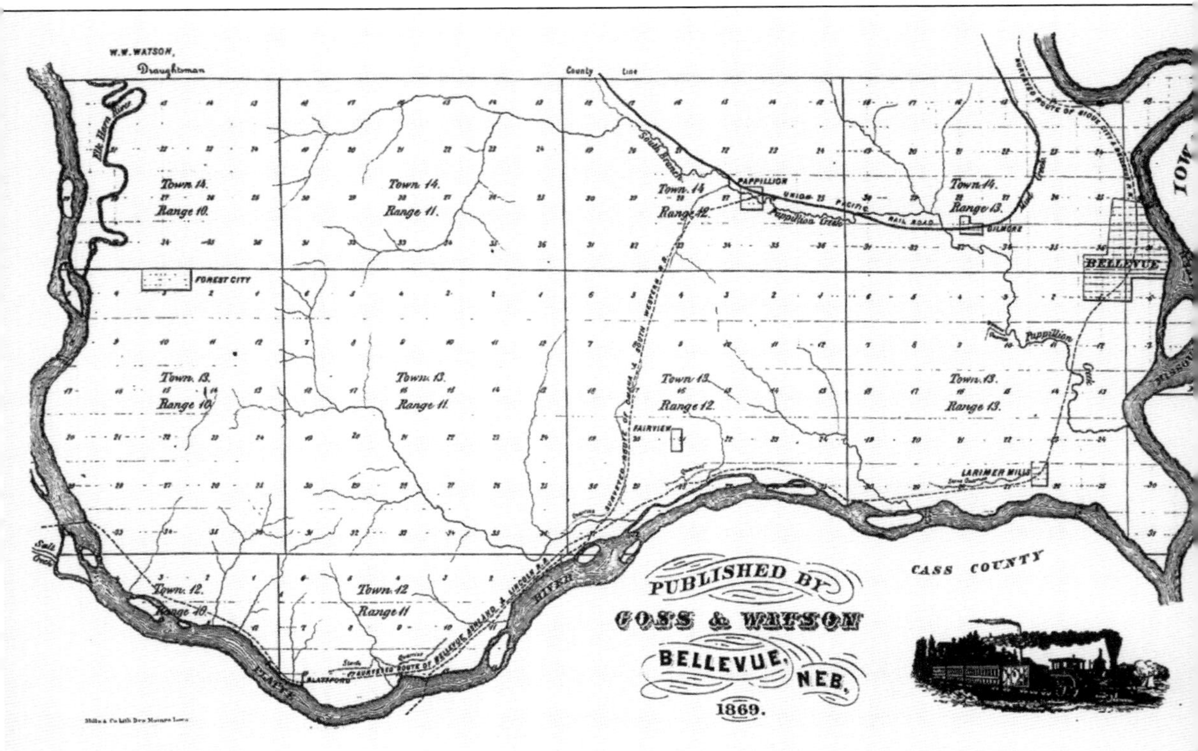

An 1869 surveyor's map shows just how small Bellevue was and yet how large it was compared to surrounding communities, many of which would collapse and fade away while others have yet to appear. Fort Crook, now Offutt Air Force Base, was a farmer's field. Perhaps most noticeable, the unique island off the coast of Bellevue has since been swallowed up by the Missouri River. (Courtesy Sarpy County Museum.)

On the Cover: This image was captured in Bellevue during the 1957 centennial celebration to mark 100 years since Sarpy County's establishment in 1857. While it appears that they partook in the latest wine, women, and song, local Bellevue citizens dressed the part with beards and ties. Prior to its emancipation in 1857, Bellevue was part of Douglas County. (Courtesy Sarpy County Museum.)

IMAGES
of America

BELLEVUE

Ben Justman of the
Sarpy County Museum

ARCADIA
PUBLISHING

ISBN 978-0-7385-7651-0

Published by Arcadia Publishing
Charleston, South Carolina

Printed in the United States of America

Library of Congress Control Number: 2011931577

For all general information, please contact Arcadia Publishing:
Telephone 843-853-2070
Fax 843-853-0044
E-mail sales@arcadiapublishing.com
For customer service and orders:
Toll-Free 1-888-313-2665

Visit us on the Internet at www.arcadiapublishing.com

*This book is dedicated to students of Sarpy County history,
past, present, and future.*

CONTENTS

ACKNOWLEDGMENTS

It has been a privilege and an honor to have the opportunity to author a work on Bellevue's history. That being said, I could not have done it without the support of others. There are a number of people who, without hesitation, offered to lend their support. They include Inez Boyd, Kay Dammast, Lloyd Dowding, Gary Garabrandt, Richard Hudson, Lowell and Linda Iske, Carol Gavin, Bob and Lorraine Jeffus, Dave Rech, Mary Stroud, Harriett Sullivan, Bette Swanson, Dennis and Becky Wilfong, Ron Woodle, Ed Wootton, and the board of directors of the Sarpy County Museum. Lastly, I wish to thank my family for their continued support.

A good portion of the photographs contained in this book come from the lifelong hard work of John Gebbie; without his efforts, the visual history of Bellevue would remain largely scattered and undocumented. It is important to acknowledge the local historians, from John Goss to Gary Iske. Their endeavors to research and document the history of Bellevue made this book possible. When I first began this project, I was unsure if I had a sufficient variety of unique quality images to document Bellevue, as I especially sought to include additional images outside of the museum archives. By the time it was finished, I felt disappointed that I could not include them all. I hope you enjoy learning about the history of Bellevue and are inspired to add to future chronicles.

—Ben Justman
executive director, Sarpy County Museum

FOREWORD

This is a book to refresh memories or offer an introduction to our neighbors. Bellevue is the oldest continuing community in Nebraska, and the city is proud of its heritage. Lewis and Clark stopped near the site on the Missouri River on their voyage to the west coast. Fur trader Peter Sarpy followed, founding his trading post on the hills overlooking the river. Moses Merrill, a missionary, arrived in 1835 and hoped to educate the Indians. He moved his mission southwest on the settlement near the Platte River. The settlement grew and was incorporated in 1855.

Fort Crook was located near the city, starting a long relationship with the military. The Martin Bomber plant during World War II experienced a burst of growth that resulted in the once-sleepy community becoming a major city. Bellevue welcomed the military families as they came to join the community.

Leaders in the city supported growing schools and were founders of Bellevue College in the early 1960s. It is now Bellevue University, educating many and contributing to opportunities in education.

I have seen and participated in the growth and changes in the community. I enjoy traveling on the JFK Freeway, having access to numerous commercial outlets, and visiting our historical sites and trails. As mayor for 12 years, the city grew to become the third largest city in Nebraska. It gives me great pleasure to look back and reminisce about those changes. We are fortunate to have Ben Justman as director of the Sarpy County Museum, as he has put together this wonderful resource for many people to enjoy.

—Inez Boyd
former mayor of Bellevue

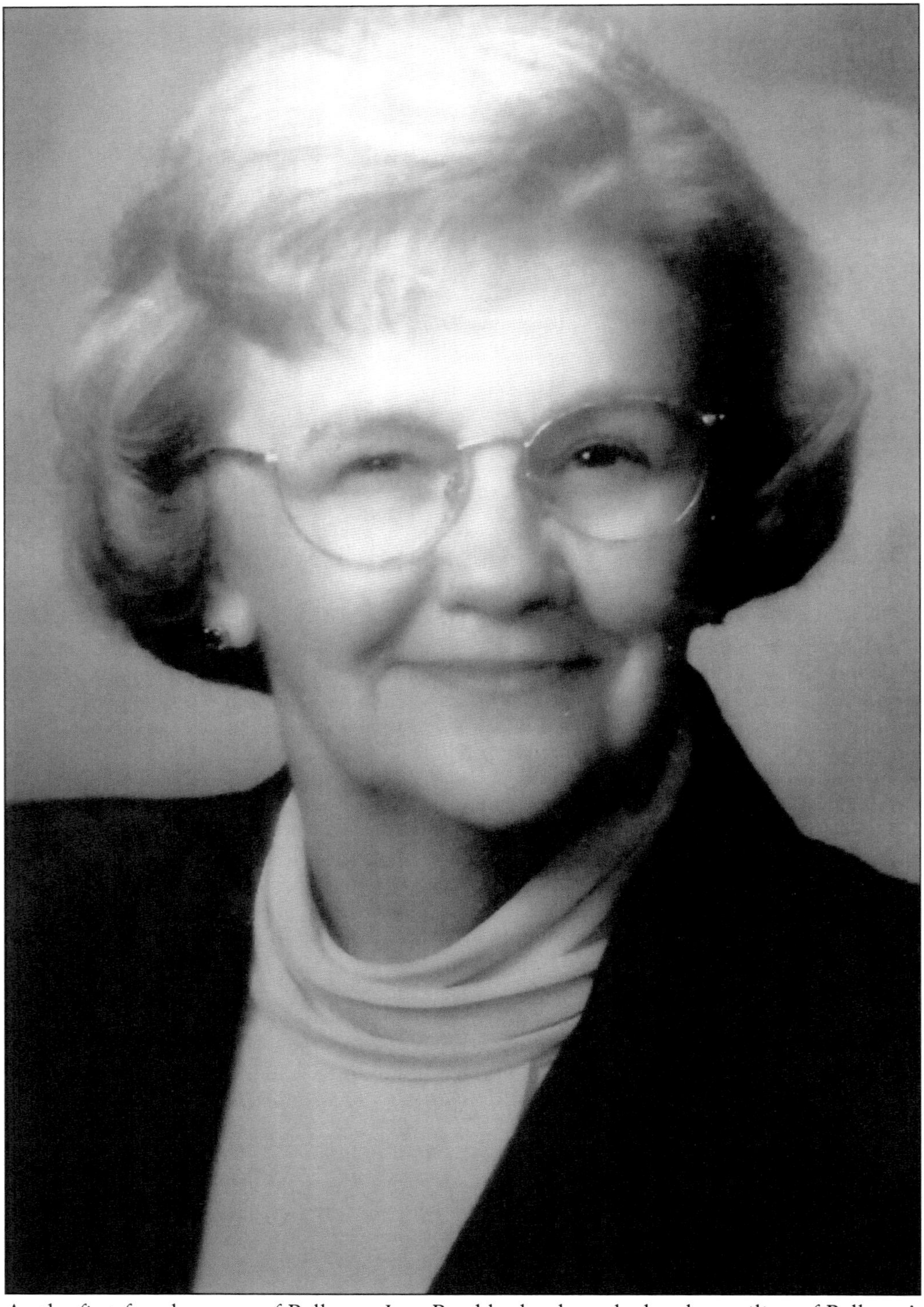

As the first female mayor of Bellevue, Inez Boyd broke through the glass ceiling of Bellevue's male-dominated political world. Serving first on the city council, she was later elected mayor in 1986. Boyd held the title of mayor for over a decade until 1998 and has continued to be active in the community today.

INTRODUCTION

One sees the history of Bellevue every day walking or driving through the community and observing the handful of structures still standing. Fontenelle Bank, the old church, and the log cabin are three easily identifiable structures. These buildings represent Bellevue's past and each has its own tale to tell. Other history is less apparent and yet still in plain sight. Betz and Childs Roads and Wake Robin School are just a few of the active assets named after people who made a difference in the community. Once prominent local figures, they today live on as spirits, even if only on a sign, but the further history of Bellevue is long gone. Perhaps rubble or a headstone remains, but in many cases, not even that is identifiable. Photographs and images bridge the gap for all three of these categories. They truly can be worth a thousand words, but in many instances, that just is not enough. When available, the information to accompany a picture is priceless. This book will highlight Bellevue's unique history through the use of our local photographs.

That history, for the town's purpose, can begin with the Lewis and Clark expedition in 1804. This event was similar to the modern-day exploration of outer space in that it created a wealth of new prospects for Americans. With the door open, the fur traders seeking lucrative rewards of an untapped region began to arrive in 1822, led by Joshua Pilcher of the Missouri Fur Company. Others followed, including Fontenelle, Sarpy, and the Merrills. The result formed a triumvirate of fur traders, missionaries, and Native Americans.

Soon, Bellevue served as a trailside stop for those seeking fortune and glory or simply a better life in the western part of the United States. Mormon pioneers heading to Utah in 1847 utilized Bellevue's Missouri River crossing, as did forty-niners seeking a gold claim in subsequent years. Many would pass through the area, and some would ultimately stay. One who would not stay for long was the first territorial governor of Nebraska, Francis Burt. In 1854, after serving two days in his new position, he died. His replacement, Thomas Cuming, would relocate to Omaha, closer to his political center.

The fruitful years would not stay gold forever. The westward expansion that helped Bellevue prosper was not exclusive to Nebraska's oldest continuous settlement. Omaha also grew and at a faster rate, dwarfing the population and economic opportunities in Bellevue. Furthermore, it squelched any political influence Bellevue might have had. The result was that when the Union Pacific railroad built a line in Nebraska, it went to Omaha and not Bellevue. Population numbers in Bellevue continued to stagnate and then decrease. When the county seat was transferred to Papillion in 1876, the fate of Bellevue as just another failed settlement was nearly sealed.

Bellevue's days as a city were numbered. This would have been how Bellevue's story played out, had it not been for the US Department of War, Congress, and Pres. Benjamin Harrison approving the establishment of Fort Crook. Additionally, higher education chose Bellevue when Bellevue College was founded in 1880. As the new century dawned, farmland became fort land and campus commons, and with it, Bellevue regained the upper hand at survival. Despite the reprieve, it would be a long, unpaved road before Bellevue would become Nebraska's third largest city, the sprawling metropolis that it is today. Population numbers would increase, but only gradually during the first half of the 20th century.

America began to retool itself from peacetime to wartime as the threat of its entry into world war loomed. Fort Crook was selected to serve as a major bomber assembly plant for the allied war effort. Starting in 1942, the Glenn L. Martin Bomber Plant churned out airplanes. It did so for the next 33 consecutive months and was always on schedule. No other aircraft assembly plant in the nation ever came close to this record. To support this superhuman feat, an army of workers was needed; many of them lived in Bellevue.

Like many cities, Bellevue mirrors the greater American chronicle of postwar life in a number of ways. The major difference was that while ex-servicemen and women settled into the community after the war, there were others who continued their military service or civilians who maintained an active role on the now-thriving military base. As America reorganized and restructured its military strength for new threats, Fort Crook became Offutt Air Force Base in 1948. In that same year, the base took on additional importance when it became the host base for Strategic Air Command. At the end of the Cold War, Strategic Air Command dissolved and US Strategic Command was formed while both Offutt and Bellevue entered a new chapter in their histories. All throughout the jet-age revolution and beyond, Bellevue continued to see population and commercial growth. Today, over 50,000 people call Bellevue, Nebraska, home.

A great deal of the history of Bellevue has been complied in a far more thorough academic monograph compiled by Dr. Jerold L. Simmons, entitled *La Belle Vue: Studies in the History of Bellevue, Nebraska*. Without it, much of the information would have been exceptionally arduous to acquire. In addition to the scholarship by Simmons, the genealogical work and historical documentation amassed over the years at the Sarpy County Museum supplemented my understanding of Bellevue. Perhaps the most important primary resource essential for this book was the *Papillion Times* and the *Bellevue Press*. Over 100 years of local newspapers have the ability to help the reader travel back in time to the day relevant events took place.

The majority of photographs can be found within the archives at the Sarpy County Museum and, unless otherwise noted, are from their collection. Many of these are the work of John Gebbie, photographer and editor of the *Bellevue Press*. Others come from a smattering of sources within Bellevue's neighborhood, including several generous community members, as well as the Fontenelle Nature Association. The pictures featured within the contents of this book are not the entirety of Bellevue's photographic chronicle. There are more images. They are in your basement, garage, attic, or crawlspace. Please consider donating them to the Sarpy County Museum where your history—and the history of Bellevue—can be preserved and shared for generations.

One

Beautiful View

There was a time when Bellevue was nothing. Wide-open lands inhabited by Native Americans was all there was to the region. The first nonindigenous people set their sights on this area in 1804. For the next 50 years, the area was not officially Bellevue. Nebraska was not a state, let alone a territory. Despite this, Bellevue's early history is an exciting one with an ensemble cast of characters, each important in the development of Bellevue. Much of this history remains fragmented and often unclear, due to poor original documentation, shortsighted record keeping, or simply as a result of the shifting sands of time. One thing that is certain is that Manuel Lisa did not name Bellevue. There is no factual evidence to support this legend that has previously been featured in the bulk of Bellevue's historiography.

The whole area that encompassed the great unknown was off limits to average Americans unless they had good reason to traverse such unfamiliar land. The three exceptions were the military, the fur trade, and the missionaries; nearly all Bellevue's early key players fell into one of these three categories. An additional category consisted of the original inhabitants of the land, Native Americans. Together, these four factions intertwined to build the foundation for what would become Bellevue. By the 1830s, it was a smattering of log buildings containing a blacksmith, trading post, and an Indian Agency. The missionaries during this time and the following decade filled in the ranks, establishing their missions where they found a mix of white and Indian civilizations.

In 1854, the Nebraska Territory was formed and, not long after, Bellevue was as well. Once incorporated, it officially became the largest town in Douglas County. Logically, big things were to come for the city, including its location as the new territorial capital. However, this was not to be.

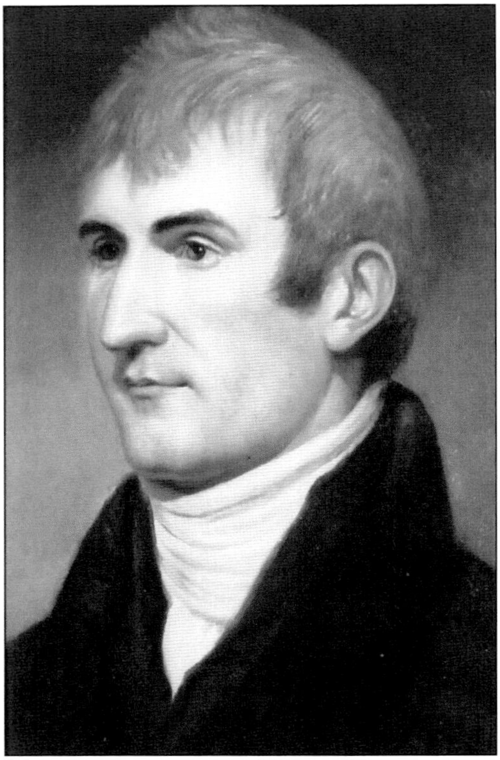

Meriwether Lewis (left) and William Clark (below) stayed here three times. The first of these visits was overnight on July 21, 1804, near present-day Catfish Lake. The pair of explorers noted that there were a number of wolves that could be heard from the campsite. The following night, they settled not far from present-day Fontenelle Forest and operated out of "White Catfish Camp" for four days before continuing westward on their journey. The camp earned its nickname simply because a member of the party caught a white catfish. During their return trip, Lewis and Clark once again stayed at the site of White Catfish Camp in September 1806.

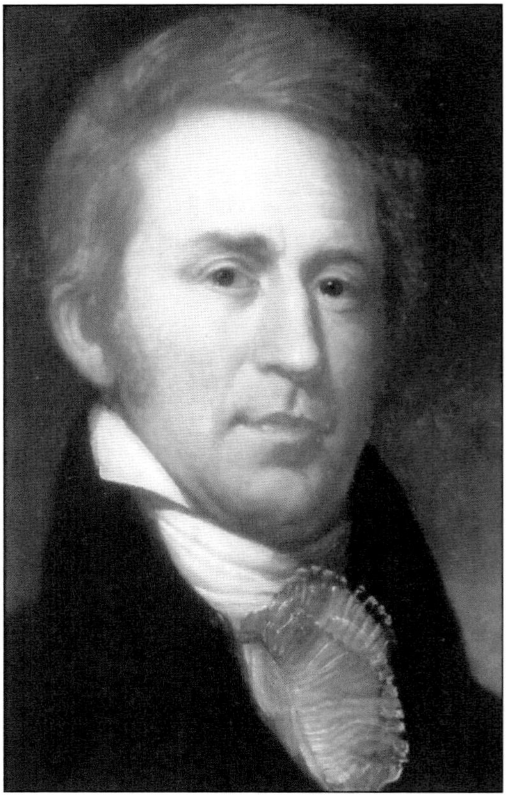

Known for his political and diplomatic skills, Chief Big Elk of the Omaha led his tribe from 1811 until his death in 1846. In a time that has been characterized as uncertain, relations between the settlers and the Omaha tribe were peaceful. On two separate occasions, Big Elk visited Washington, DC and met with two US presidents.

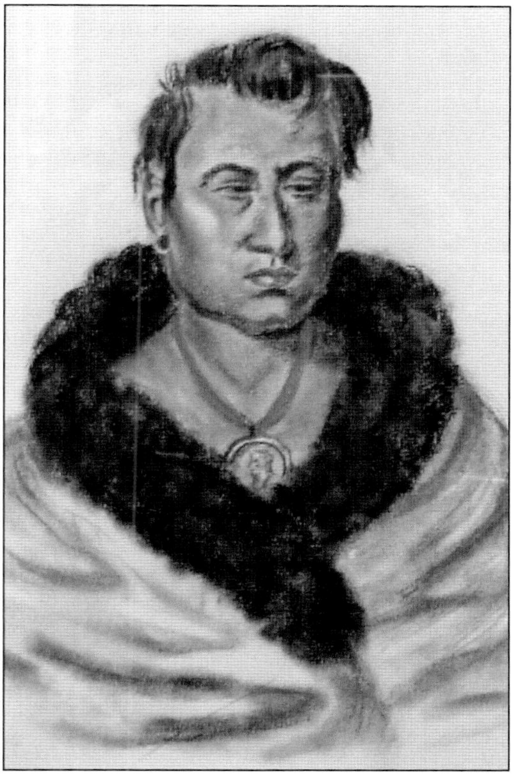

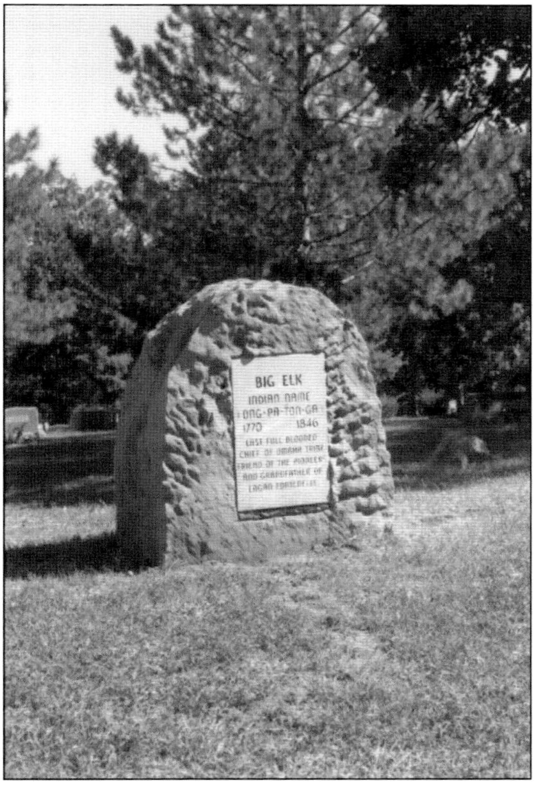

After his death in 1846, Big Elk was buried on a high hill in Bellevue known as Elk Hill. Near the end of the 19th century, the land was needed, so Big Elk was reburied in one grave with 14 other tribesmen. His remains were once again dug up before he was finally interred at Bellevue Cemetery in September 1954 with about 1,000 people in attendance.

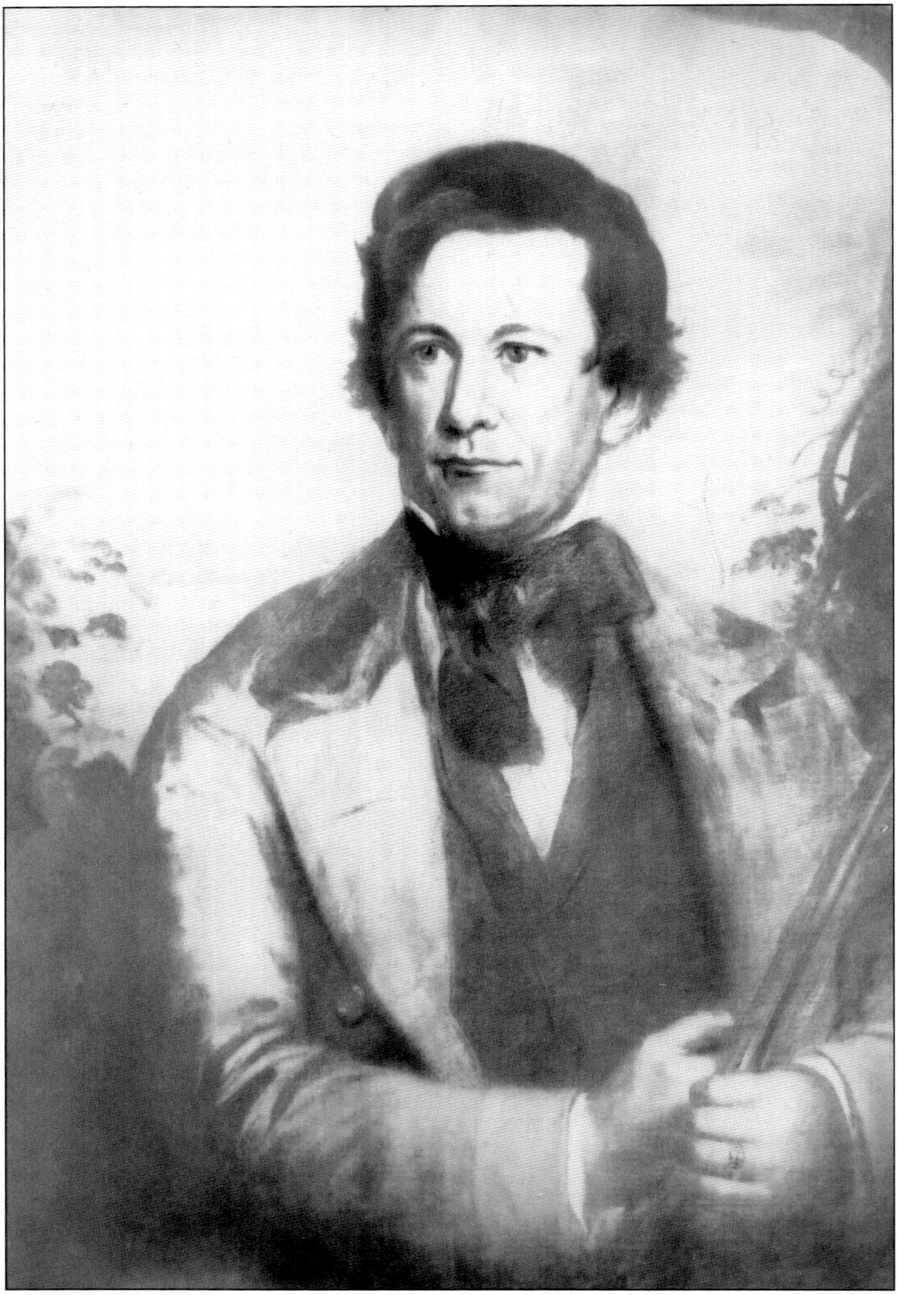

Fur trader, trading post operator, ferry operator, and businessman Peter Abadie Sarpy is not only the namesake of the county, but the man responsible for Bellevue. Sarpy first came to the area in 1824 as part of the American Fur Company. In 1847, he transported Mormons en route to Utah across the Missouri River at his trading post. Sarpy repeated this a few years later when gold-seekers were passing through on their way to California. Both Logan Fontenelle and Joseph LaFlesche, two important figures in Bellevue's history, worked for Sarpy's ferry service. In 1855, Sarpy organized the first Masonic lodge in the Nebraska Territory in the upper rooms of his trading post. Eventually, Sarpy decided Bellevue was becoming too large for his liking and moved to the nearby town of Plattsmouth. He died there on January 4, 1865.

The daughter of Ioway chief Hard Heart and the Omaha-Otoe mother, Kazawin, Nicomi (1808–1888) married Army surgeon Dr. John Gale of Fort Atkinson. Together, they had Mary. After Gail's death, Nicomi would later marry Peter Sarpy, and the two would raise Mary until she married Joseph LaFlesche, successor to Big Elk as chief of the Omaha Tribe. Their child, Suzette LaFlesche Tibbles, also known as Bright Eyes, would become a champion for Native American rights. (Courtesy Washington County Museum.)

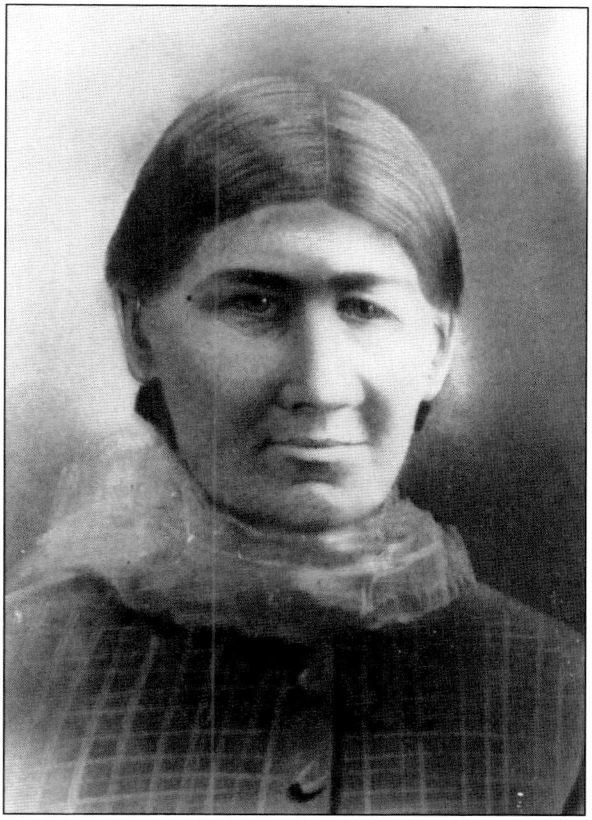

In 1833, German prince Maximilian of Wied visited Bellevue during a trip to the new world. Accompanying him was Swiss painter Karl Bodmer. While here, Bodmer painted the Indian Agency, former location of Fontenelle's Trading Post. Bodmer's work has been noted for its great detail and realism. In all likelihood, his depiction of Bellevue would have not differed too far from reality.

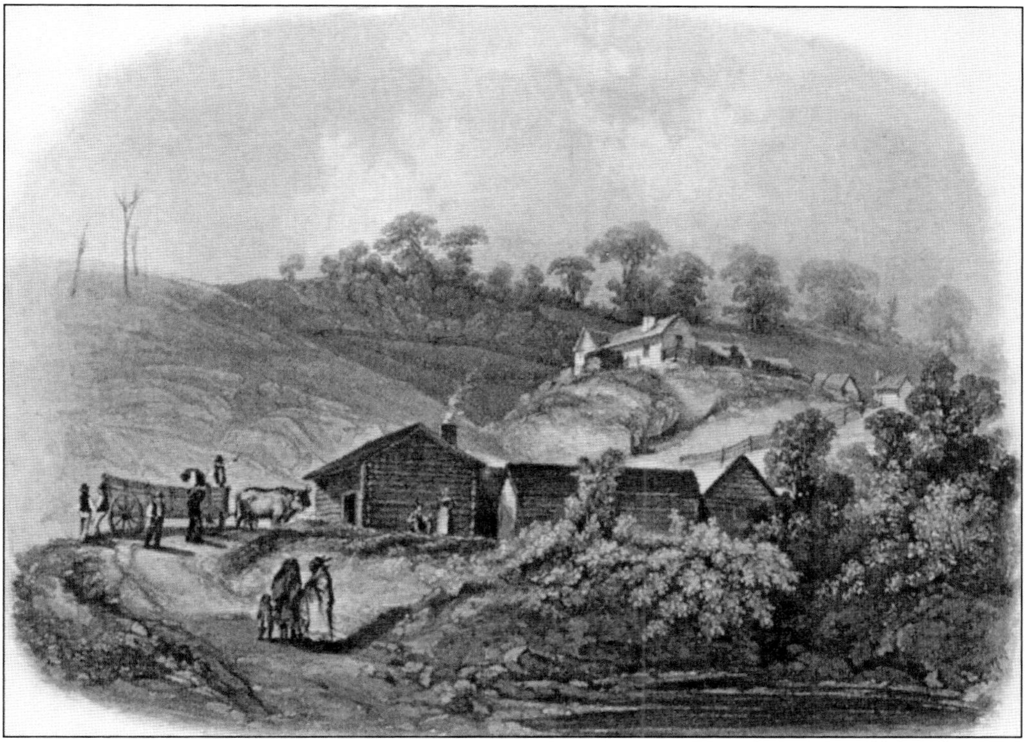

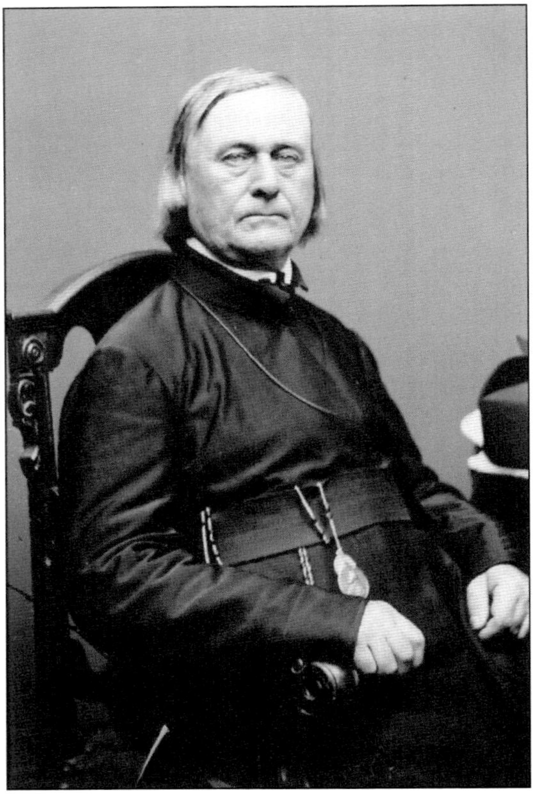

Jesuit priest Fr. Pierre-Jean De Smet was a man with an expansive history. A Catholic missionary from Belgium, he traveled through much of the early United States for the better part of 30 years. In addition to spreading his message, he served as an explorer, cartographer, and arbitrator, ultimately gaining the respect of both white and native populations. In Bellevue, De Smet officiated at the funeral of Lucien Fontenelle.

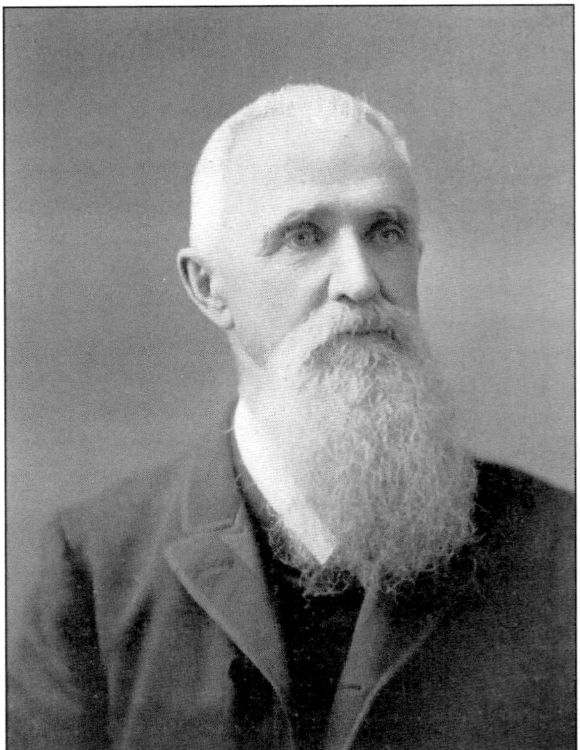

A native of Somersetshire, England, the Honorable John Q. Goss arrived in Bellevue in 1859, joining his brother, Methodist missionary Rev. Charles C. Goss. John Goss used his skills and knowledge to serve as county attorney, county clerk, county school superintendent, and county examiner. Prior to enlisting in the Union army in 1862, he spent three years in the territorial legislature.

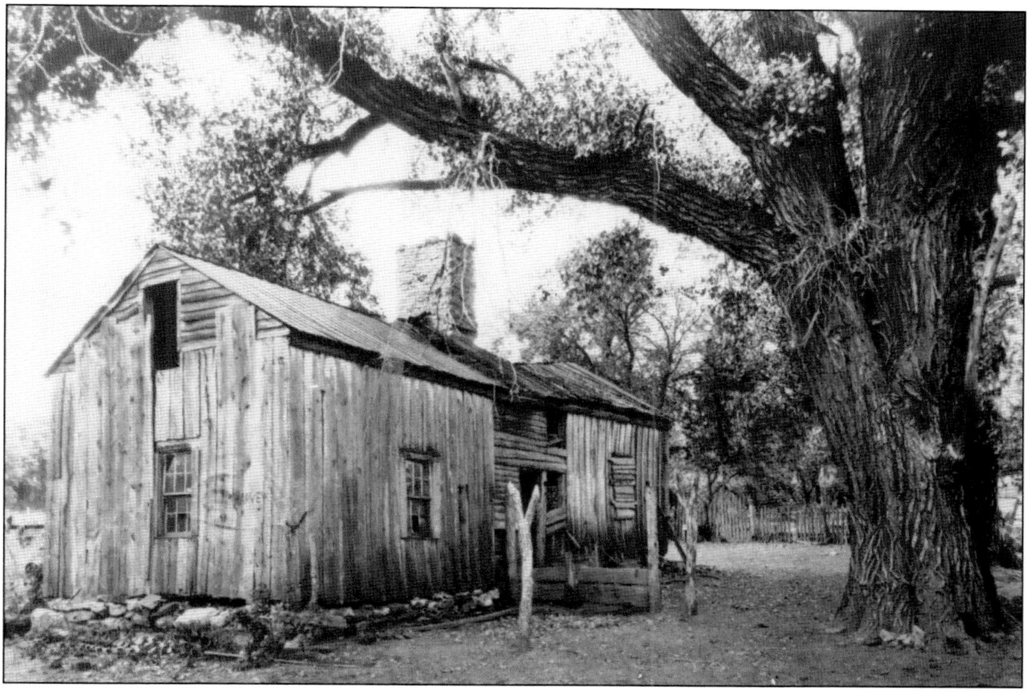

Arriving in Bellevue in November 1833, Moses and Eliza Merill hoped to bring salvation and education to the local Indians. Having approximately 20 students at a time, the missionaries taught them how to read and write, as well as provided a hefty dose of religion and temperance. At the age of 36 in 1840, Moses died from tuberculosis. His last words were a request that someone take his place in educating the Indians; however, no one did. Shortly after his death, Eliza and her young son packed up and left. These photographs taken in 1922 show the ramshackle structures. Today, the only trace of the Baptist missionary is a single chimney.

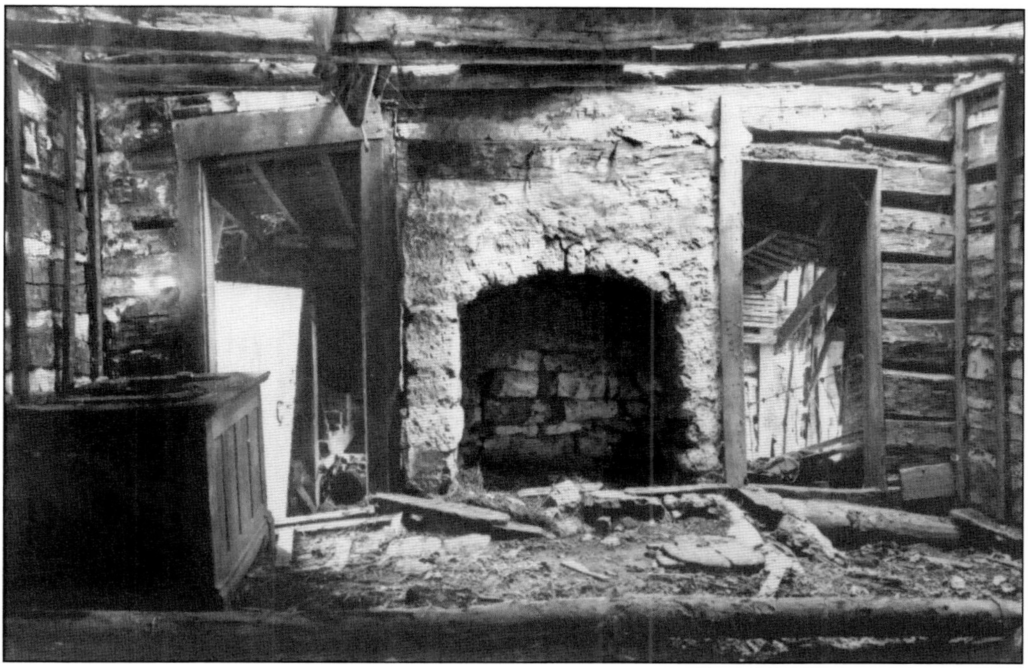

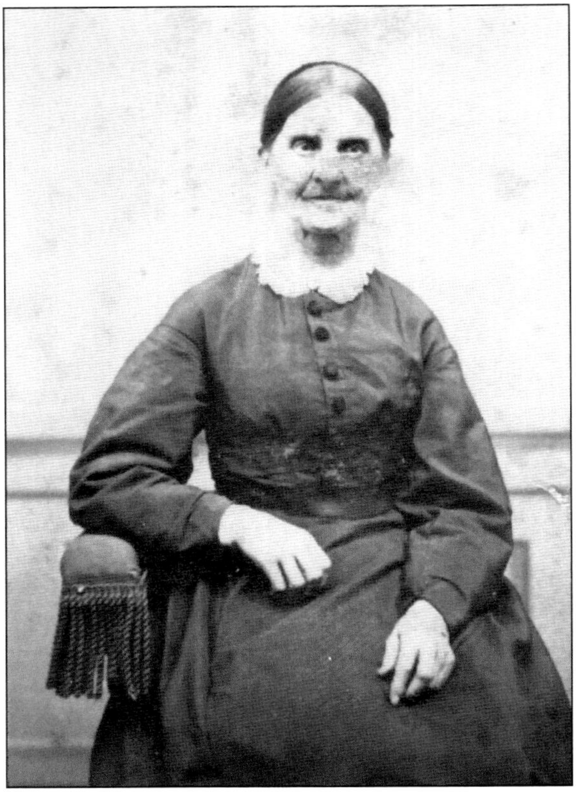

Samuel Allis and partner John Dunbar were other early missionaries to grace Bellevue. Accompanying them to Bellevue in 1834 was Indian agent John Dougherty. In 1836, Samuel married Emaline Palmer, and together, they continued their missionary work with the Pawnee. Despite good relations, the majority of the tribe were not interested in converting. Samuel and Emaline, as well as their son, are buried in Bellevue's Wall Cemetery.

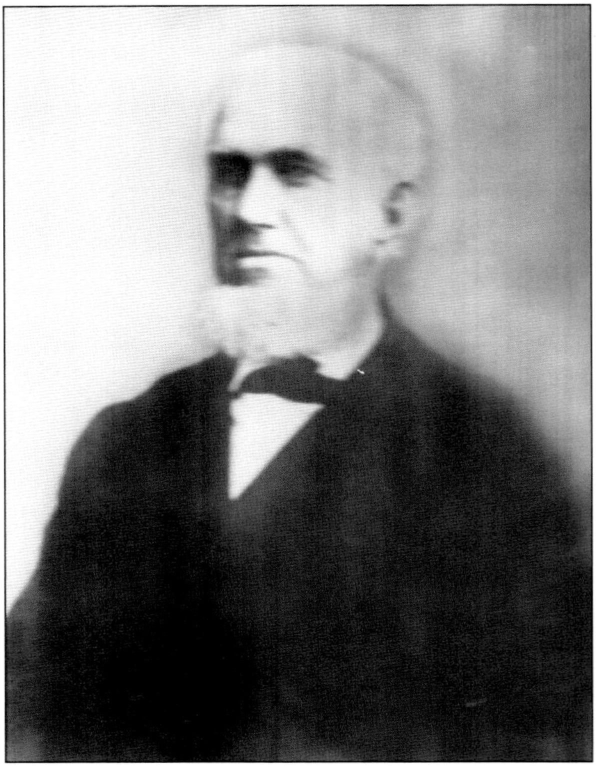

Born August 1, 1811, Presbyterian reverend William Hamilton had been doing God's work for quite some time, including a 15-year stint in Kansas with the Iowa and Sac Indians before finally coming to Bellevue in 1853 to head a new missionary for the Otoe. Hamilton would continue working closely with Indians until his death on September 17, 1891, at the age of 80.

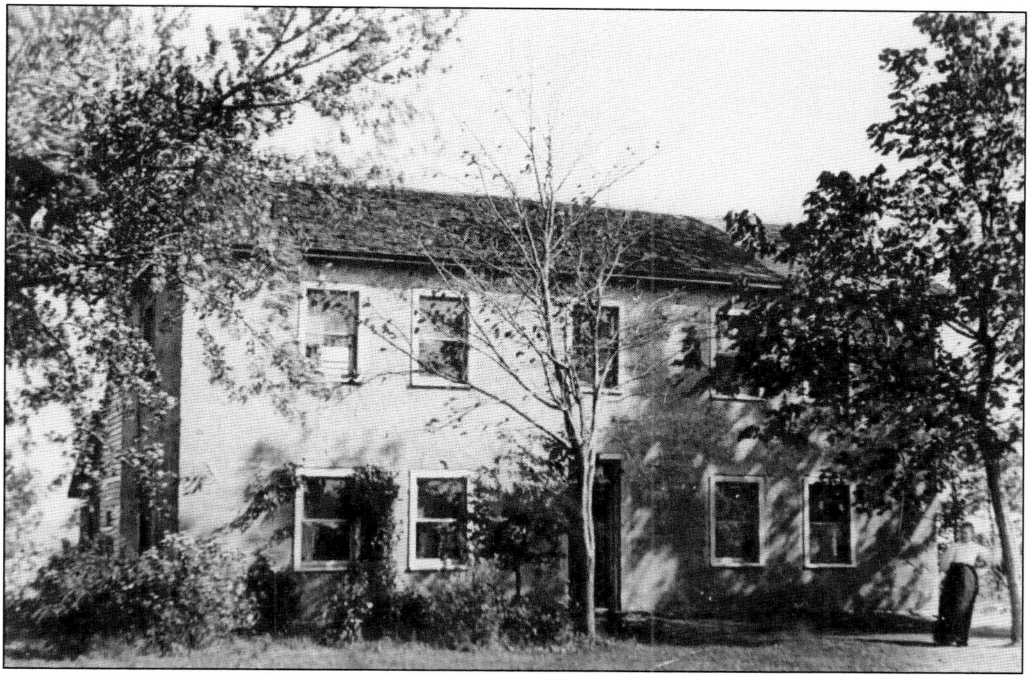

The Hamilton House was nearby the Indian mission and was operated by Rev. William Hamilton and his wife. The school intended to educate pupils by adhering to the common notion that there was civilizing to be done in order to "kill the Indian while saving the man." The house is also the place where Nebraska's first territorial governor, Francis Burt, died.

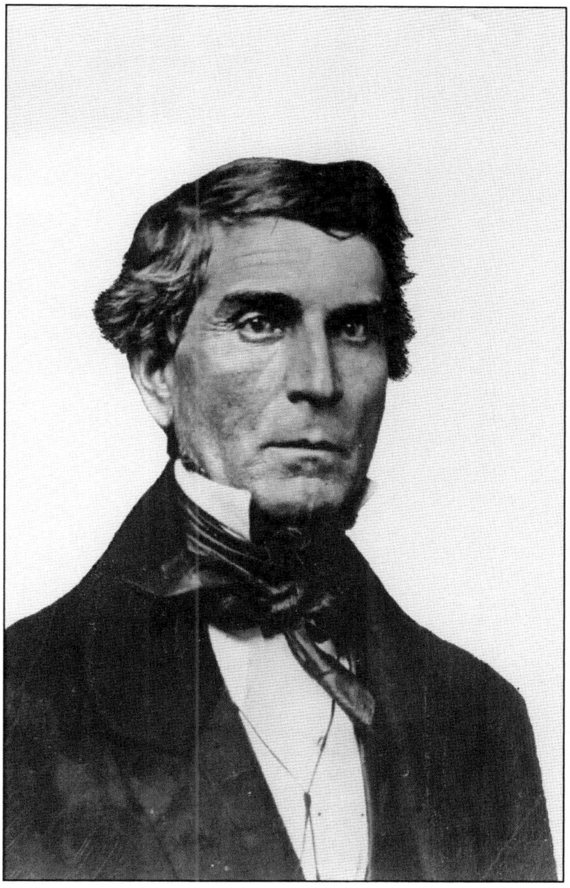

Francis Burt could have been the man to ensure that Bellevue would have served as the first territorial capital of Nebraska. With Burt at the helm, perhaps it might have even one day become the state capital. It remains unknown what greatness Burt could have offered to Bellevue, because on October 18, 1854, two days after his arrival and swearing in, he died.

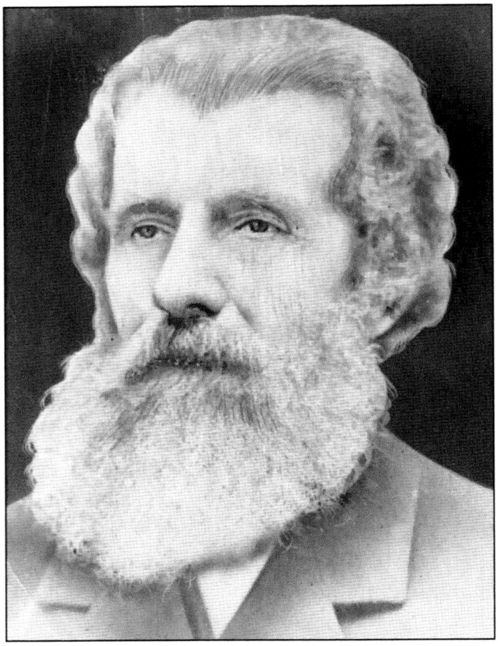

Arriving in Bellevue with his family on November 10, 1852, Mitchell Jonas was commissioned by the government to serve as a blacksmith for the Omaha Indians. Jonas was born in Manchester, England, and learned his trade as an apprentice before relocating to America. Despite a rough first night in Bellevue that entailed sleeping in Peter Sarpy's warehouse, several of his eight children would continue to call Sarpy County their home.

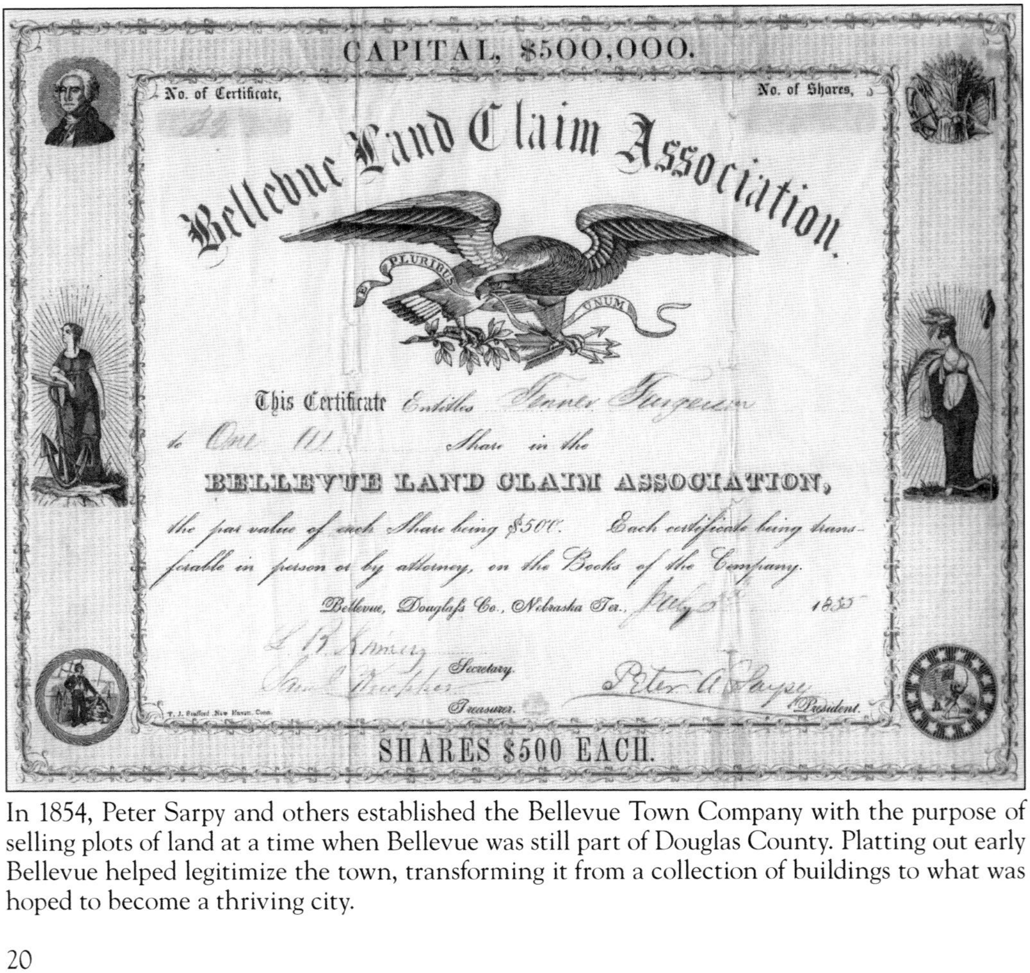

CAPITAL, $500,000.

No. of Certificate, No. of Shares,

Bellevue Land Claim Association.

This Certificate Entitles [illegible] to One (1) Share in the

BELLEVUE LAND CLAIM ASSOCIATION,

the par value of each Share being $500. Each certificate being transferable in person or by attorney, on the Books of the Company.

Bellevue, Douglass Co., Nebraska Ter., July 1855

Secretary.

Treasurer.

Peter A. Sarpy President.

SHARES $500 EACH.

In 1854, Peter Sarpy and others established the Bellevue Town Company with the purpose of selling plots of land at a time when Bellevue was still part of Douglas County. Platting out early Bellevue helped legitimize the town, transforming it from a collection of buildings to what was hoped to become a thriving city.

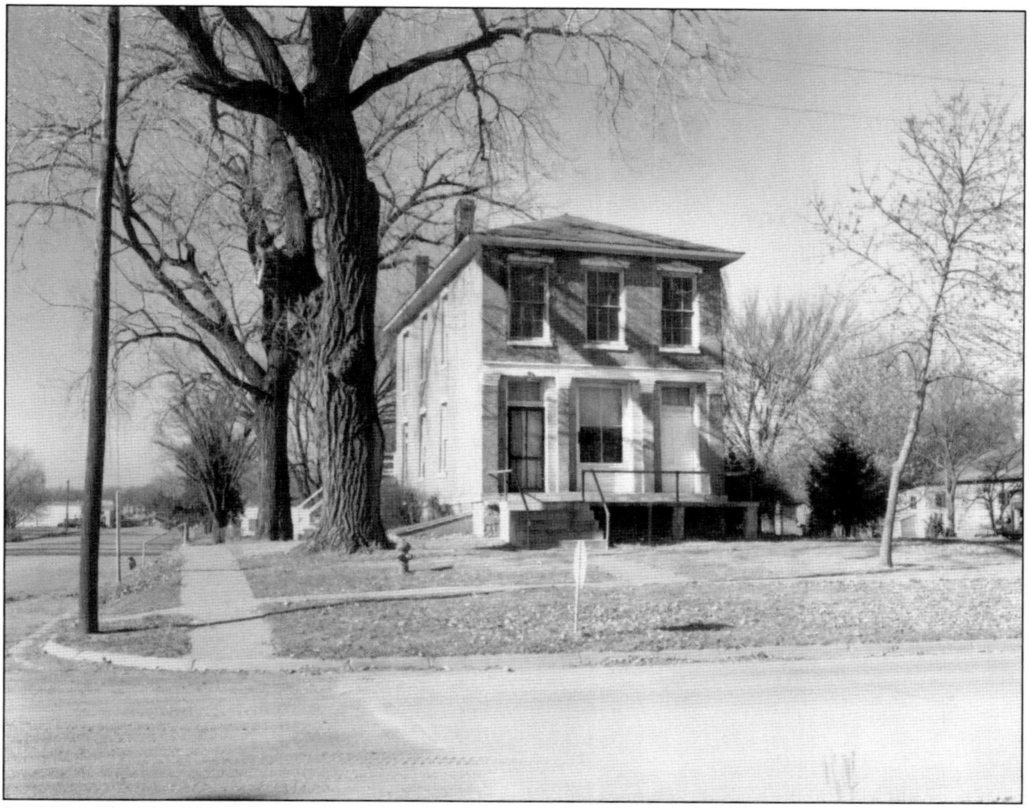

In 1856, this building was constructed to function as the Fontenelle Bank of Bellevue, but by the following year, the bank had failed during the Panic of 1857, so it was turned into the county courthouse. When the county seat was relocated to Papillion, it served as the town hall for the next 75 years.

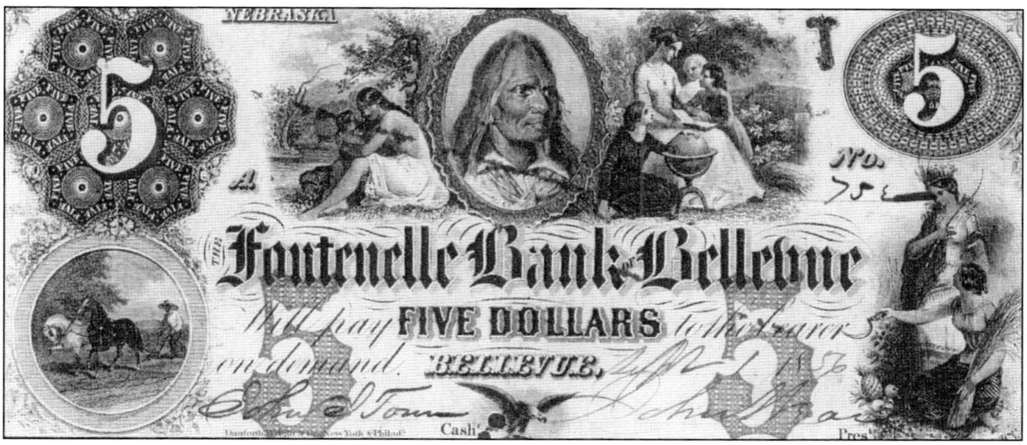

Those who had traded in their greenbacks for Bellevue dollars enjoyed colorful pieces of paper with wonderful artwork. Unfortunately, that is about all they enjoyed as their money was gone, leaving them with an unusable local scrip. Based on the consumer price index and adjusted for inflation, $5 in 1856 would be a little more than $133 today.

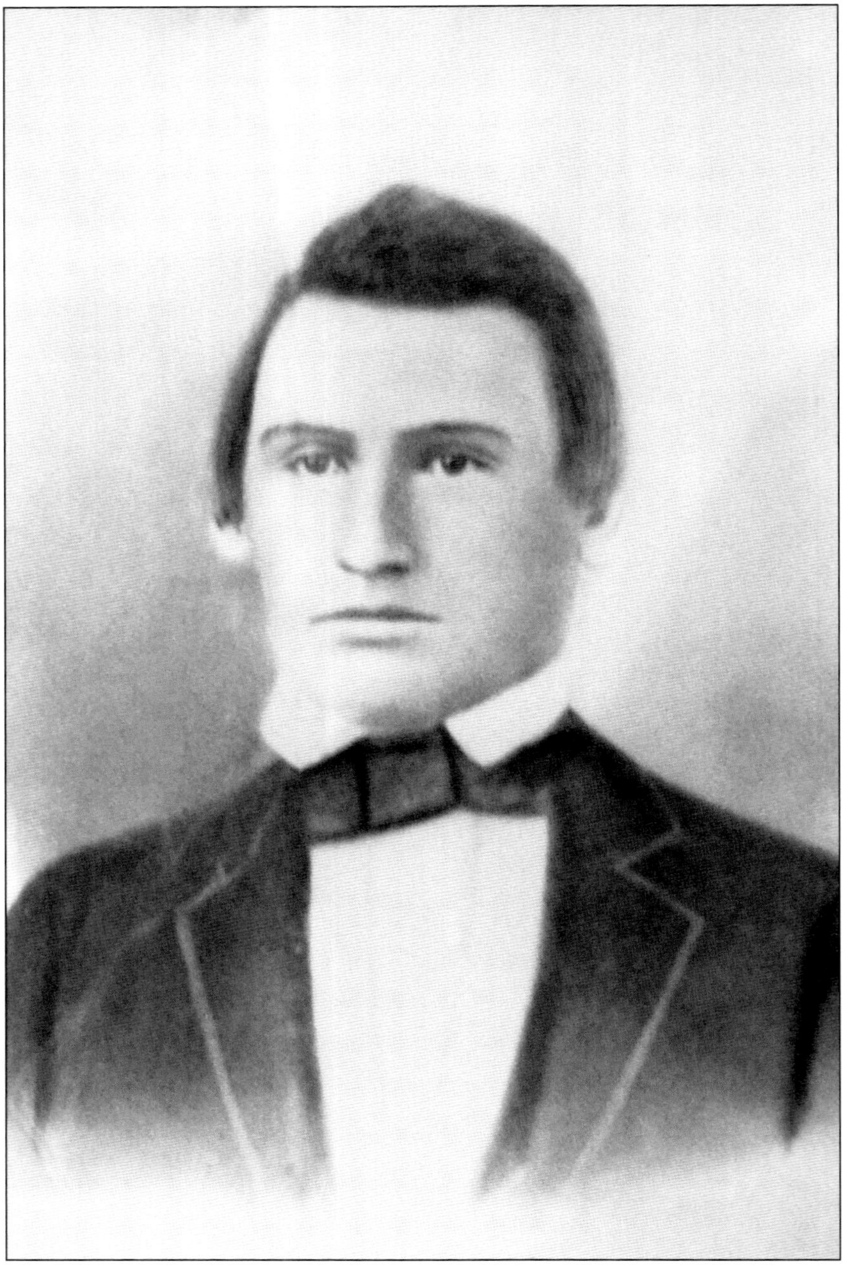

Half Omaha Indian Logan Fontenelle, the son of Lucien Fontenelle, took part in the Treaty of 1854. The treaty allowed the United States to acquire the present-day Nebraska region spanning from the Missouri River to the Sand Hills and from the Niobrara River to the Platte River. For many years, Logan served as an official interpreter for the US government. This position was somewhat ancillary to his role as chief of the Omaha, a role he served for two years from 1853 until 1855. Logan was attacked and killed by Dakota Sioux near Beaver Creek, north of the Loup River in Boone County, Nebraska, during the summer buffalo hunt of 1855. Following his death, his body was returned to Bellevue and buried on present-day Fontenelle Nature Association (FNA) property. In addition to the forest, schools, roads, hotels, public housing, and towns also bear the name of Logan Fontenelle.

Two

Exploring Nebraska's Birthplace

Digging deeper into the history of Bellevue, one will find that there is far more than fur traders, Indians, and missionaries. Discovering the people, places, and events that have made this community what it is today is essential to understanding the history of Bellevue. This includes the pioneers of Bellevue, of course, but there is another dimension to the history of Bellevue as well. It includes people like Jim Baldwin, commonly known as "Jim the Hermit." It includes places such as the town of Fort Crook, now part of modern-day Bellevue. Not to be forgotten are events that have made a mark on life in Bellevue, such as the 1957 Sarpy County Celebration, or quite literally, the 1908 tornado.

All of this and more can be found in Bellevue, a community with a rich past. It is just a matter of bringing much of this history to the surface. Local history can be found not far from one's very own yard in Bellevue. In every alley, within every church pew, and behind every doorway is history waiting to be told. This chapter attempts to do that. Perhaps not all of it will make its way into the pages of a classroom textbook; nonetheless, it is the history of this community and should not fall by the wayside. Exploring Nebraska's birthplace beyond the textbook narrative can provide a certain unmatched depth in aiding the understanding of just what has made Bellevue great.

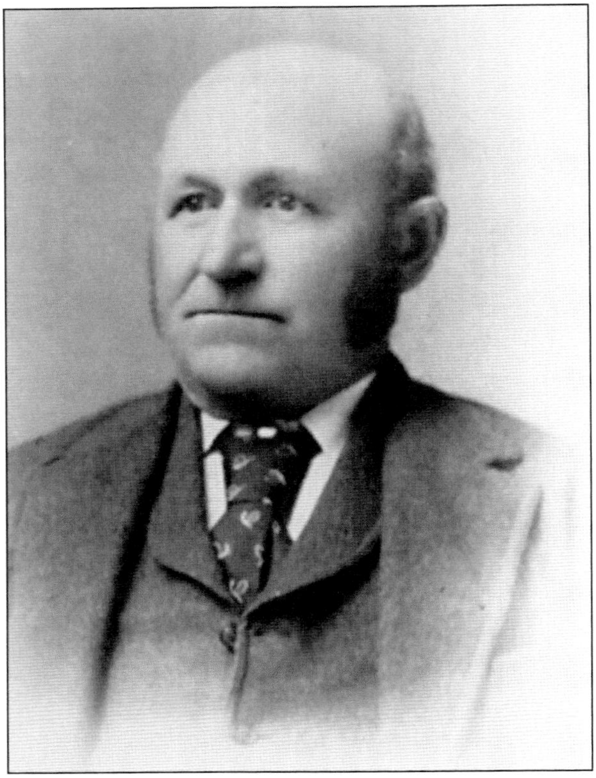

Amos Gates and his wife settled near Thirty-sixth Street and Cedar Island Road in present-day Bellevue, purchasing a 160-acre tract of land that, up until then, had never been plowed. By 1872, Amos had expanded his property to 505 acres. County taxes that year amounted to $120.76. Not just a farmer, Amos served four terms in the territorial assembly and another four terms in the Nebraska legislature.

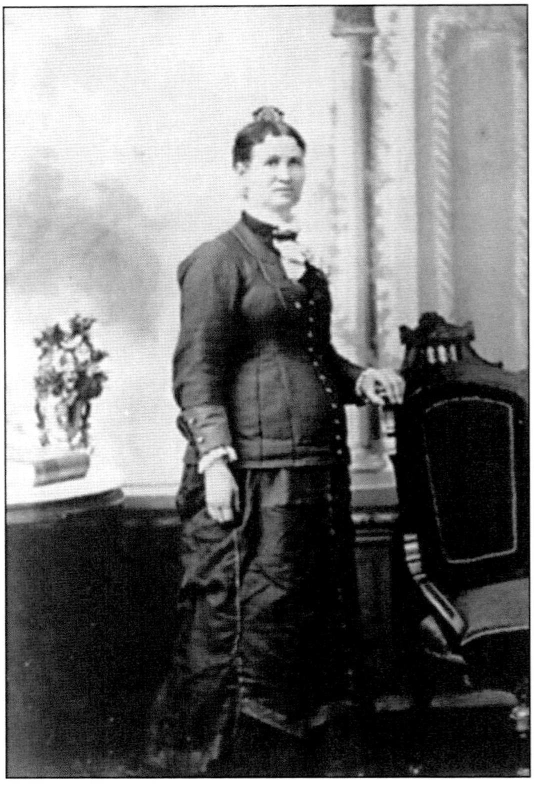

Samantha Gates, an early pioneer, came to the area in 1855 with her husband, Amos, settling in the town of Gilmore, another of Sarpy County's unsuccessful towns encompassed over time by annexation. The couple had eight children, 28 grandchildren, and 28 more great-grandchildren. In 1893, with $800 collected in a family pool, they were instrumental in the founding of Anderson Grove Church.

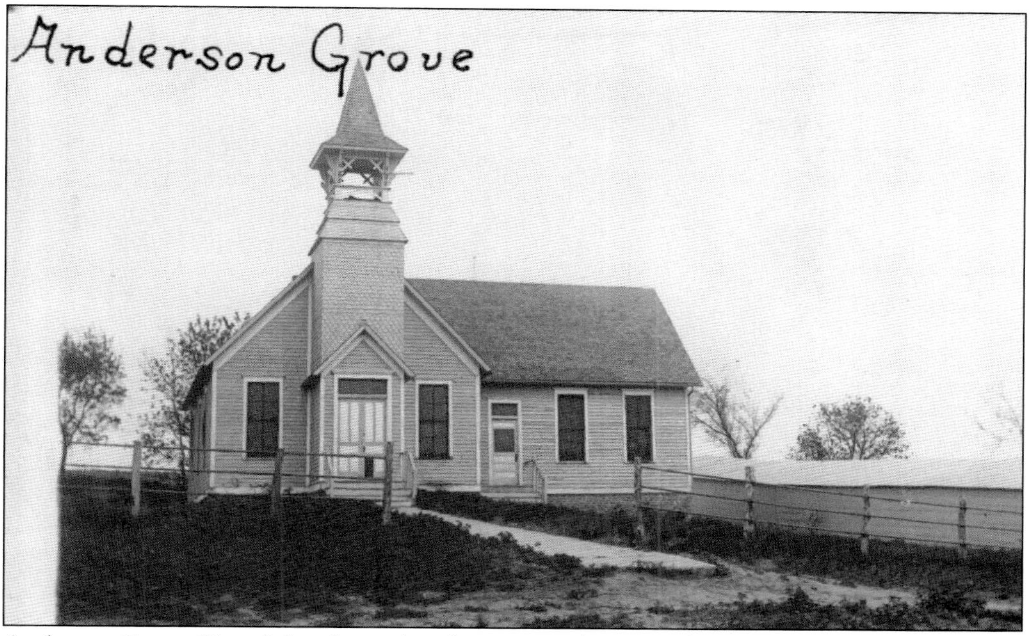

Anderson Grove Church has long played a part in this area's history. Built in 1893 for those who lived too far from First Presbyterian and the handful of other area churches, it still retains much of its physical appearance as seen in this 1920s photograph. It has, however, undergone several improvements since its construction, including a second wing in 1912 and the addition of a furnace and basement.

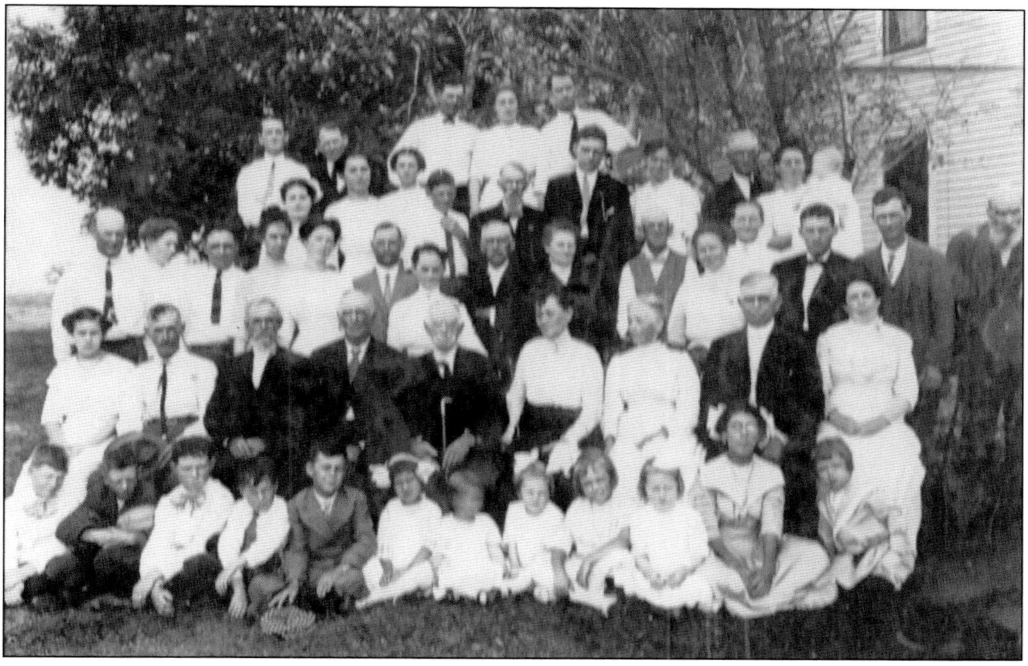

This is an early photograph with many of the Bellevue residents at the time, including a very elderly Judge James Gow (with cane). The image was captured in the backyard of the Storr family home. The great big white house would be located today at 24th and Clay Streets had it not ironically been seized and demolished to make way for the Sarpy County Museum.

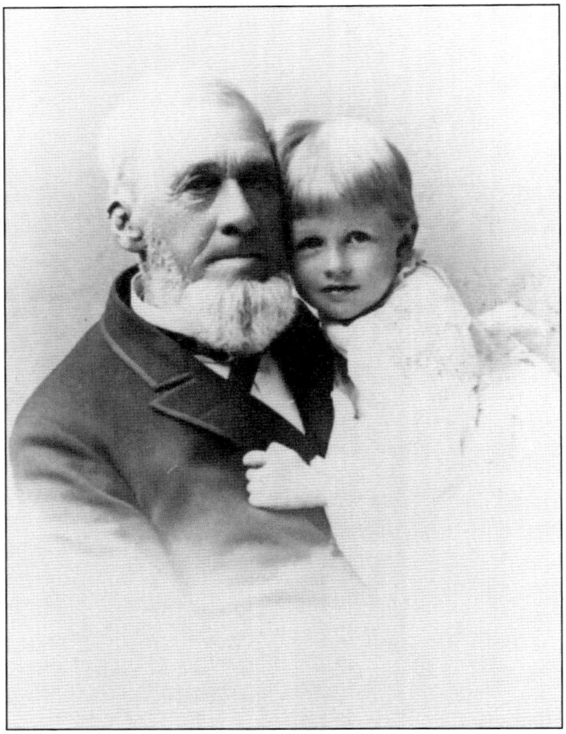

Charles Childs is pictured here with his grandson Charles Everard Childs in about 1895. Childs, an early pioneer in Bellevue, built a mill in the area in 1856. He resided on his Bellevue property until he relocated to Omaha in 1873. Despite his business ventures and historical importance to the region, Childs died destitute in 1903. (Courtesy FNA.)

Charles Childs's sawmill would have looked very similar to this one from nearby Richardson County, Nebraska, in the 1870s. Despite the advancement of steam power to improve the efficiency and production of mills at the time, Childs fell into financial troubles and was forced to sell off the property to his son's father-in-law, Everard D. Ferguson. (Courtesy FNA.)

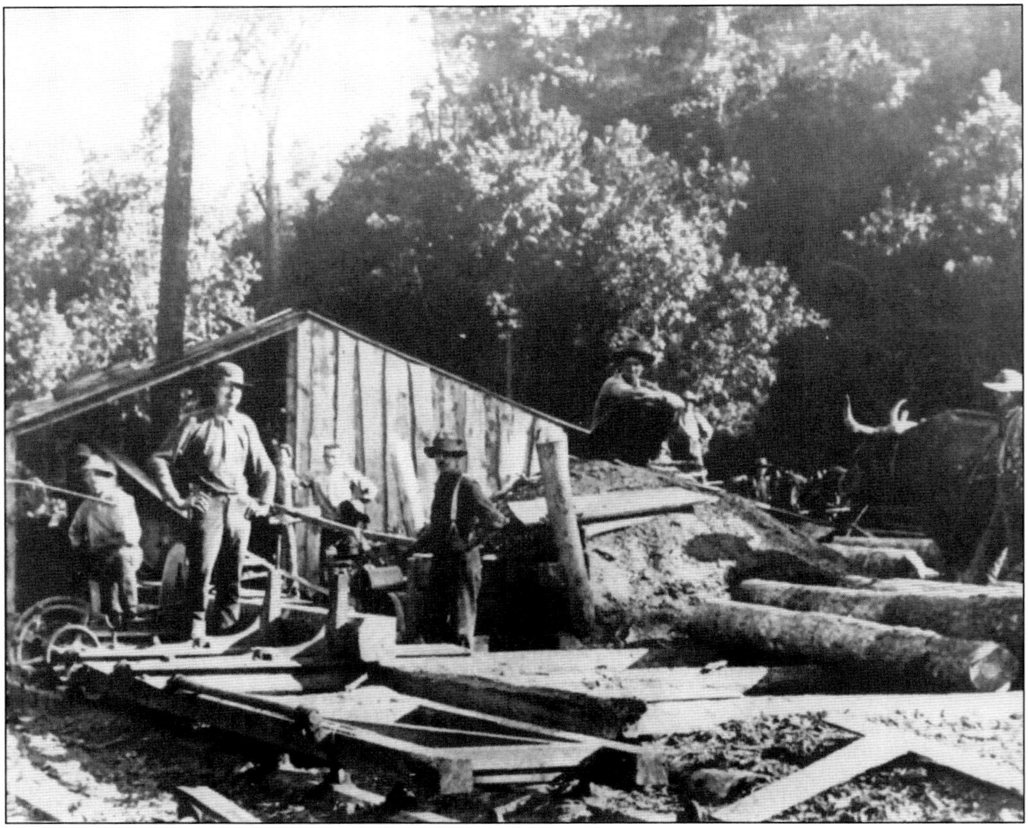

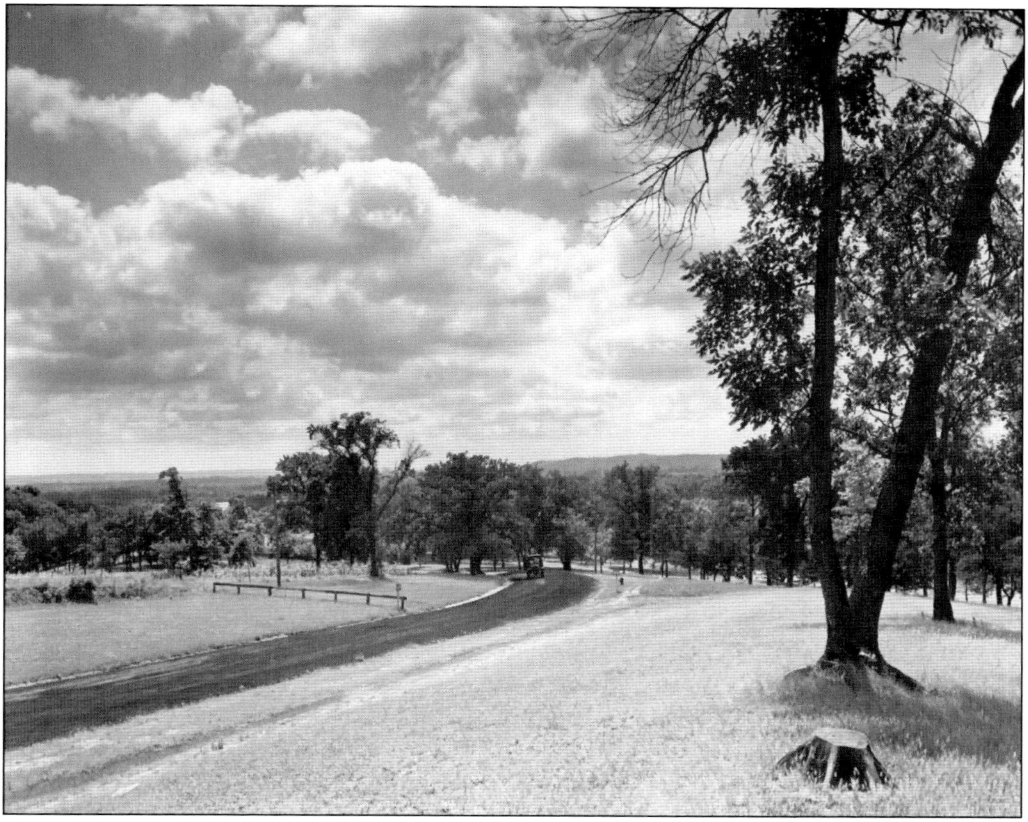

Childs' Point, part of expansive property Charles Childs once laid claim to, was where the Missouri River made a wide bend, allowing the land to jut out, hence the name. Childs' Point was a popular bird watching spot, dubbed one of the best regions in the state for the activity by *Bird Lore* of the Audubon Society in 1908. (Courtesy FNA.)

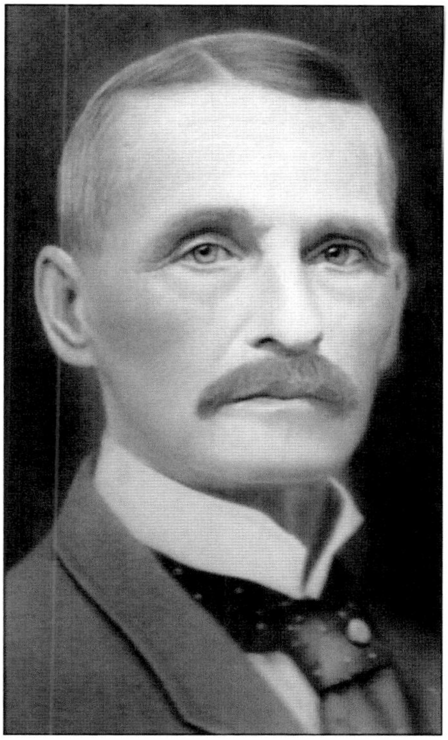

Originally from New York, William Clark McLean, like many, found the grass to be greener on the other side of the Missouri River. During the Civil War, McLean took part in Chancellorsville, Gettysburg, and Sherman's march to the sea. After the war, he settled in Bellevue, married Mary Osler, had four daughters, and served as postmaster of Bellevue from 1869 to 1872.

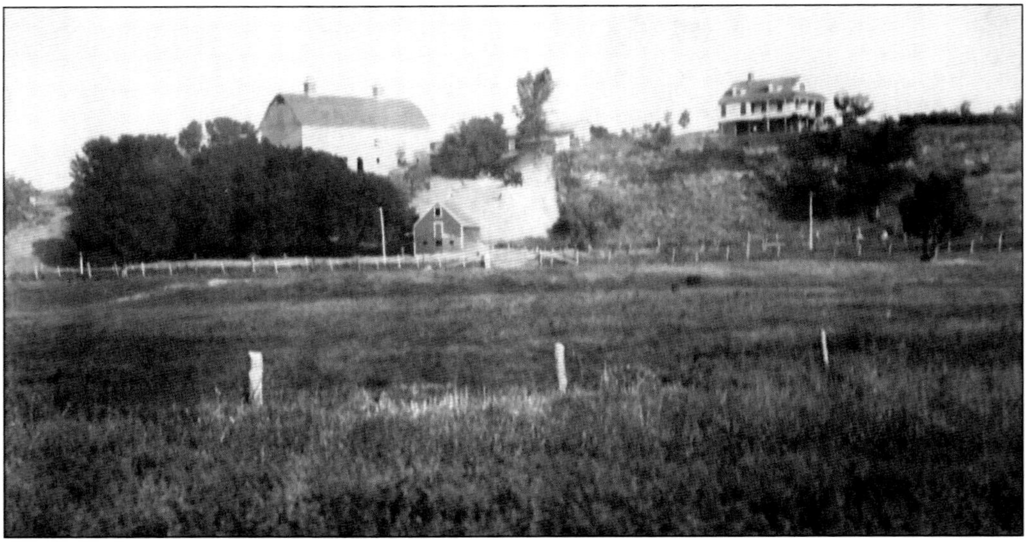

Prior to their relocating to South Omaha, the Stouffer family resided at their Bellevue farm home for nearly 20 years from February 13, 1881, until March 9, 1900. The open farmland seen here presents a very different picture than that of the Bellevue of today, and while the great big barn still stands, additional residences have since encircled the building.

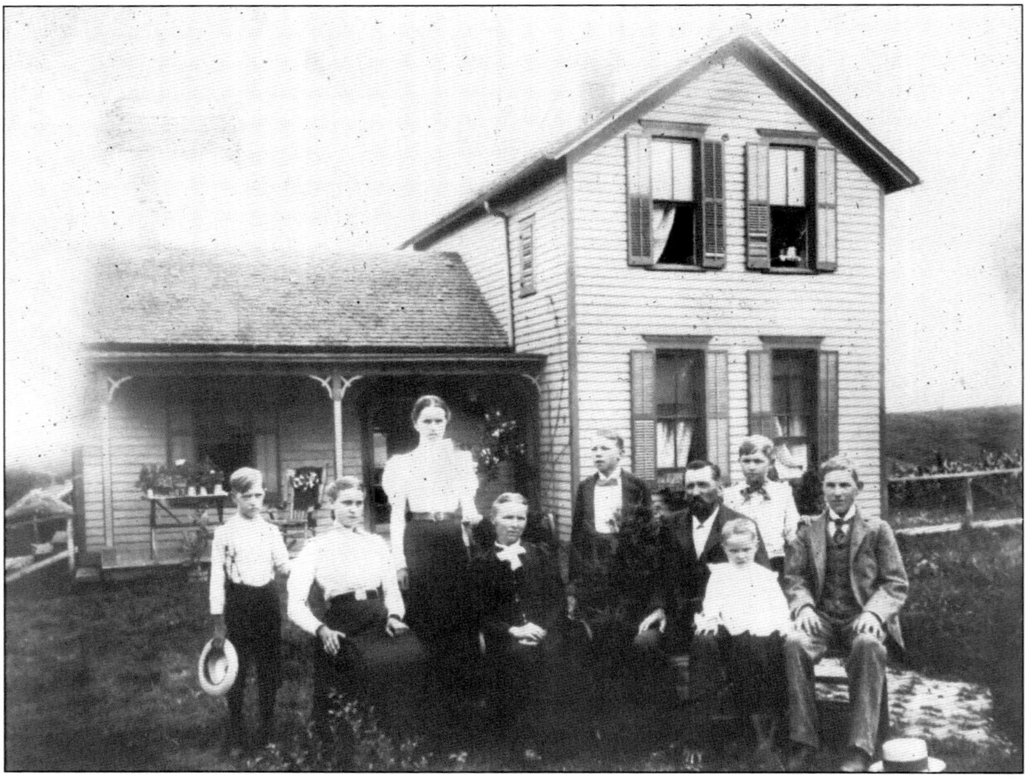

The Schlekaus were another family to arrive in Bellevue in the mid-1880s. Featured in the family portrait at their farmstead are Henry and Minnie Schlekau. Together, they had sons Henry, Charles, Ed, Frank, and Fred and daughters Anna and Clara. At one time, the Schlekaus were one of the most extensive landowners in the county.

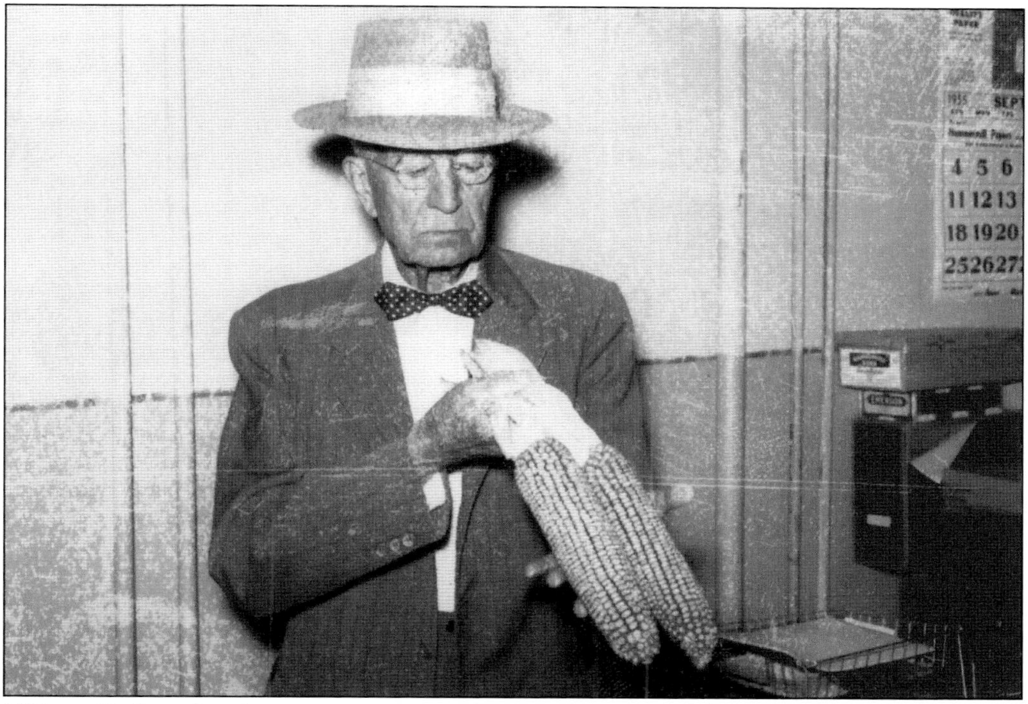

William R. Patrick, a longtime attorney and one-time justice of the peace for Bellevue, served in a number of capacities including a seven-year stint as Sarpy County attorney and as a state senator beginning in 1907, prior to the implementation of the unicameral system. A true jack-of-all-trades, he also sold vehicles for the Holman Automobile Company. Patrick passed away in 1962 and is buried in Bellevue Cemetery.

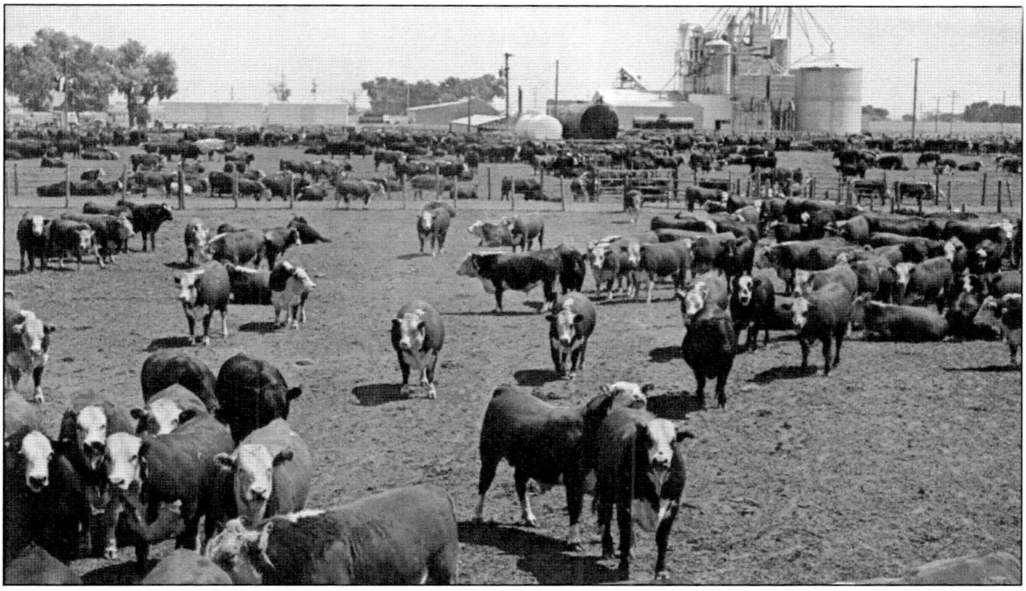

While slaughterhouses and butcher shops are associated with Omaha, feedlots were a common site in Bellevue. Thousands of cattle roamed the land now used as streets and stores, awaiting their final destination as a steak on someone's table. Nebraska earned the nickname "the beef state," and in no small way has Bellevue's history contributed to that moniker.

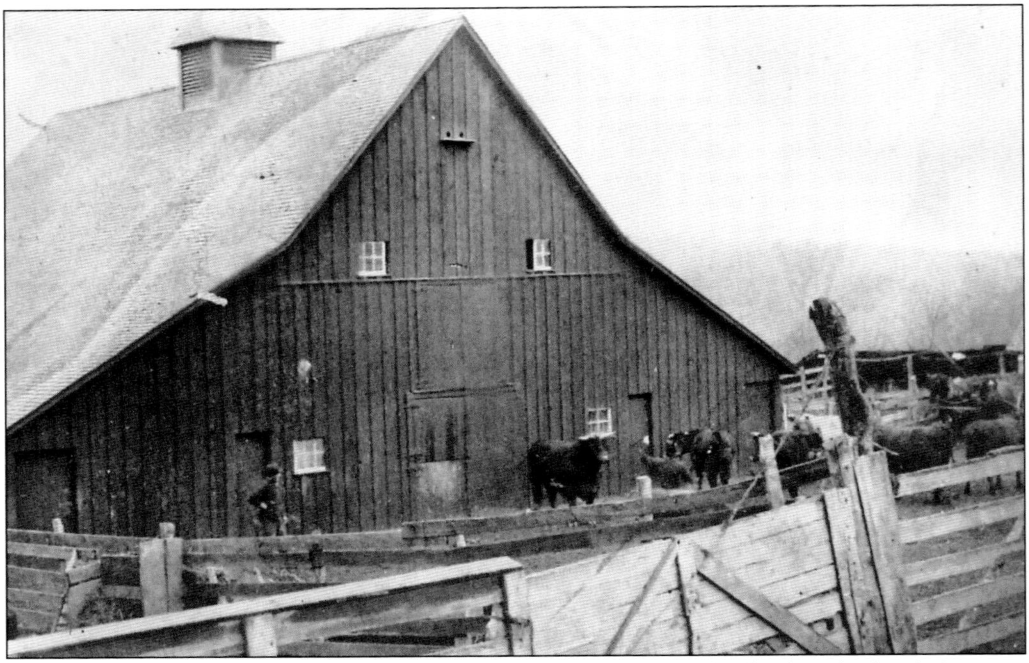

Barns were once a common site in Bellevue and the surrounding land. The Iske family barn on 36th Street is long since gone, replaced by modern urban residential and commercial centers. The Iskes were just a handful of families who occupied the rich rural land along 36th Street between the 10-mile Bellevue-Papillion corridor. Over time, many of these neighbors would become family. (Courtesy Iske Family.)

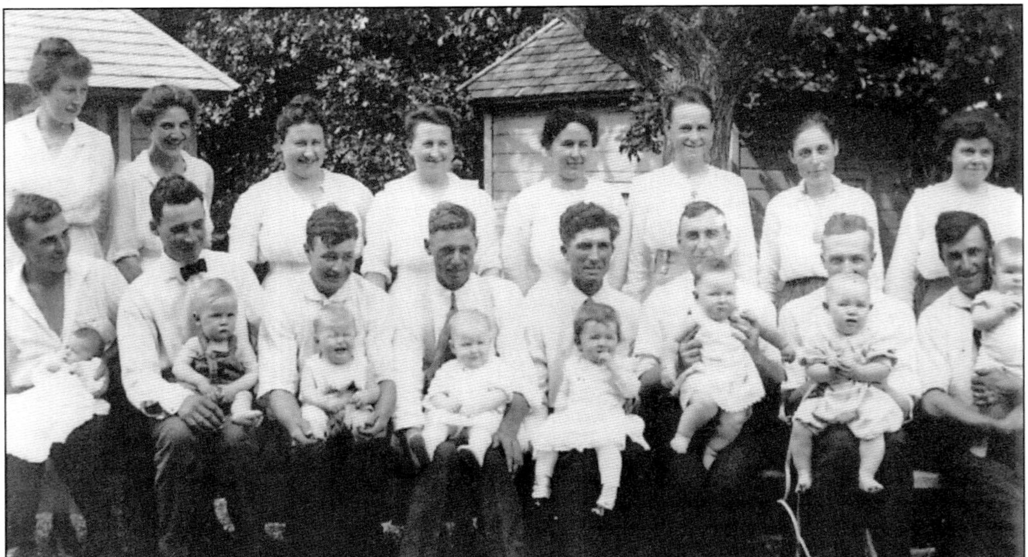

Lined up on their fathers' laps with their mothers standing behind, these eight infant cousins gathered—with a little help from their parents—for this family photograph in 1917. From left to right (listed back to front) are Lora, Harold, and Mildred Gates; Gertrude, Harry, and Ralph Gates; Gertrude, Clarence, and Evelyn Iske; Mildred, Ben, and Ruth Whitted; Inez, Leo, and Dorothy Hood; Mayme, Henry, and Marjorie Rosencrans; Anna, Paul, and Ralph Duel; and Marie, Fred, and Marion Gates. (Courtesy Iske Family.)

Augustine H. Hood, his wife, and one of their three sons, possibly Thomas, pose in the parlor together for a family portrait. Tragedy would strike in 1933 when 49-year-old son Leo took his own life rather than face continuing poor health. As sworn in by his certificate of election, Augustine served as an elected justice of the peace for Bellevue as early as November 1896 until 1919, if not later. As justice of the peace, he would have been able to officiate marriages, mediate low-level conflicts, and serve in a constabulary fashion. The Hood family could trace their linage all the way back to Thomas Hood, born in 1455. Augustine himself was born in 1850.

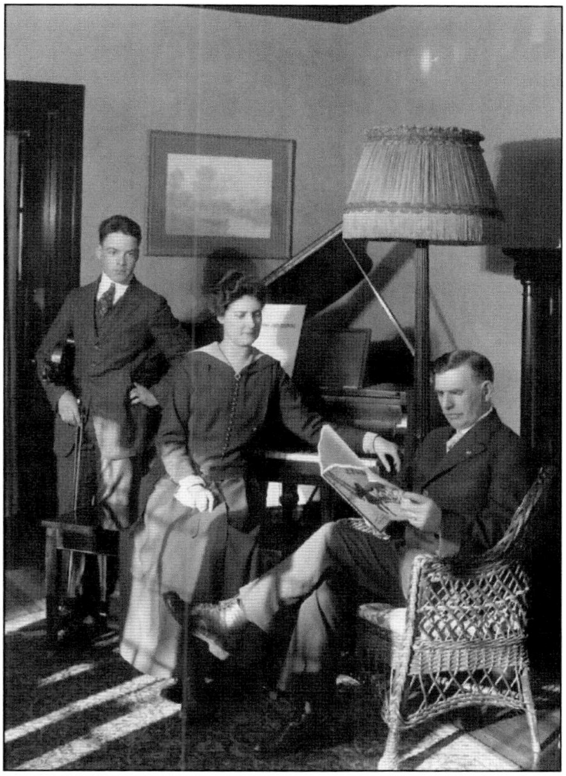

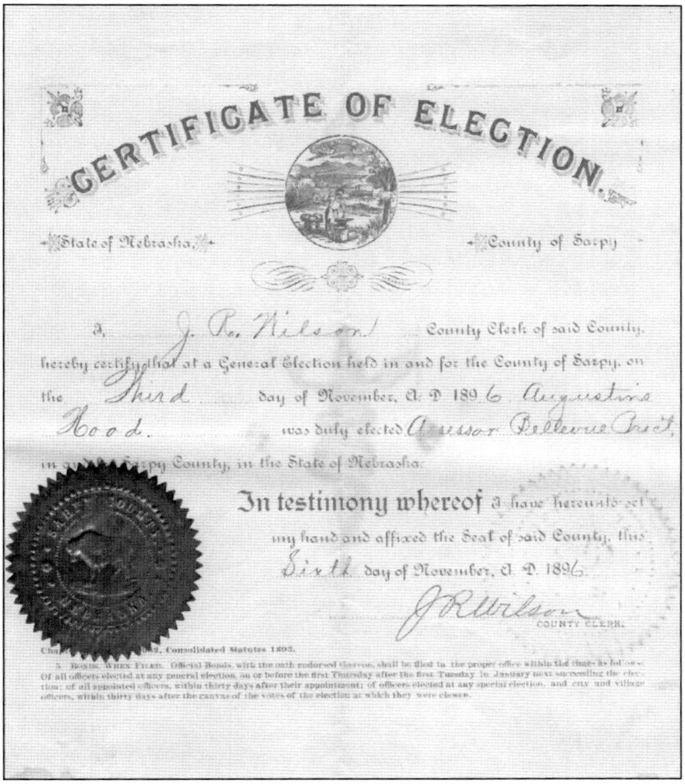

CERTIFICATE OF ELECTION.

State of Nebraska, County of Sarpy

I, J. R. Wilson County Clerk of said County, hereby certify that at a General Election held in and for the County of Sarpy, on the Third day of November, A. D. 1896 Augustine Hood. was duly elected Assessor Bellevue Prect, in and for Sarpy County, in the State of Nebraska.

In testimony whereof I have hereunto set my hand and affixed the Seal of said County, this Sixth day of November, A. D. 1896.

J R Wilson
COUNTY CLERK.

Consolidated Statutes 1893.

5. BONDS, WHEN FILED. Official Bonds, with the oath endorsed thereon, shall be filed in the proper office within the times as follows: Of all officers elected at any general election, on or before the first Thursday after the first Tuesday in January next succeeding the election; of all appointed officers, within thirty days after their appointment; of officers elected at any special election, and city and village officers, within thirty days after the canvass of the votes of the election at which they were chosen.

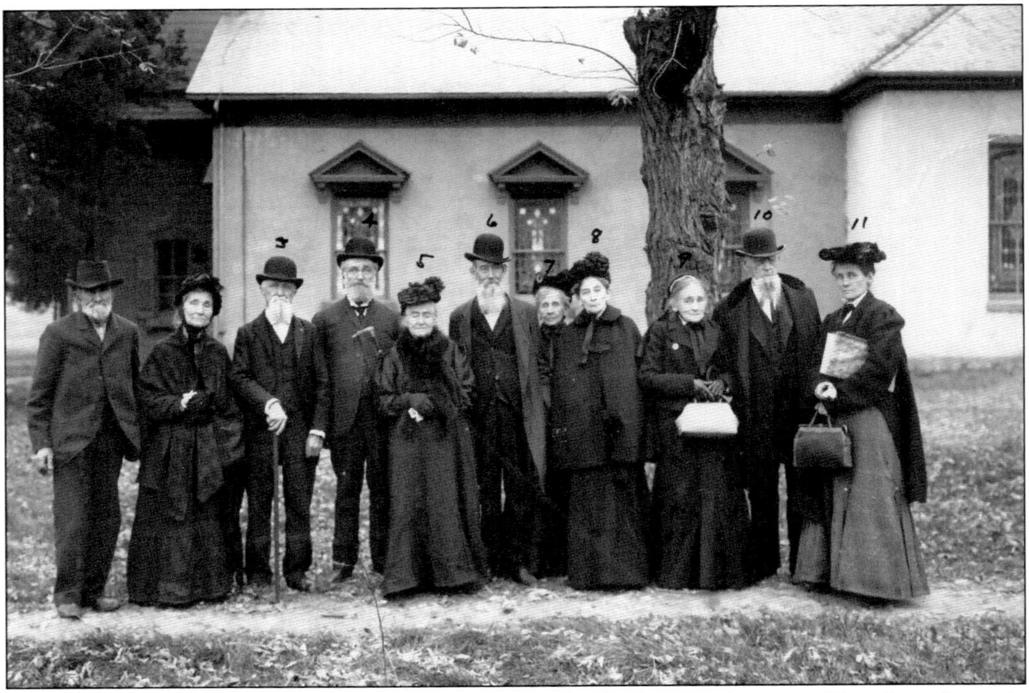

Bellevue pioneers gather for a group photograph outside the First Presbyterian Church in the early 1900s. These were some of the first residents of Bellevue. They are, from left to right, Dr. Joseph and Helen Betz, John Q. Goss, Henry T. Clarke, Mrs. Slightam, George Burtch, Mrs. Leach, Mrs. Chaffee, Mrs. Allen, Judge James Gow, and Mrs. Bradley.

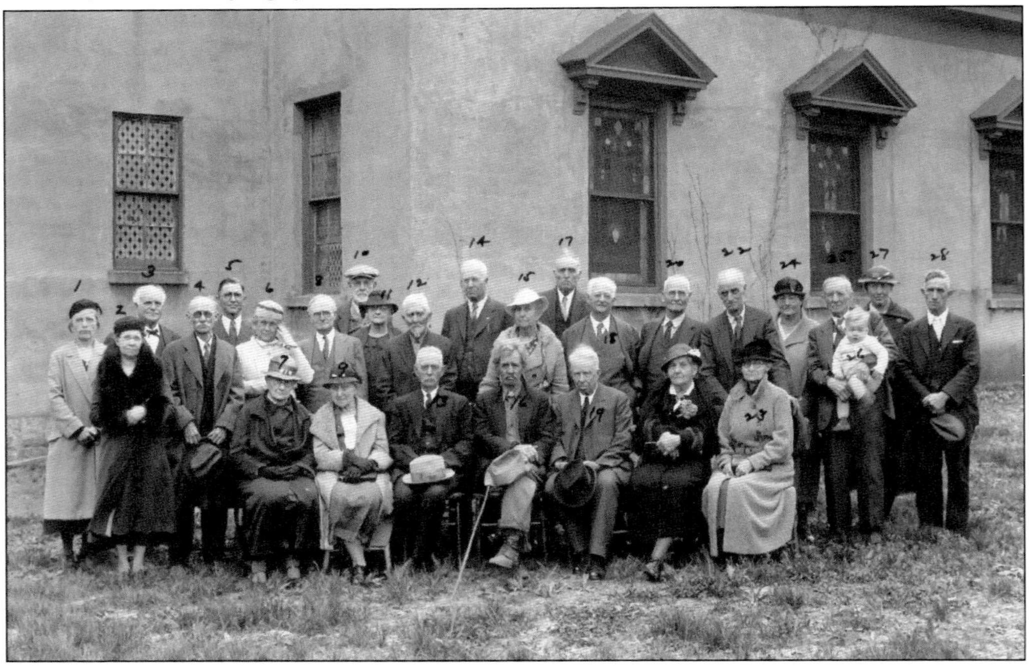

Obviously a popular backdrop, a number of Sarpy County's influential people gather on May 2, 1936, for a group photograph outside the First Presbyterian Church. Bellevue residents include Dr. and Mrs. Robert Gilder, Mr. and Mrs. Gates, Rev. W.D. Stambaugh, and James Gow.

A pair of horses with carriage waits out front of the First Presbyterian Church sometime prior to the 1908 tornado. In 1846, Reverend McKinney arrived in Bellevue to serve as the first overseer of the mission that Father Hamilton would later supervise. On December 26, 1850, McKinney met with five others to form the first congregation. Eight years later in 1858, the oldest church in Nebraska would be completed.

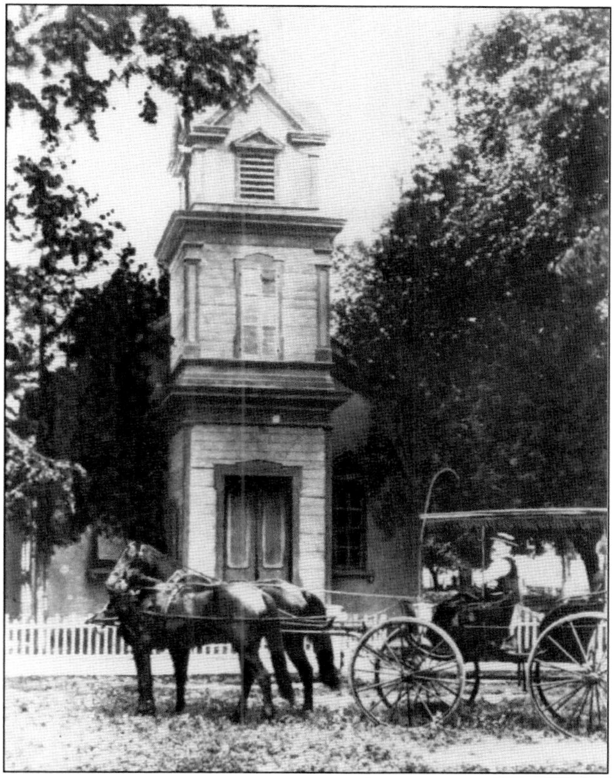

Men, women, and children exit the old First Presbyterian Church into the Nebraska wind during Mother's Day on May 10, 1953. Minister Phelps addressed them with the message of the day, "honor thy mother." Near the end of the assembly, all mothers received corsages presented by the Mariners Club. (Courtesy First Presbyterian Church)

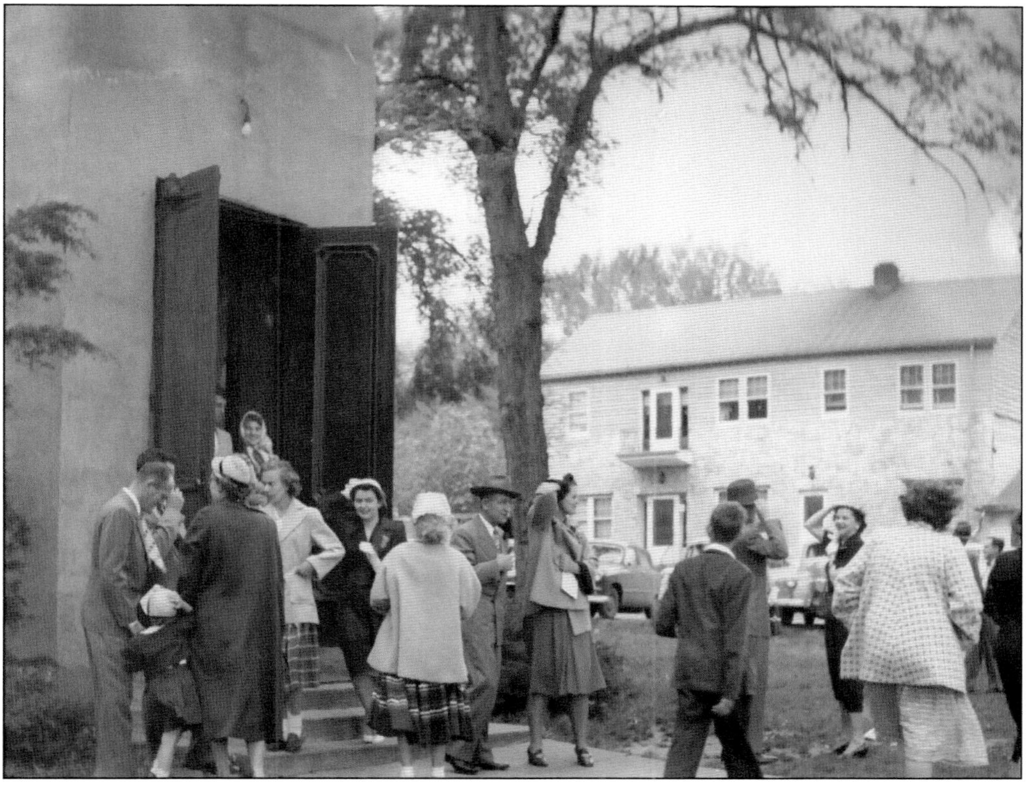

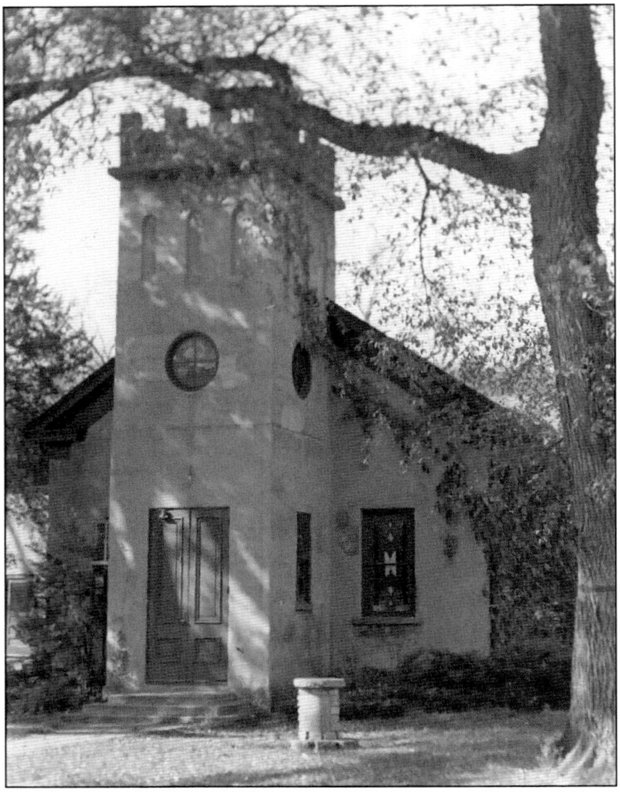

The small church of 100-plus years had served its congregation well during the Great Depression and two world wars, but by the mid-20th century, it was determined that a new church would be needed to meet the needs of the future congregation. Exactly 100 years after the completion of the old church, work began on a new church located on Bellevue Boulevard.

On September 7, 1958, several months after the ground breaking, the cornerstone of the new church was laid. Rev. S.A. Hanke led a dedication service that included reading *Ephesians 2:20.* In attendance were Bellevue architect and church member Willis Regier; Joseph Morgan, chairman of the finance committee; and Hugh Campbell, chairman of the building committee. (Courtesy First Presbyterian Church)

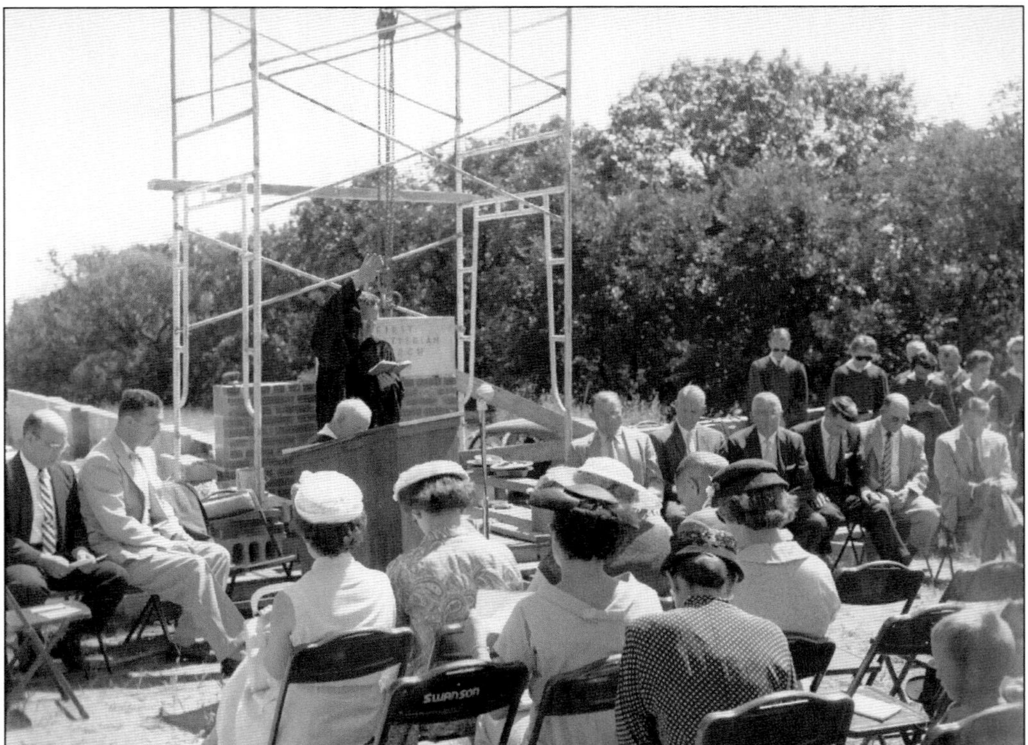

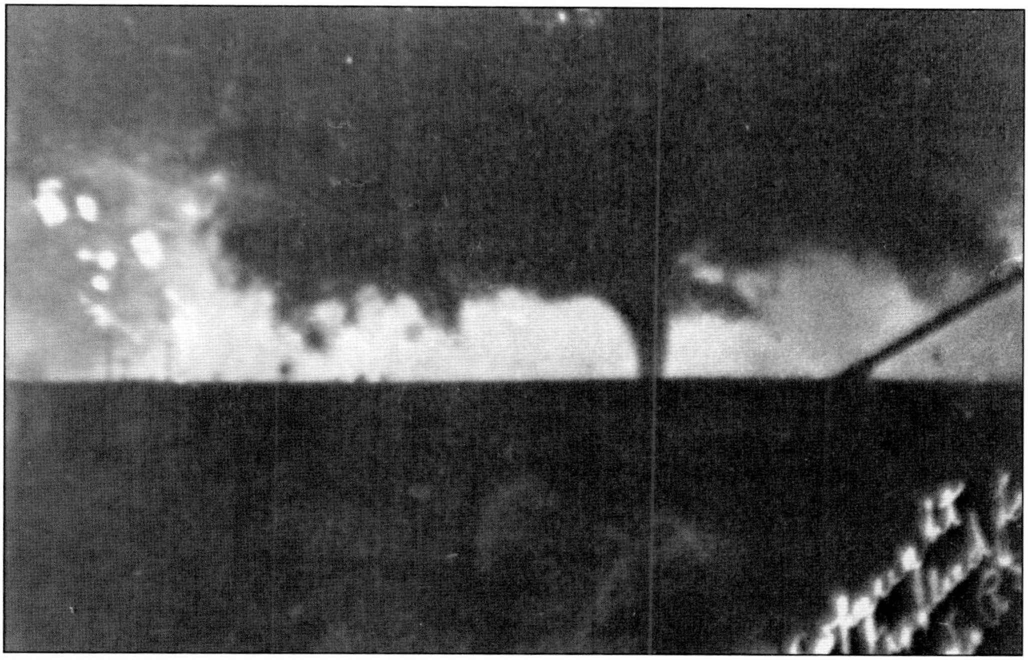

Given the camera technology at the time, this photograph of the May 12, 1908, tornado is especially unique. The tornado touched down in Bellevue in the afternoon as many residents were going about their day. Many of the students from Bellevue College had gathered to watch a baseball game. It wasn't long though before the skies darkened and the weather changed.

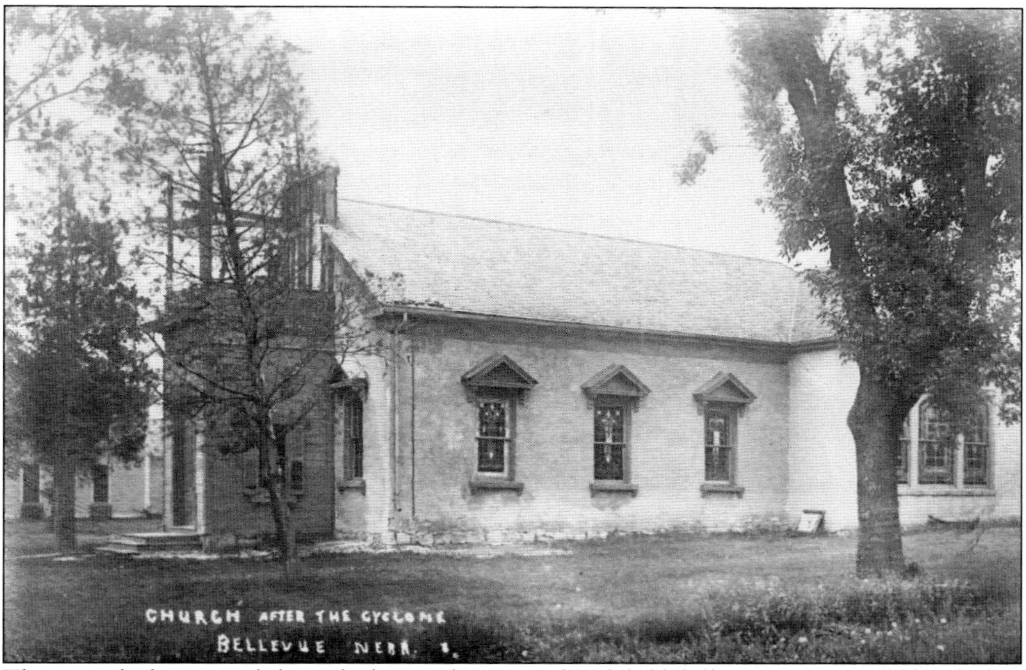

The tornado first ripped through the nearby town of Richfield, killing an 11-year-old boy before mortally wounding Bellevue resident Edward Miller. Windows were shattered at the college, the roof of Clarke Hall was ripped off, homes and barns were flipped on their sides, and the steeple of the Presbyterian church was torn off.

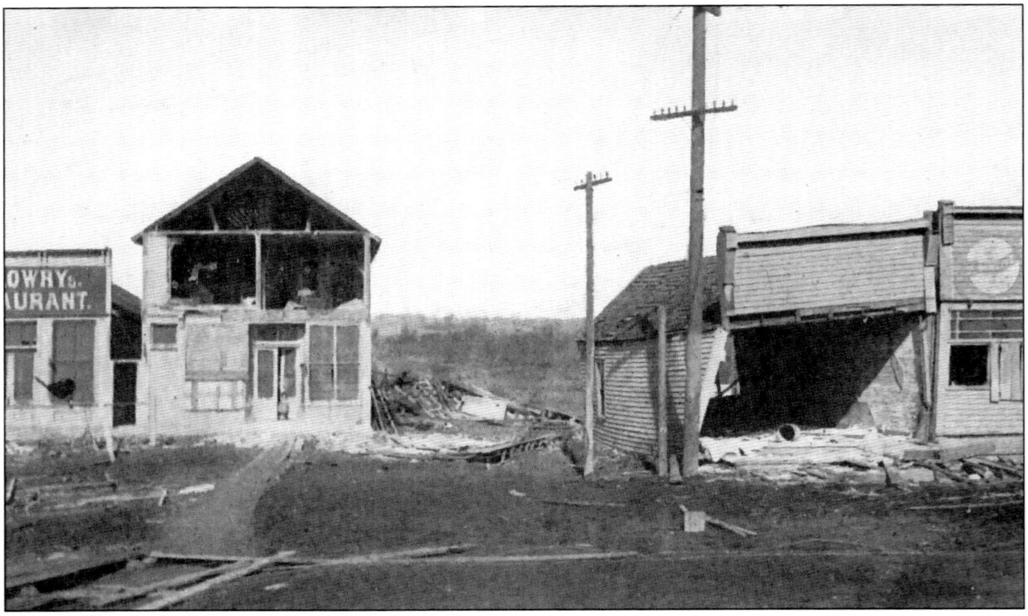

The town of Fort Crook suffered extensive damage, and as a result, some structures such as the town hotel lost their entire front facade. The actual fort suffered further damage at a loss valued at $80,000. Although the damage to the buildings was severe, there were no deaths and not even a single reported injury.

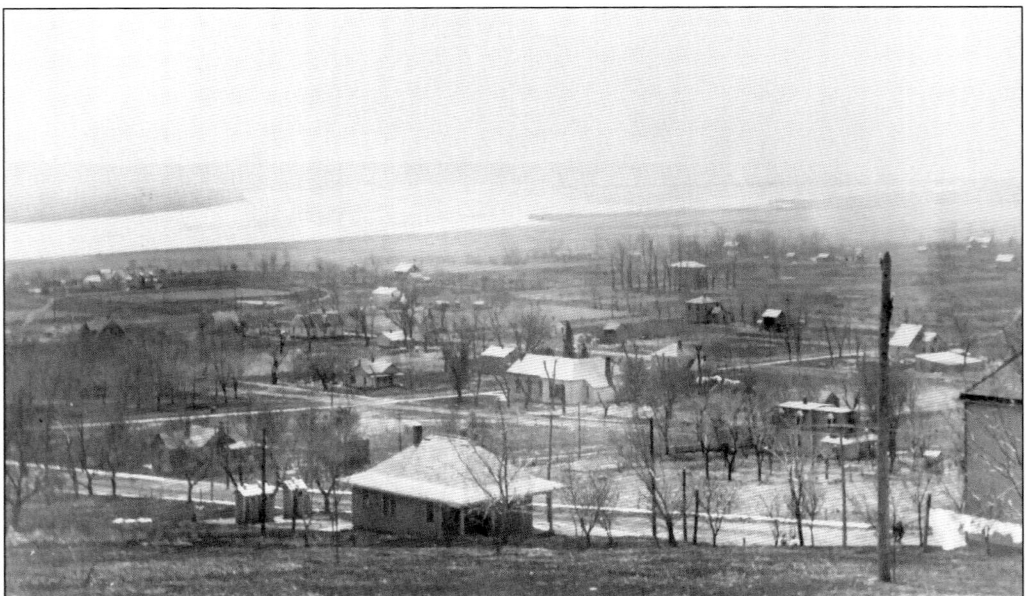

Bellevue looks small, cold, and deserted in this panoramic photograph taken from Elk Hill, depicting a common unfriendly Nebraska winter scene. In all likelihood, this was taken during the winter of 1908, as indicated by the lack of a steeple on the church. In the foreground is the Omaha and Southern interurban depot.

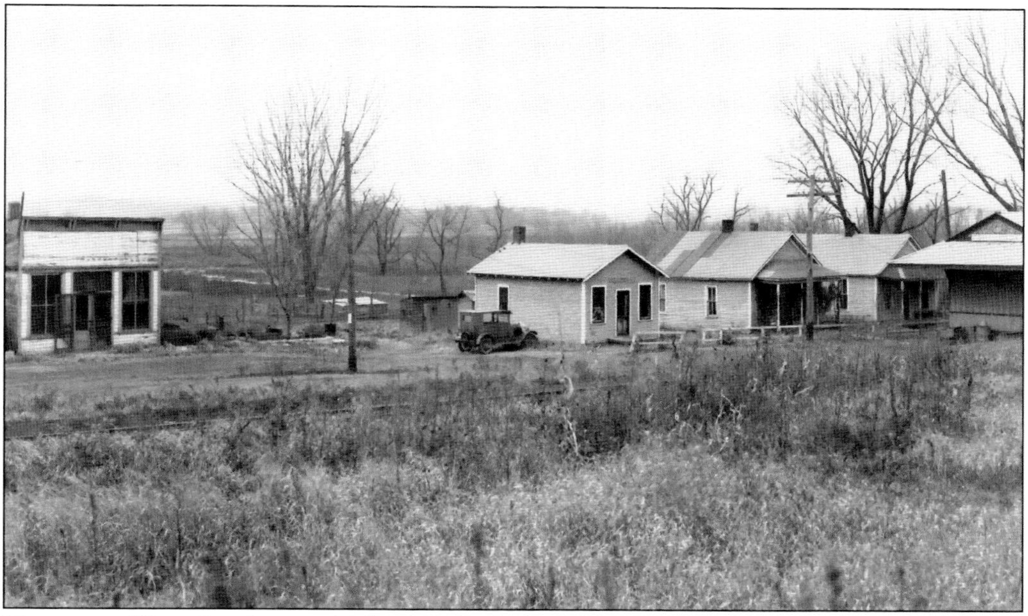

The town of Fort Crook is not Nebraska's birthplace; however, it is part of Bellevue today. Now a ghost town, the settlement suffered from five major floods, fires, a tornado, and high taxes that forced the town to fold. At one time, Fort Crook had several restaurants, five taverns, a blacksmith, barbershop, dance hall, and a two-story hotel. Established in 1897 as its own separate entity from both the nearby military installation and Bellevue, it was a fully functional community. But by 1960, the last resident had left and has since passed away, making Fort Crook a true ghost town. (Above, courtesy the Bostwick-Frohardt Collection, owned by KM3TV and on permanent loan to the Durham Museum.)

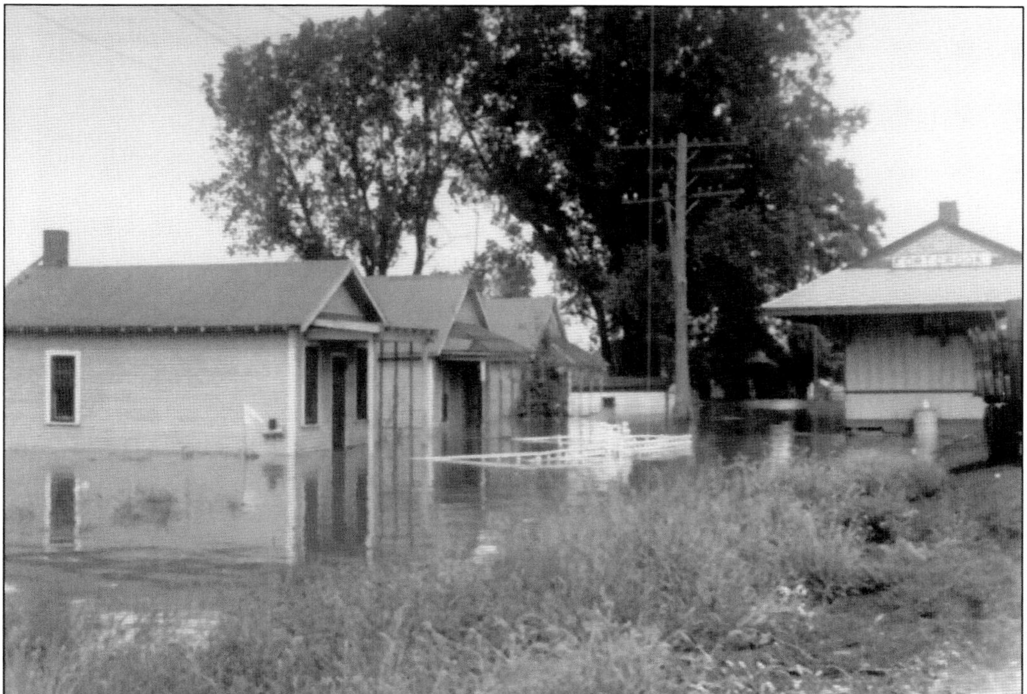

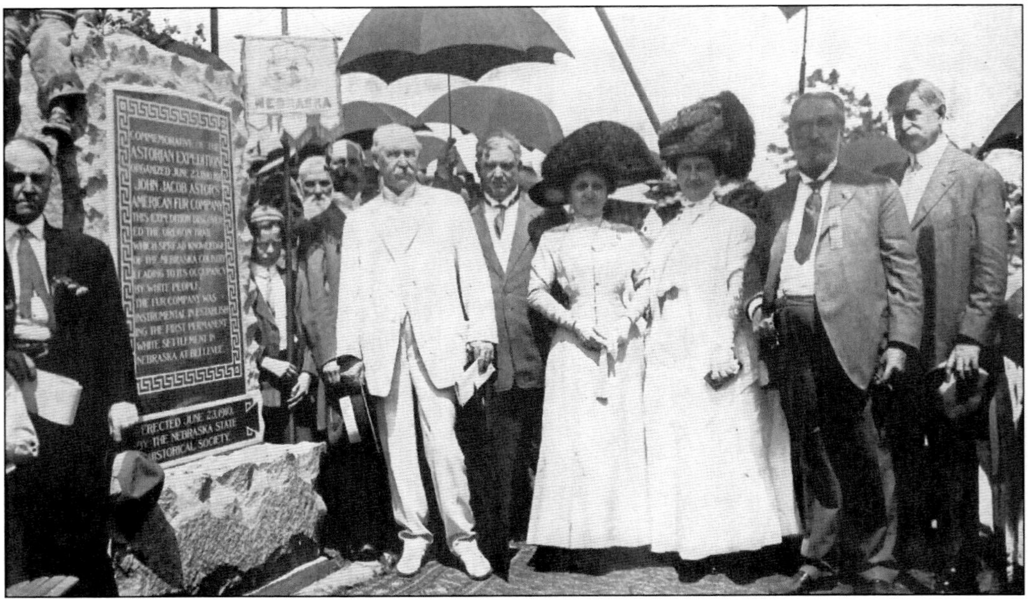

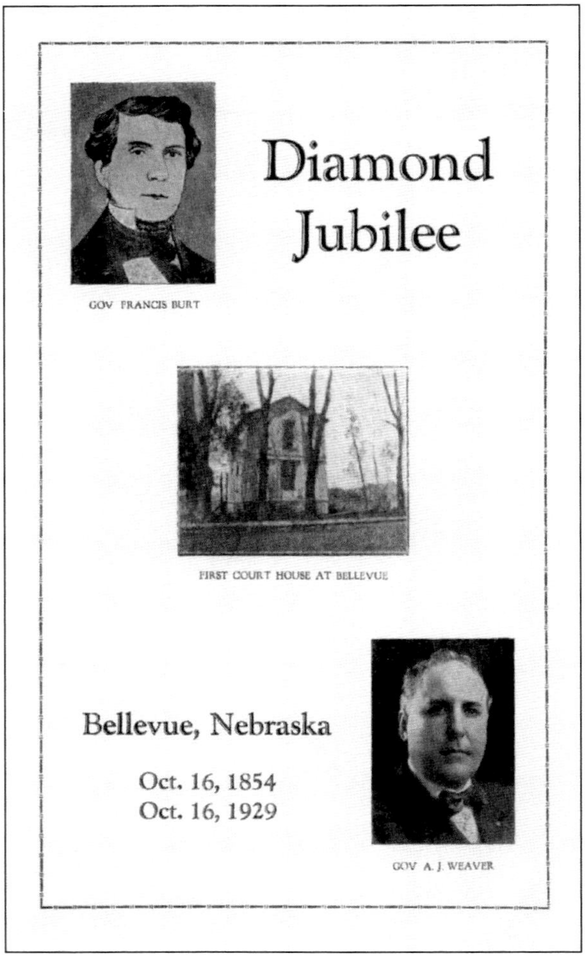

Bellevue has ties to the Astor family, owners of the Pacific Fur Company, which was a partial subsidiary of the American Fur Company, the company Peter Sarpy was originally employed with. On June 23, 1910, a dedication of the Astorian Monument was held with Gov. Ashton C. Shallenberger present. John Lee Webster, the president of the Nebraska Historical Society (in white suit), commemorated the occasion with a historical address. (Courtesy Nebraska State Historical Society.)

The celebration of the diamond jubilee marked 75 years since the inauguration of Francis Burt. In attendance to mark the event was Gov. A.J. Weaver and members of the Nebraska Supreme Court, including Chief Justice Goss, as well as hundreds of onlookers. A true community effort, the event was coordinated by the Bellevue Men's Club, with food provided by the Bellevue Ladies Aid Society and music by the Cardinal Orchestra.

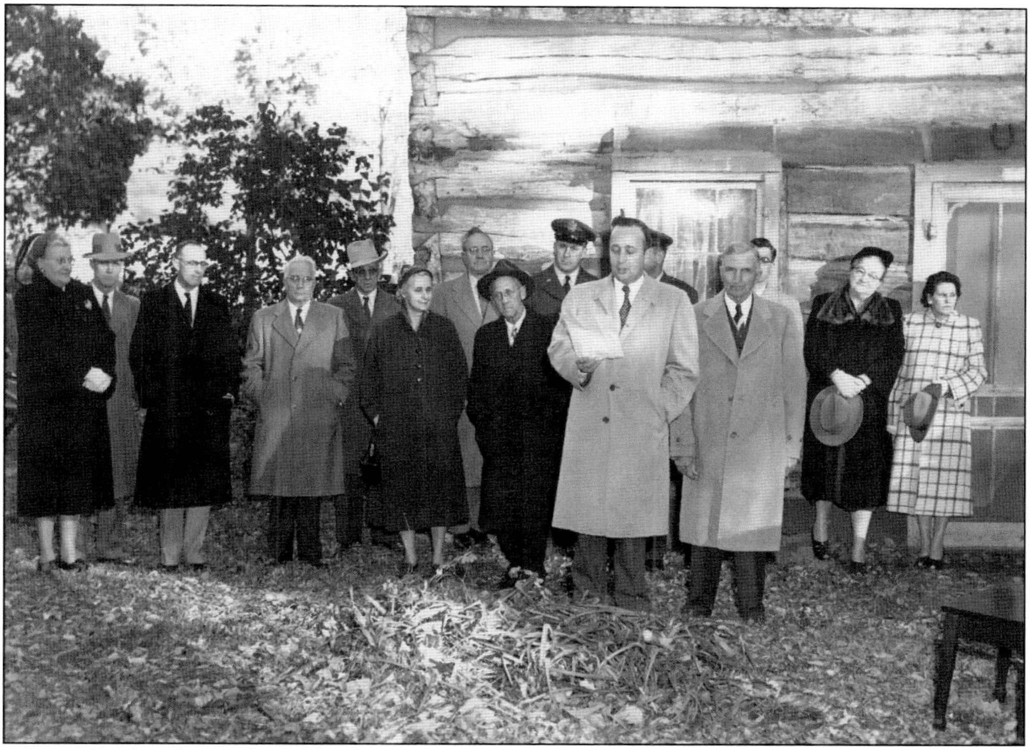

Many of Nebraska's political leaders have recognized the importance of Bellevue within their state. Governor Crosby is one of the many to visit the community, issuing a Thanksgiving proclamation on November 2, 1954, to mark the 100-year anniversary of the first such proclamation. Behind Crosby are members of the Sarpy County Historical Society and Bellevue's log cabin.

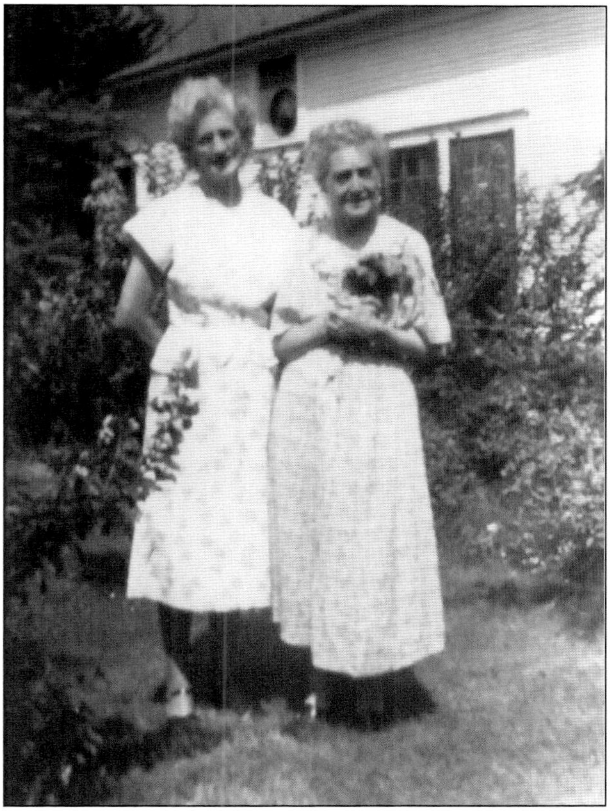

The log cabin has become synonymous with the history of Bellevue. It is said to be not just the oldest building in Bellevue, but also the entire state, dating back to about 1835. Today a historical landmark, the cabin was occupied well into the 1950s by Josephine Mountain, affectionately nicknamed "Grandma Mountain," who lived to be nearly 100 years old. This photograph of her alongside her daughter was taken in 1948.

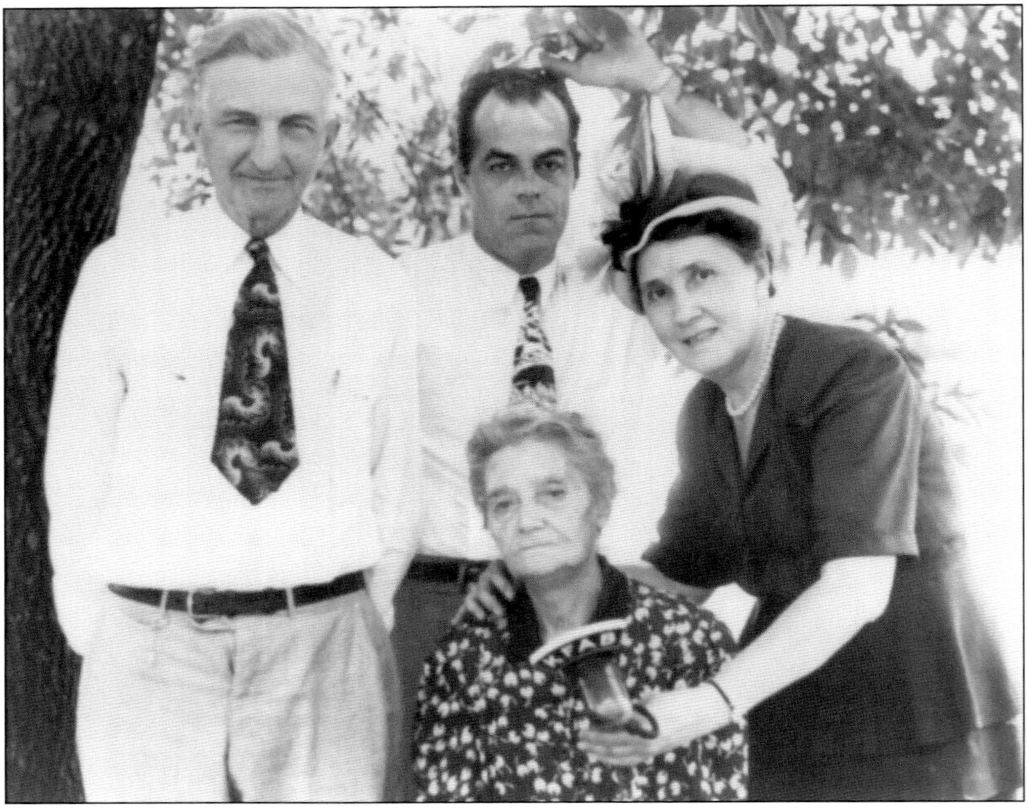

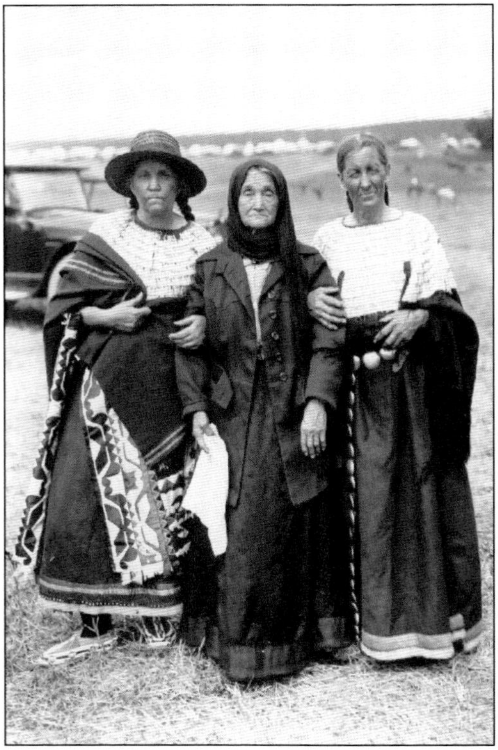

Pictured here with Josephine Mountain (seated) are, from left to right, William Shallcross, John Gebbie, and Ruth Daly Neuhaus of KFAB. Shallcross was Belllevue's local writer and historian. A graduate of the 1900 class of Bellevue College, he was passionate about the history of Bellevue, penning *Romance of a Village* in 1954 in an attempt to document the origins and early history of his community. Other books written by Shallcross include *A Boy's Way of Life* and *The Fallacy of Communism*.

Taken August 21, 1921, a reported 106-year-old Emily Fontenelle, wife of Henry Fontenelle Sr., stands between Mrs. Heneke (left) and Mrs. Hamilton. Henry was the brother of Logan Fontenelle, who was considered the last chief of the Omaha. Initially serving as an official interpreter for the United States in 1858, he would go on to fight for Indian rights, partially with the Ponca in Oklahoma. (Courtesy the Bostwick-Frohardt Collection, owned by KM3TV and on permanent loan to the Durham Museum.)

Cecilia Fawn Nichols resided in the Presbyterian Mission House after it became a private residence. It was once occupied by her grandparents Charles and Harriet McGinley. The McGinley family would own and renovate the house from 1899 until 1942. Pictured here in her youth in 1936, Nichols, an accomplished author, was also a lifelong educator, serving as a public school teacher and civil service instructor with the military.

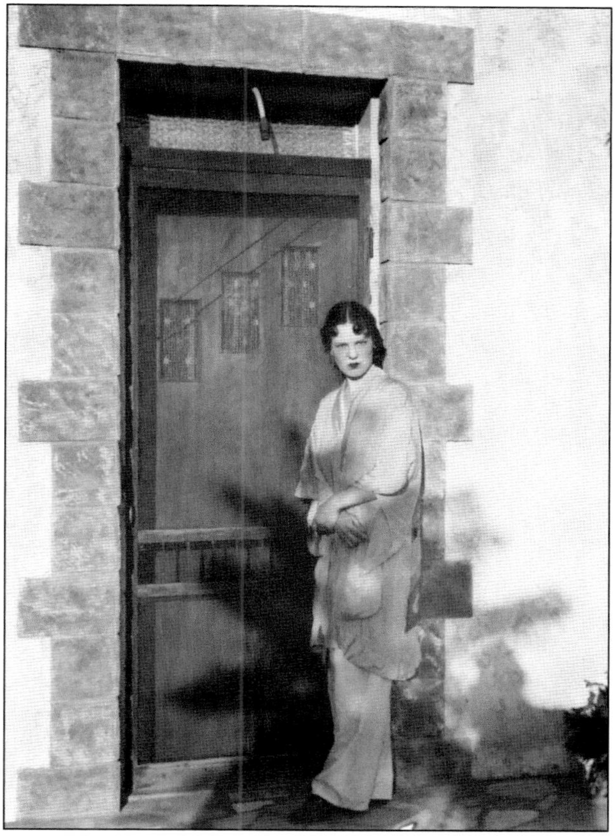

Despite its proximity to Omaha, Bellevue, even during the 1920s, was still a world away from the bustling city. Cattle can be seen grazing in a field as a motorist drives past city hall in the background. At the time this image was captured on June 14, 1924, Bellevue had survived doubts about its extinction. (Nebraska State Historical Society.)

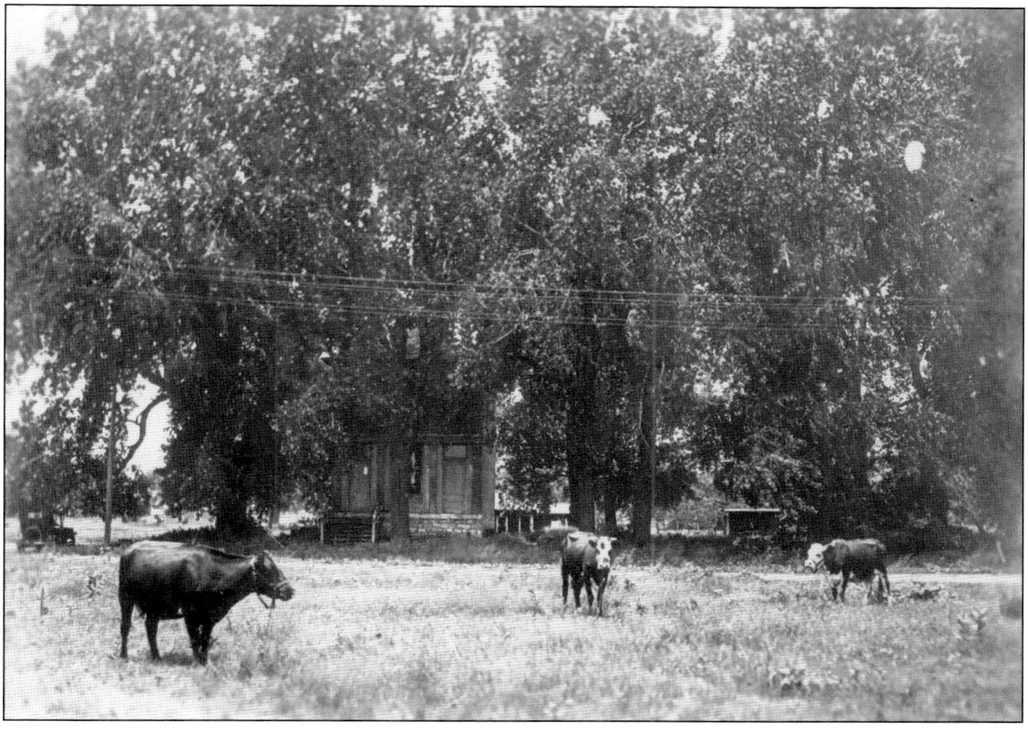

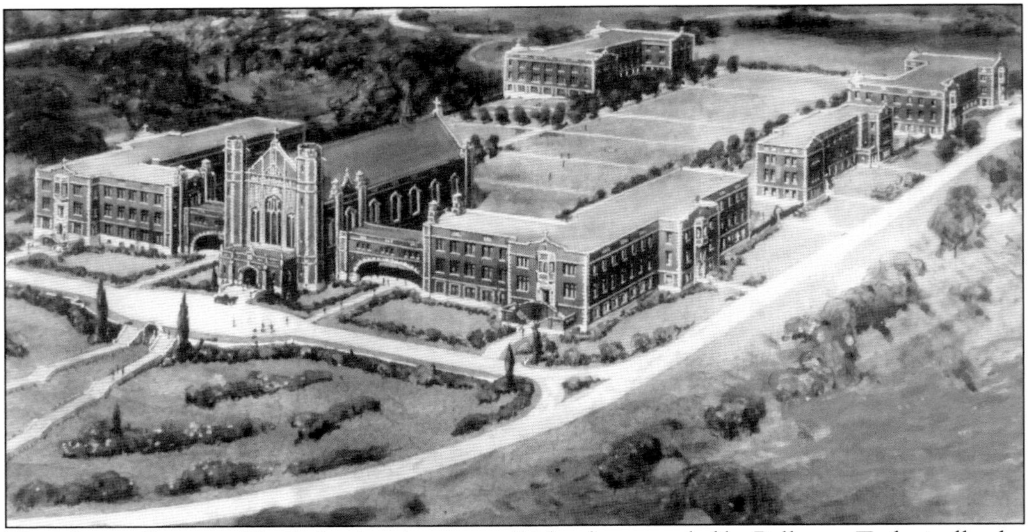

The Mission Society of St. Columban is a tranquil island surrounded by Bellevue. Technically, the headquarters of the Mission Society of St. Columban is a separate entity, complete with its own zip code and post office. Established in 1918, the Columban fathers have served as missionaries throughout much of Latin American and the Far East. While their work has been rewarding, it has occasionally proved dangerous. (Courtesy Paul Hartnett.)

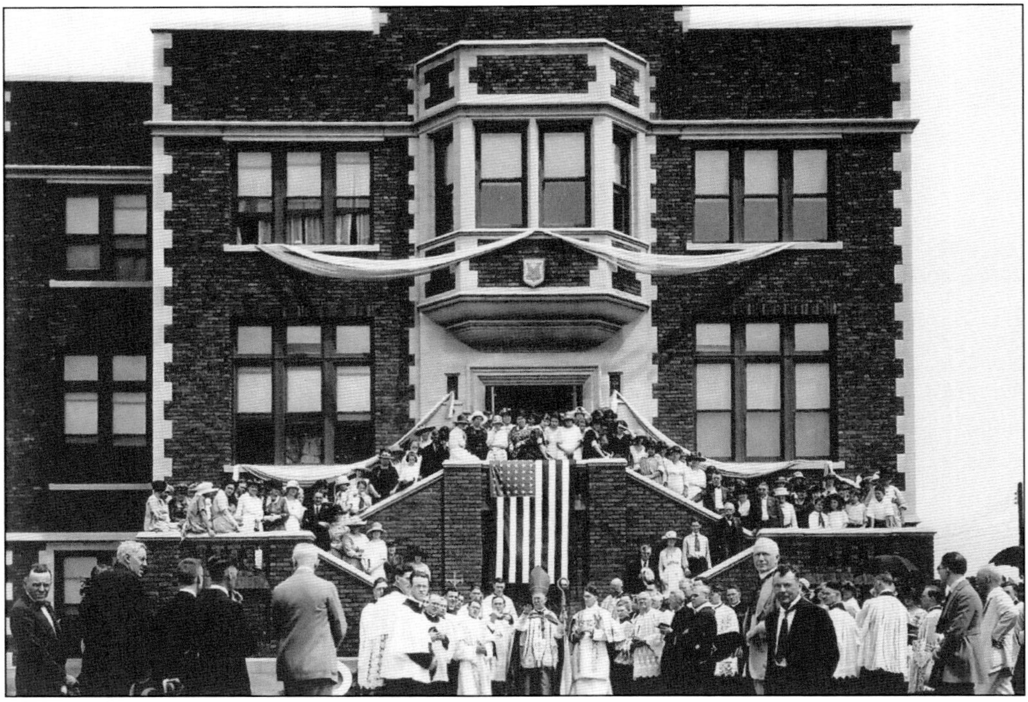

While the previous photograph shows the grand envisioned concept, the actual buildings and grounds were not to be as elaborate. Still, they would continue to serve as the North American headquarters. On September 1, 1921, the cornerstone of the building was laid. Less than a year later, on June 29, 1922, the formal dedication ceremony for the new building took place. (Courtesy Columban Fathers.)

Two Irish priests, Father Edward Galvin (left) and Father John Blowick, were the founders of the Mission Society of St. Columban. Father Blowick devoted his efforts to further organizing the society. In 1920, Father Galvin led the Columban Father missionaries to China. There, they would serve through much turmoil and strife, but remained until 1954, when they were forcibly expelled. Today's Galvin Road was named for Father Galvin. (Courtesy Columban Fathers.)

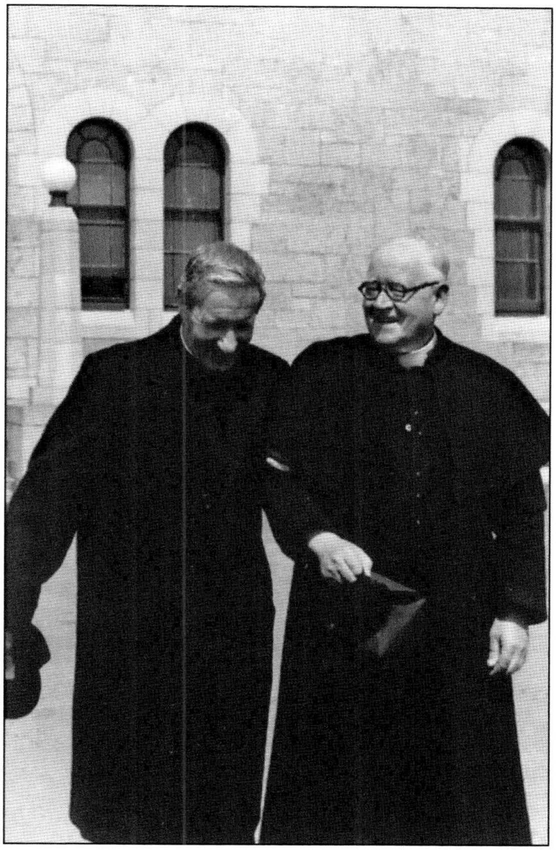

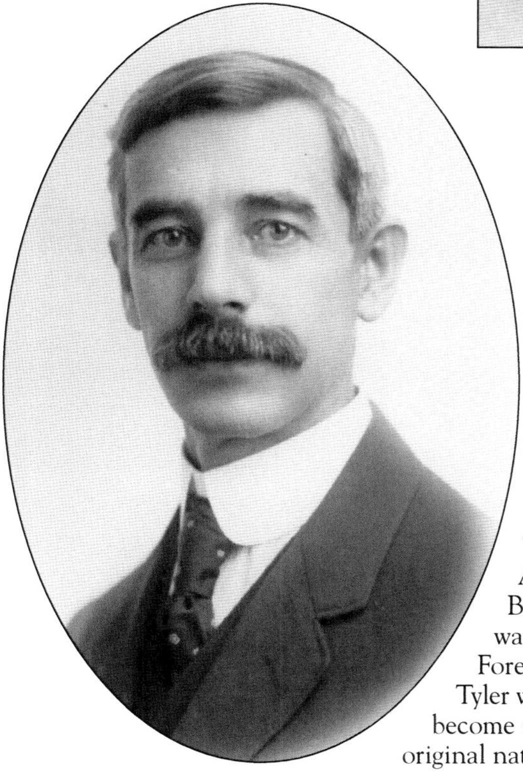

The founder of Fontenelle Forest, Dr. Ansel August Tyler was a professor of biology at Bellevue College and a dedicated naturalist. It was in part through his efforts that the Fontenelle Forest Association could establish itself in 1913. Tyler worked hard to ensure that the forest would not become a campground but would be maintained in its original natural form. (Courtesy FNA.)

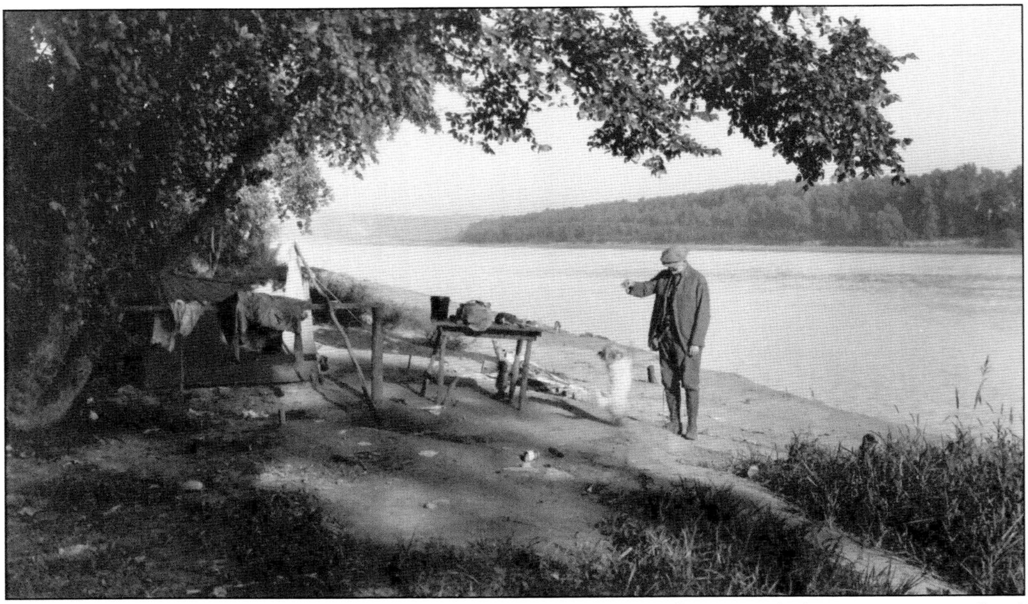

Seen here with Muggings the dog is Dr. Harold Gifford Sr. in about 1925. A prominent medical doctor and philanthropist, Dr. Gifford, along with his heirs, donated about 400 acres of land and monetary gifts to the association. Being very fond of hilltop views, he wanted to share his estate so others would have the opportunity to view the beautiful landscape. (Courtesy FNA.)

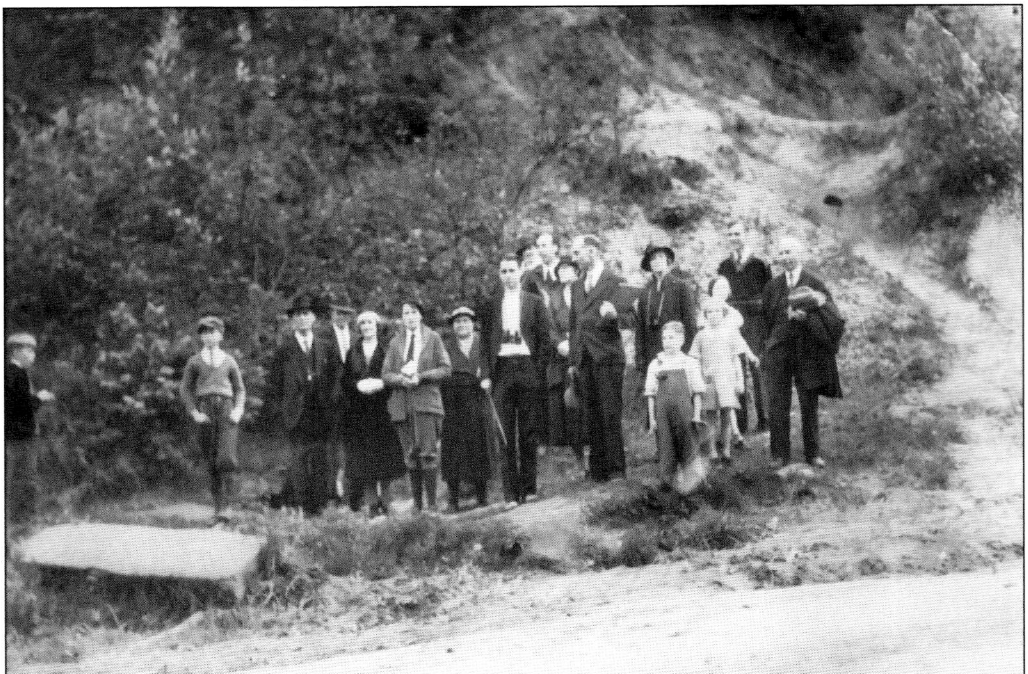

Shown here in 1932, Coffin Springs was the site of a small spring where Pennsylvania Limestone rock that bore resemblance to a coffin was located, hence the name. Known as "the lady in the coffin," the rock featured in the photograph was actually made of cement by Camp Gifford Boy Scouts. The elaborate slab was built with a face and contained a water pipe protruding from its mouth. (Courtesy FNA.)

Looking rather disheveled, Jim the Hermit became something of a local legend within the community. Bellevue resident Jim Baldwin was once a clean-shaven, tough-looking young man before he retreated from society to become a recluse. Upon returning from his service in World War I, Baldwin moved into a shanty-cave home in nearby Fontenelle Forest.

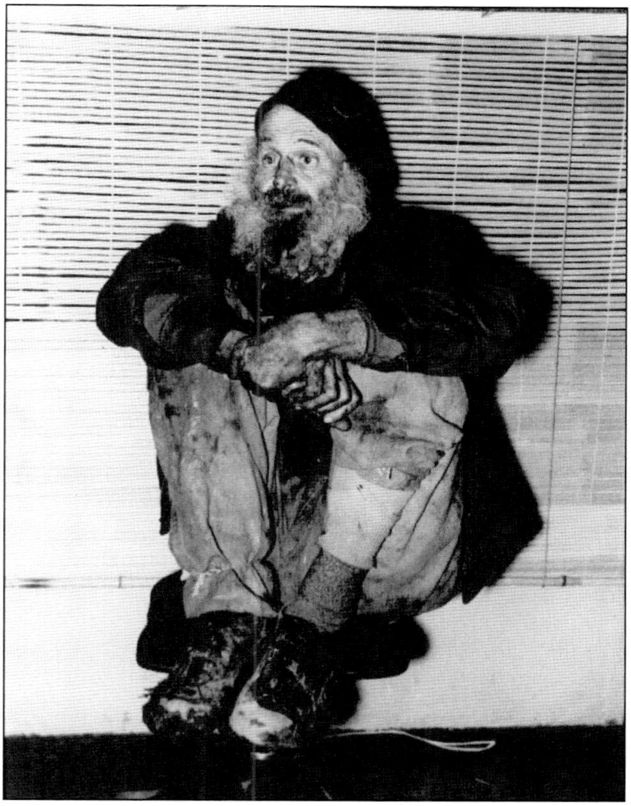

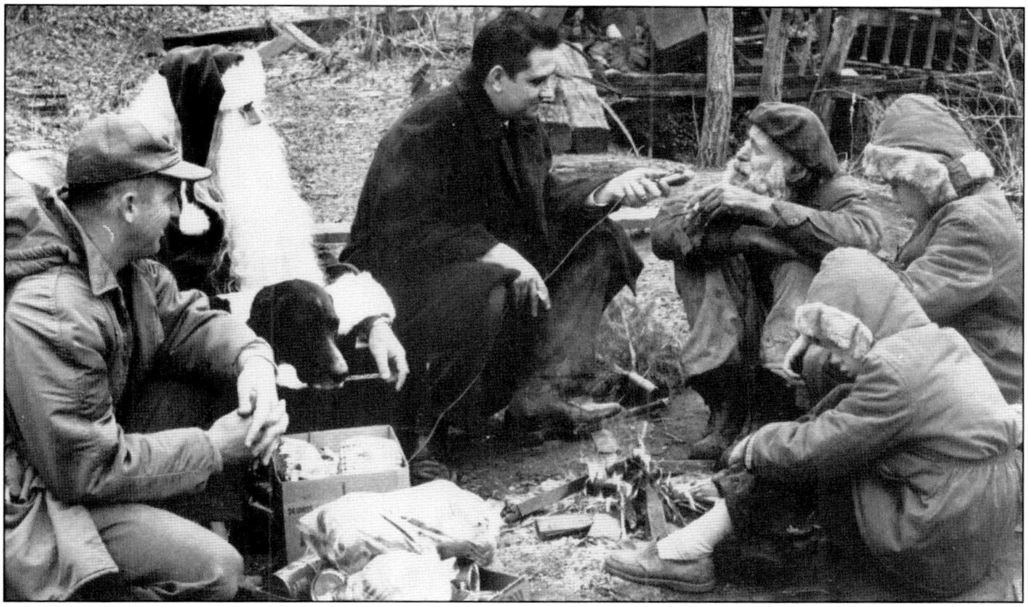

Despite his eccentric lifestyle, Jim Baldwin was mostly well received by the rest of society. Nebraska winters could be especially tough, especially once Baldwin got older and had to rely on the occasional supplies donated to him. In addition to the humanitarian aid, he often had visits from local curiosity-seekers who wanted to hear his tall tales. One year, even Santa Claus, played by Bob Roberts, dropped in to visit.

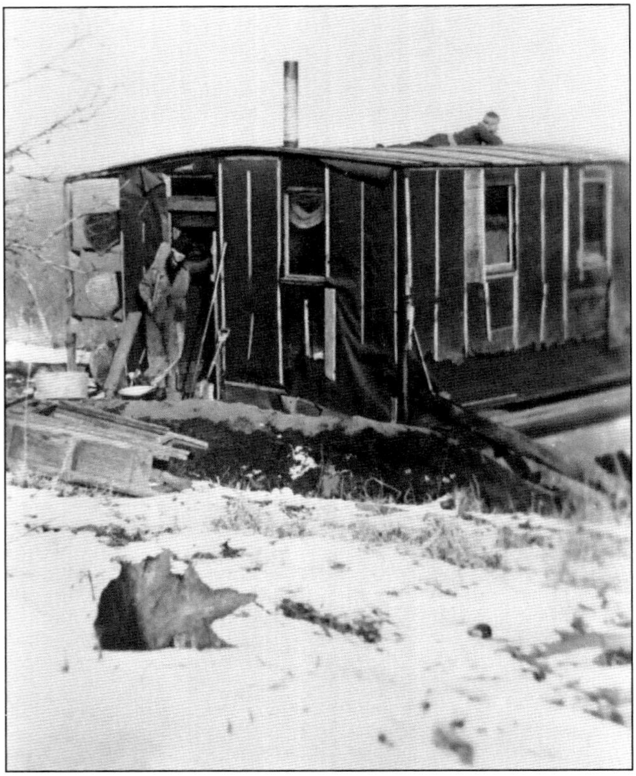

Taken by photographer Bill Koons, this early image shows Jim Baldwin's forest mansion. A layer of tarpaper provided minimal insulation from the elements. The shack was built on concrete piers in the front and was supported by wood pilings in the back. While the shack is gone, the concrete still exists. (Courtesy FNA.)

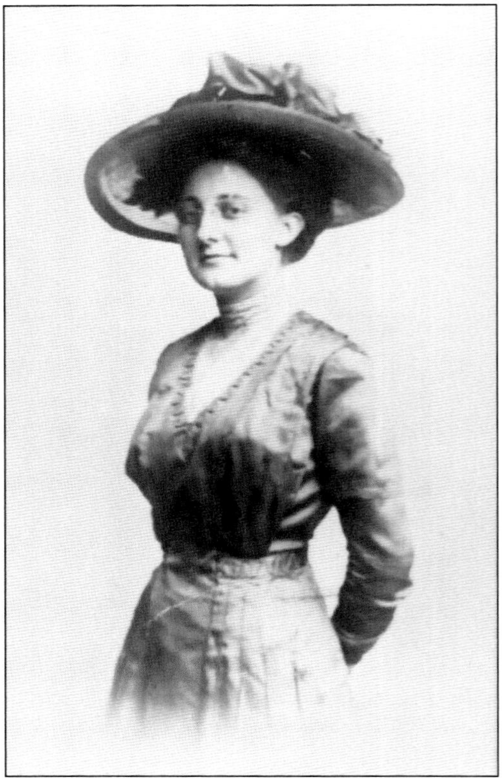

Known as the "Donut Lady," Bessie Morgan made sugary treats to sell to customers who visited Fontenelle Forest, such as Boy Scouts and members of the Omaha Walking Club. She was best known for her potato donut, which sold for 30¢ per dozen. Morgan lived and worked with her family out of a cabin in the woods provided by Dr. Gifford until her death in 1930. (Courtesy FNA.)

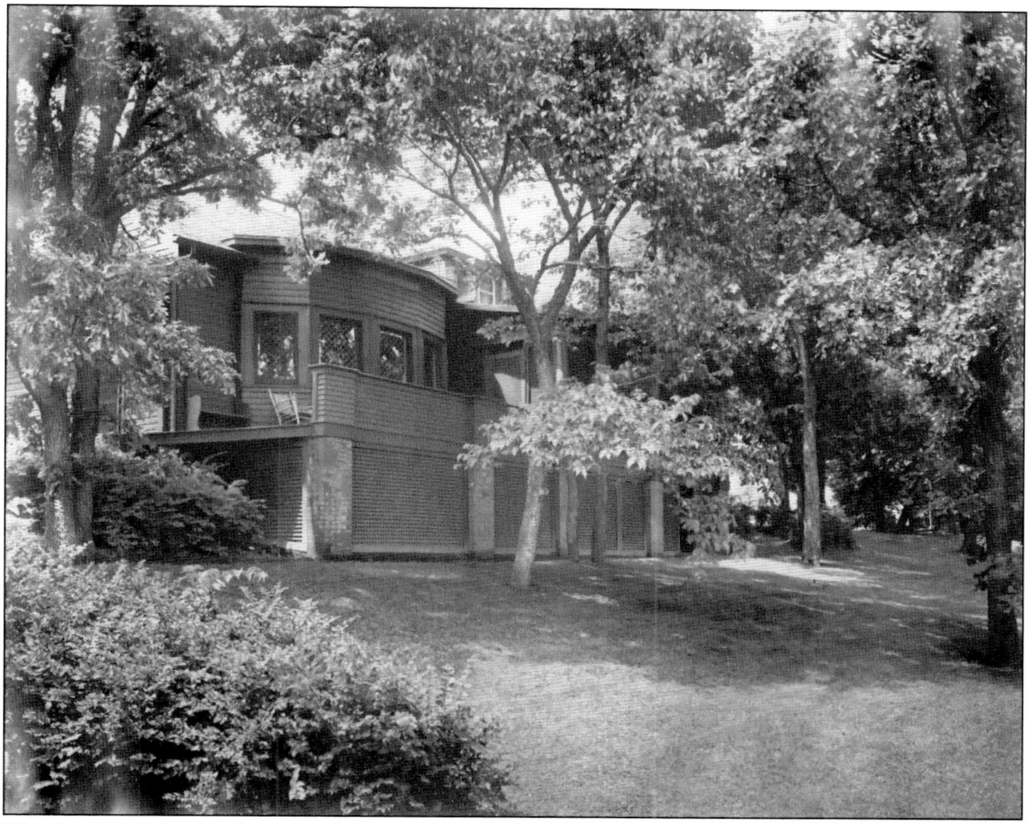

Charles Childs's son, Lowrie, along with his wife, Hortense, and their son, resided at Maxwellton, a spacious estate near present-day Fontenelle Nature Center. The Childs family eventually left Nebraska in 1918, relocating to Troy, New York, once Charles had passed away and his financial matters were settled. Two of Charles's daughters from a prior marriage remained in Omaha. (Courtesy FNA.)

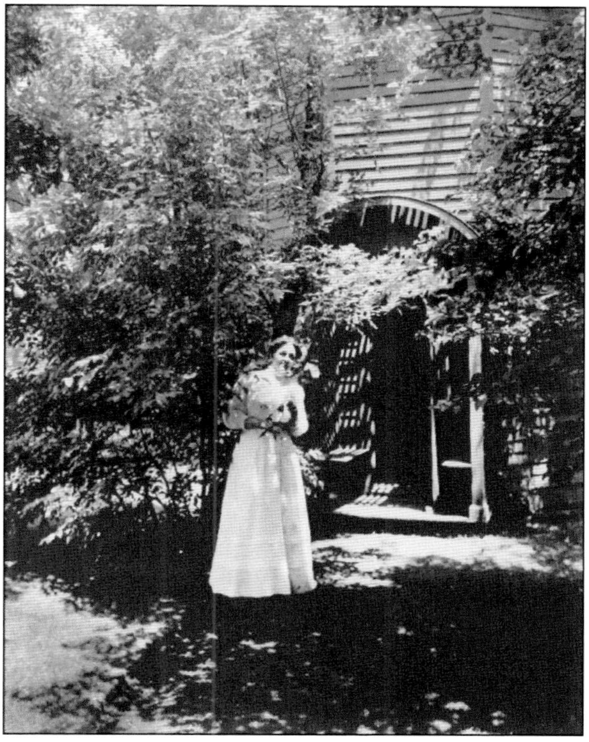

Hortense Childs, wife of Lowrie Childs, could often be found in the gardens. In this c. 1909 photograph, she is in front of the water tower at Maxwellton. The property had a well-manicured garden that was prominent enough to be featured in the March 1910 issue of *Country Life in America.* (Courtesy FNA.)

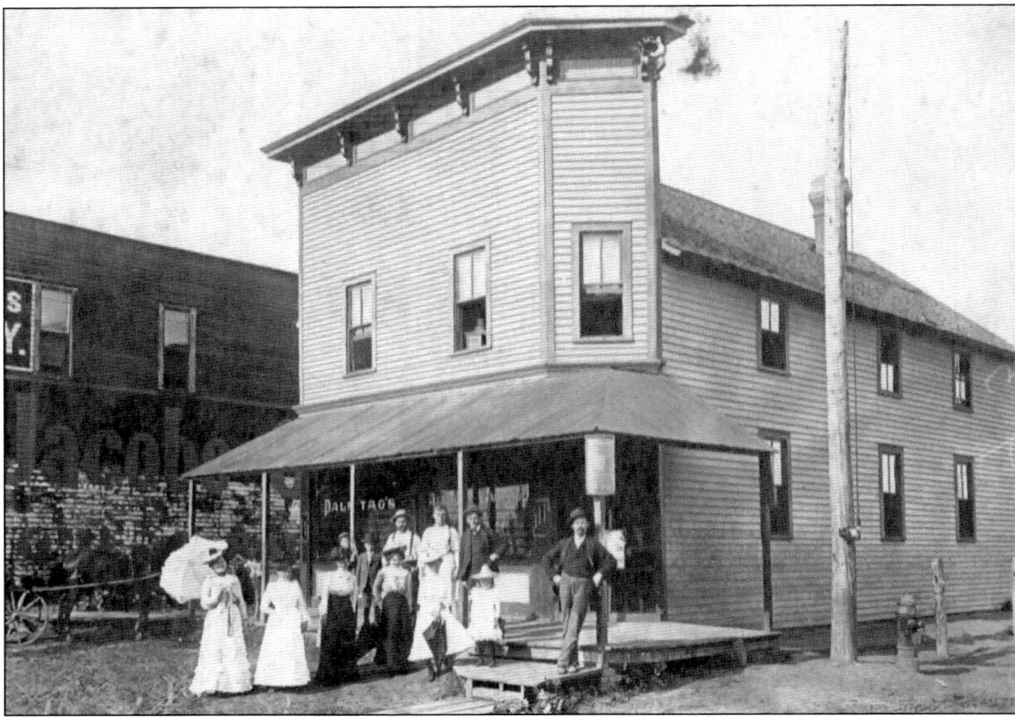

Bellevue has never had a centrally located downtown business district. During the early 20th century, a cluster of buildings near 19th Avenue and Main Street consisted of the telephone exchange, a Red and White grocery store, and later, a lumberyard. While the women could stroll with their parasols, they were not immune to the dirt roads. In some areas of town, as seen here, wooden planks served as sidewalks. (Courtesy Mary Stroud.)

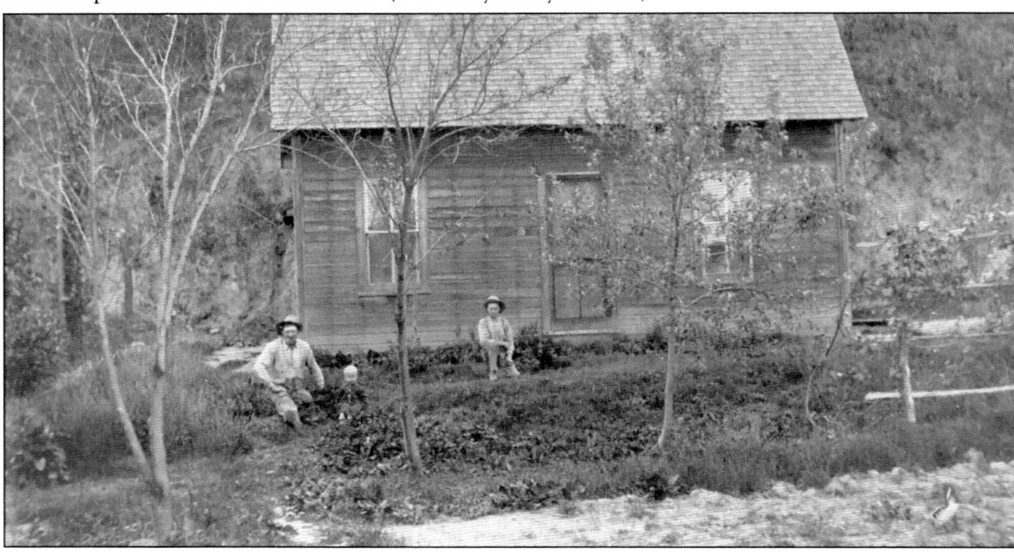

The Beckstead family log cabin would today sit near Front Street, not far from the Missouri River. In front of the cabin are Frank Vannornam and two children. Adeline Cayou was romantically involved with outlaw Jules Beni before his demise, and after her relocation to Bellevue, she married William Beckstead. Following William's death, she married his brother Elton, an employee of Peter Sarpy's trading post. (Courtesy Mary Stroud.)

St. Mary's Catholic Church already had a beautiful building dating from the 1920s, but with Bellevue's wide growth, the structure was too small by 1956. Ground broke in June of that year for the new 520-seat church. Marble from Portugal was imported, as were stained glass windows from France. Today, the original is still used for offices and meeting space. (Courtesy St. Mary Catholic Church.)

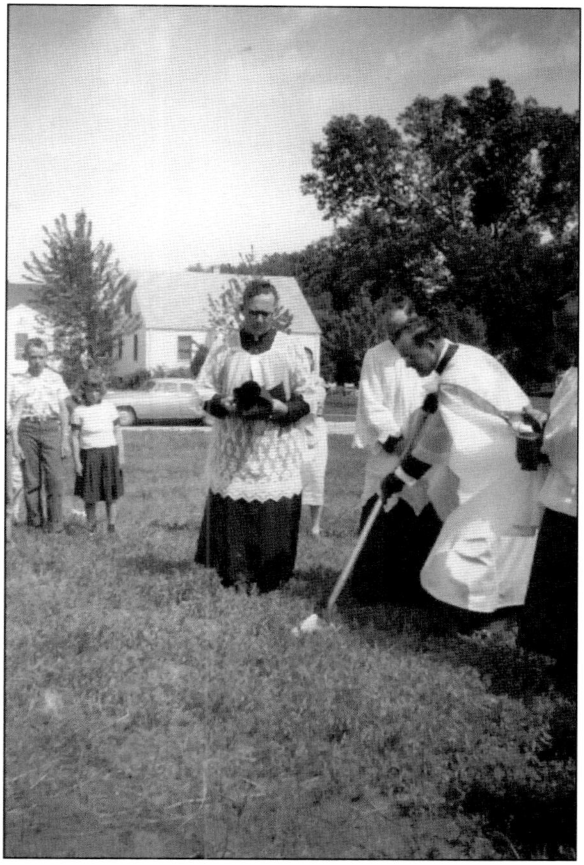

John W. Peters came to Bellevue in 1856. In 1903, the 77-year-old farmer lived in the home seen here. In an interview with the *Omaha Daily News Magazine* from September 12, 1915, Peters told the reporter, "Air, lad, air. I have traveled in 16 states. Never have I found elsewhere such air as we enjoy in this spot, Bellevue."

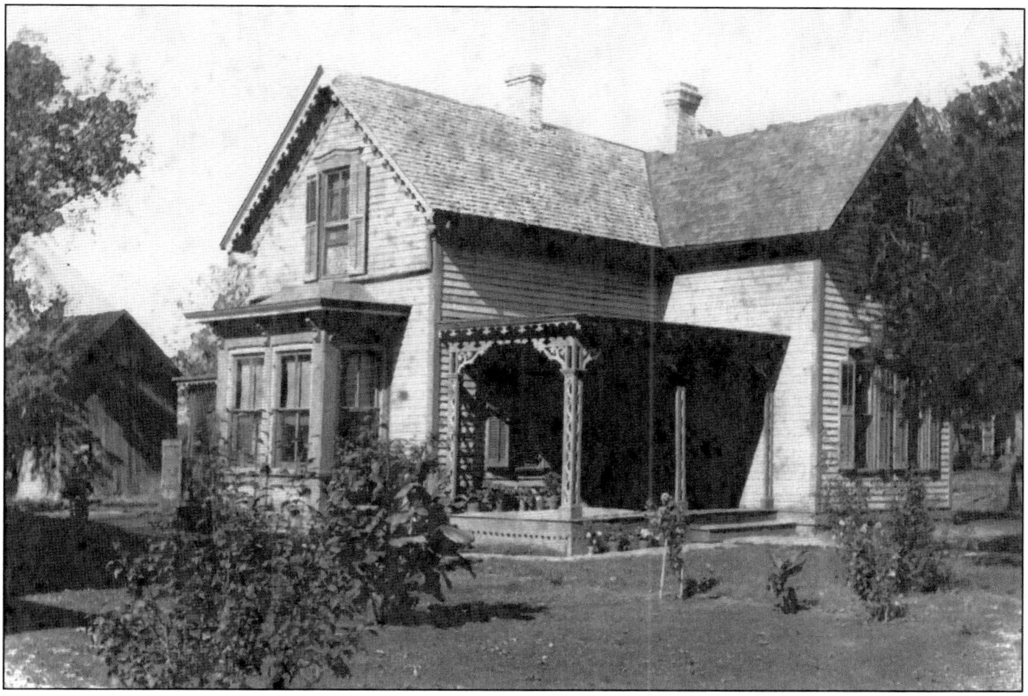

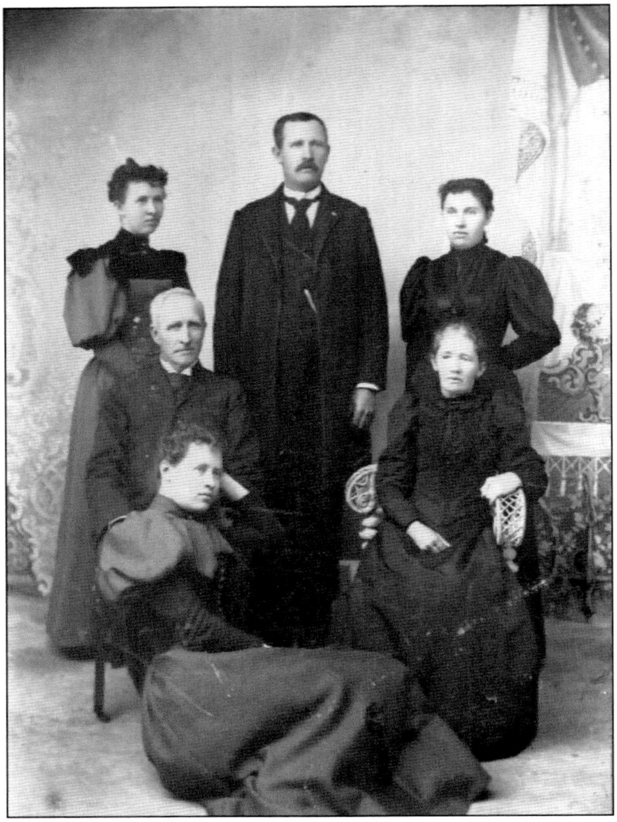

Zalmon and Rose Storrs (seated, second row) arrived in Bellevue in 1897 after a stint in Wisconsin. Zalmon was a skilled carpenter who would help construct the pews in the Presbyterian church. Their land, the same land the Sarpy County Museum sits on today, was purchased from the Stouffer family. Zalmon and Rose's daughter taught school in Bellevue for 30 years. (Courtesy Harriet Sullivan.)

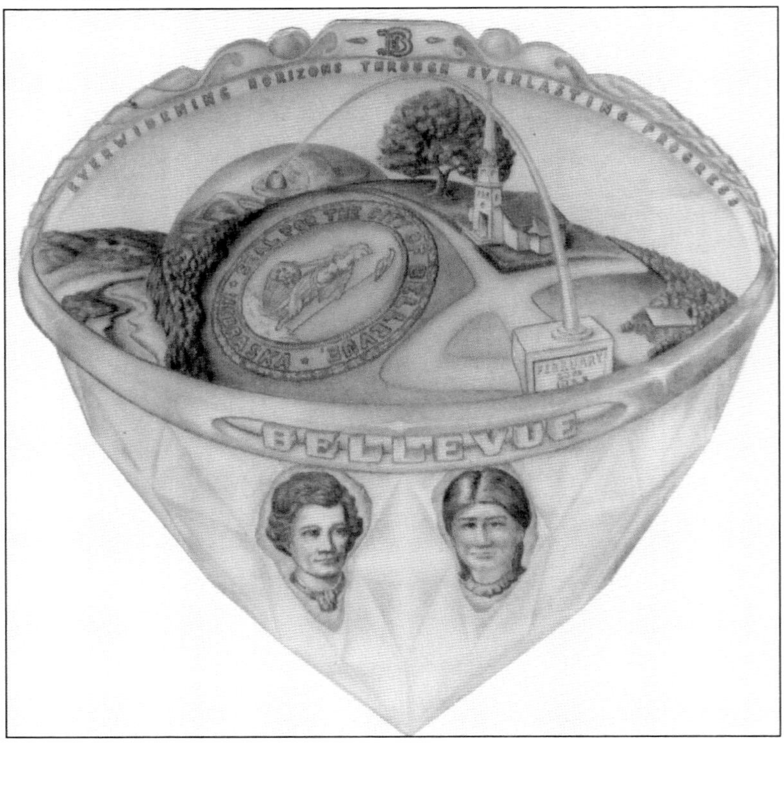

The legend of Peter Sarpy's diamond was, is, and always will be lore, not history, conjured up by J. Sterling Morton. The yarn spoke of Bellevue's progression to become a great city and required that the diamond be passed down and worn by each generation. The only problem was that there never was a diamond. In recent times, the jewel of Bellevue has been awarded to an outstanding citizen.

Three

On the Move

Since the beginning, Bellevue has had a connection to transportation. Influential in westward expansion, the community served as one of the gateways to the west during the years of Manifest Destiny as the United States grew from sea to shining sea. Situated next to the Missouri River, a lucrative ferry crossing kept the coffers refilled with outside funds until, of course, the river flooded and washed the operation downstream; however, it would be rebuilt. By the 1850s, ferries were becoming more technologically advanced. Despite Lewis and Clark passing through the area in 1804, it would not be until 1869 that the first bridge crossed the "Mighty Mo."

As people moved west, the railroads were quick to follow. In 1862, President Lincoln signed the Pacific Railroad Act, establishing a transcontinental railroad that would also pass through Nebraska. Initially in the running to be an important hub for Union Pacific, Bellevue was passed by in favor of Omaha. This was not necessarily because of land or location, but more an issue of the power and influence in Omaha rather than Bellevue.

Without the much-needed clout that Omaha had to lubricate the tracks, Bellevue's prospects of bringing the railroad to town became increasingly minimal. The result was that the spoils went to the victor and a fatal blow went to Bellevue. Despite the setback of not taking part in the transcontinental railroad line, the Bellevue-Offutt community has been home to its share of trains, planes, and automobiles, many of which are pictured in this chapter.

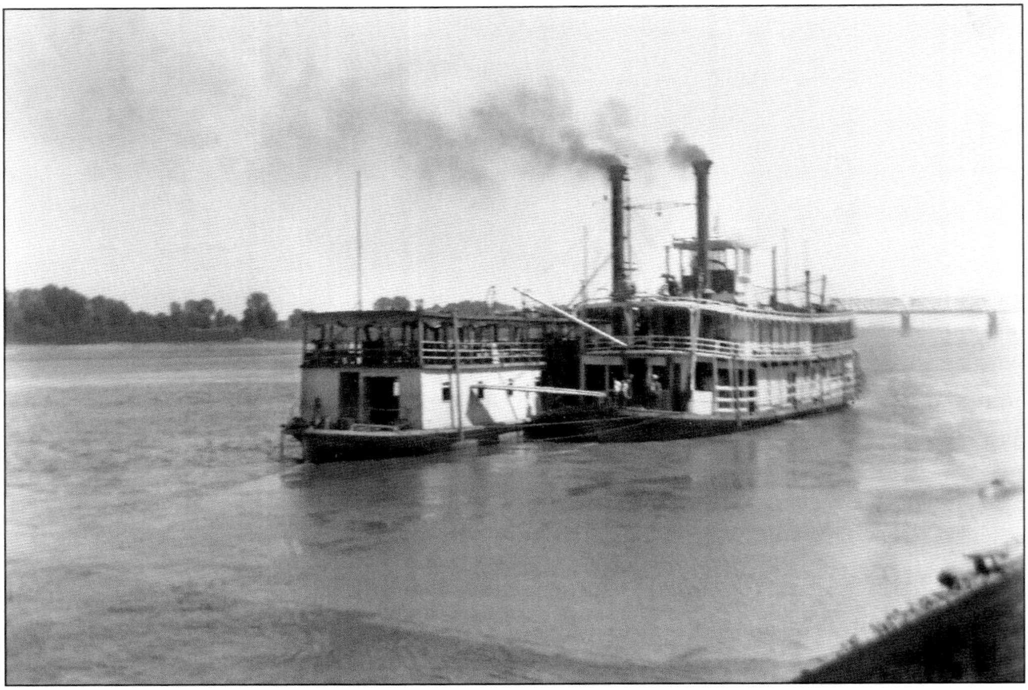

Ferryboats, steamboats, and other waterway transportation were once a common site along the Missouri River. One of those was the steamer *US Grant*. She sunk on March 22, 1866, with all her goods, but no loss of life. All that was saved was the ship's bell. The mighty river has since changed location, leaving the ship to remain undiscovered deep under Bellevue's soil.

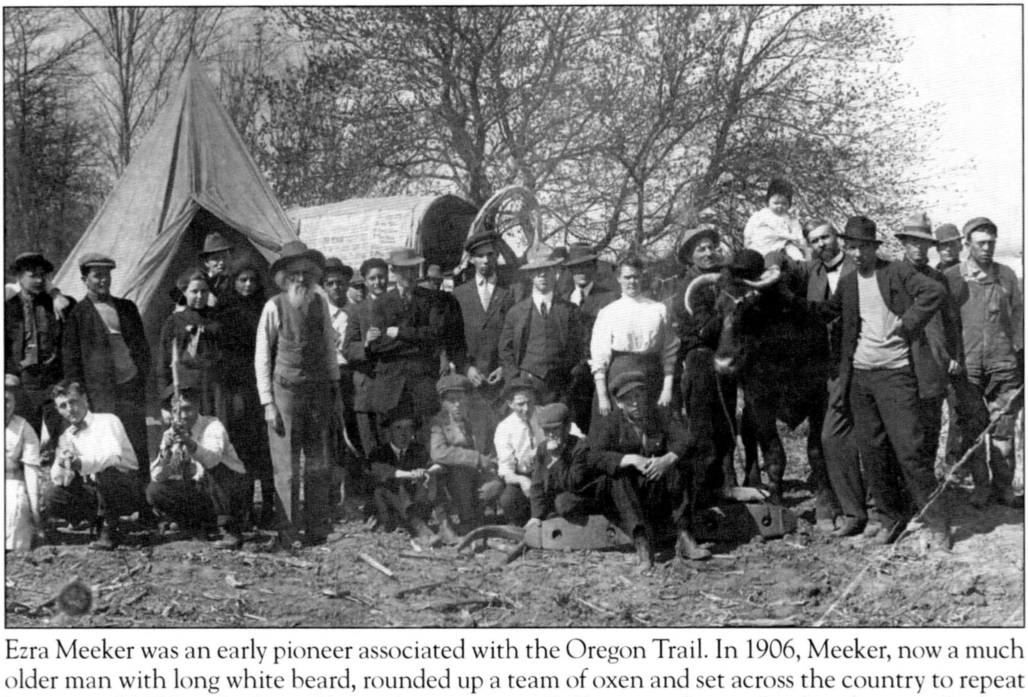

Ezra Meeker was an early pioneer associated with the Oregon Trail. In 1906, Meeker, now a much older man with long white beard, rounded up a team of oxen and set across the country to repeat his original 1850s trek. One of his early stops was in Bellevue, gathering for this photograph along the banks of the Missouri near Ernie Collins's ferry.

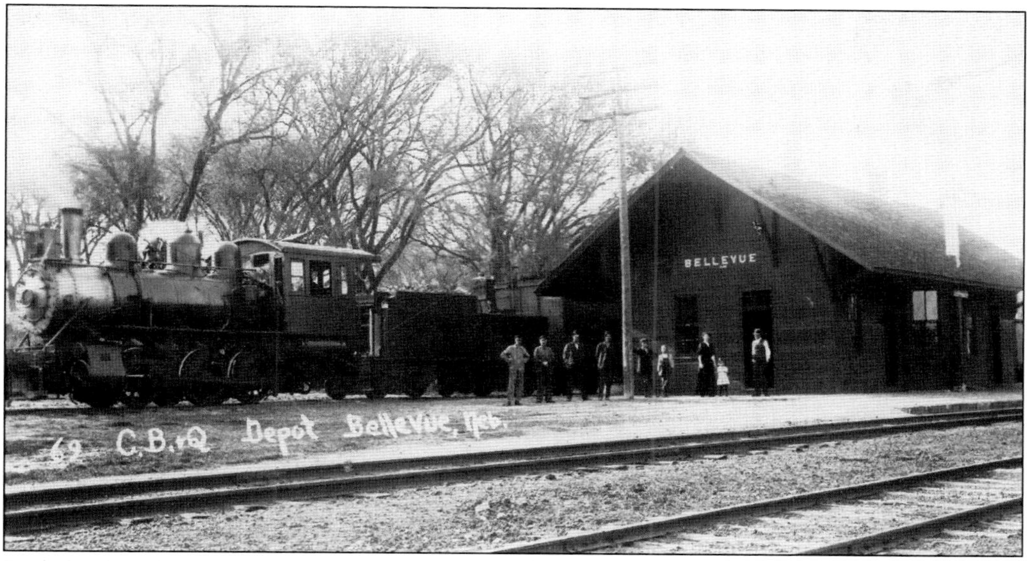

Built for the Chicago, Burlington and Quincy Railroad (CB&Q) by Henry T. Clarke in 1869, the Bellevue train depot serviced passengers along a spur line through several area communities. It also routinely brought mail and goods through and operated a Railway Express agency out of the station. The stationmaster not only worked at the depot, but actually lived within the building as well.

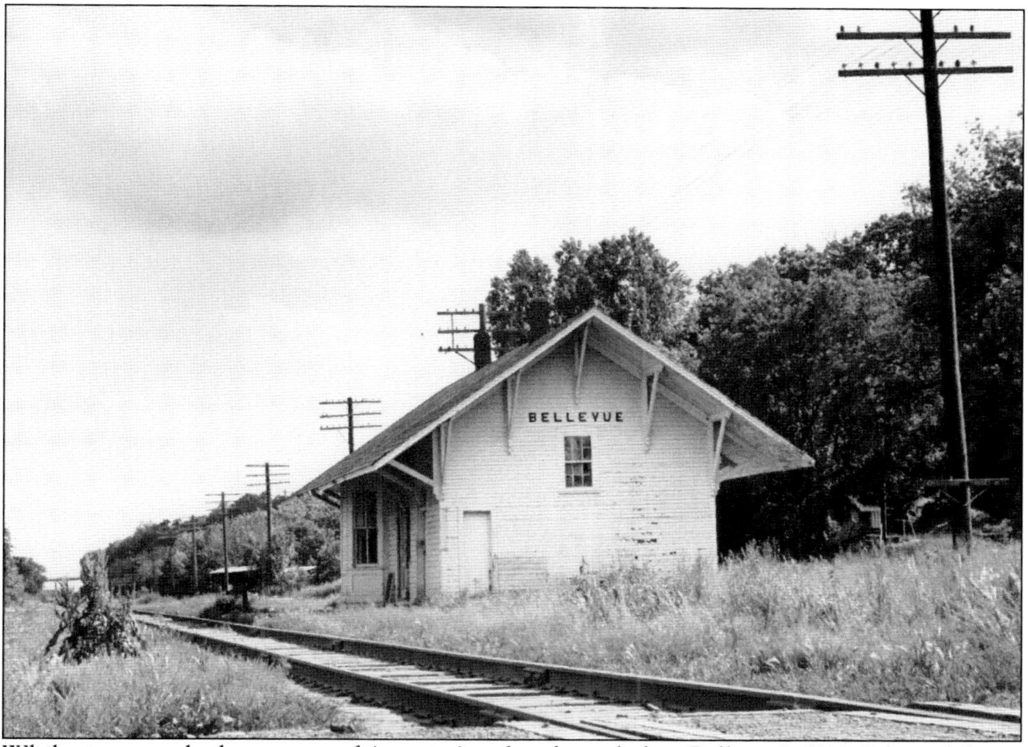

While time marched on, many of America's railroads, including Bellevue's CB&Q line, did not. By the time the line closed, a number of the communities that it was originally intended to service had dried up and folded, including Fort Crook and Gilmore. The days of an abandoned Bellevue station were numbered.

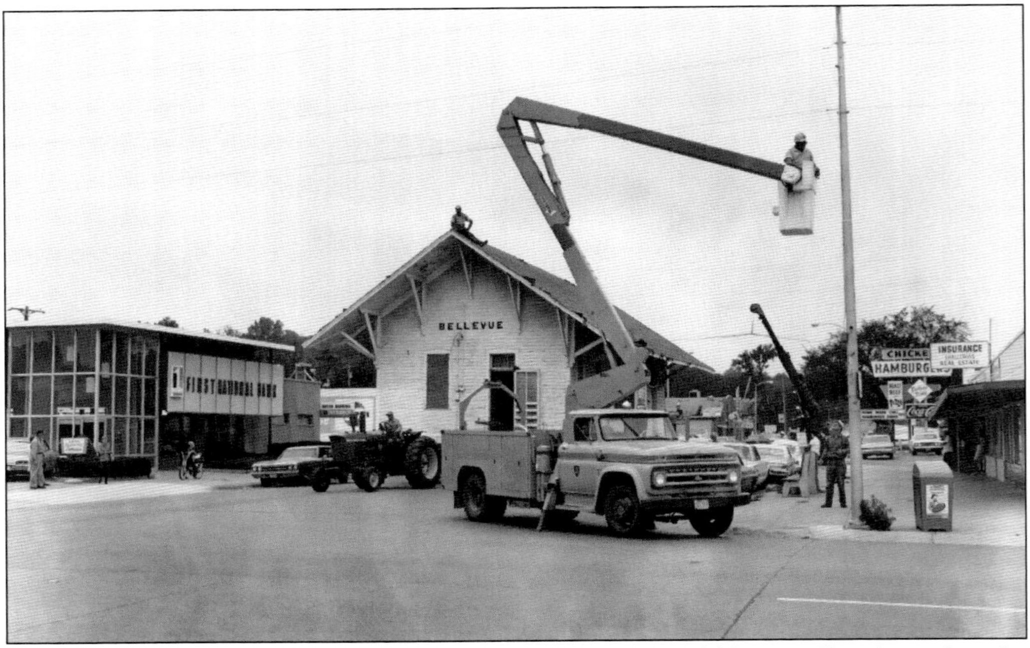

Eventually, it was proposed to move the station. The depot would be initially relocated to the corner of Mission and Main Streets, across from the Fontenelle Bank. On September 17, 1969, the entire building was picked up and moved 16 blocks. Its second location was Haworth Park. The building currently sits in Gemini Park, across from the Sarpy County Museum.

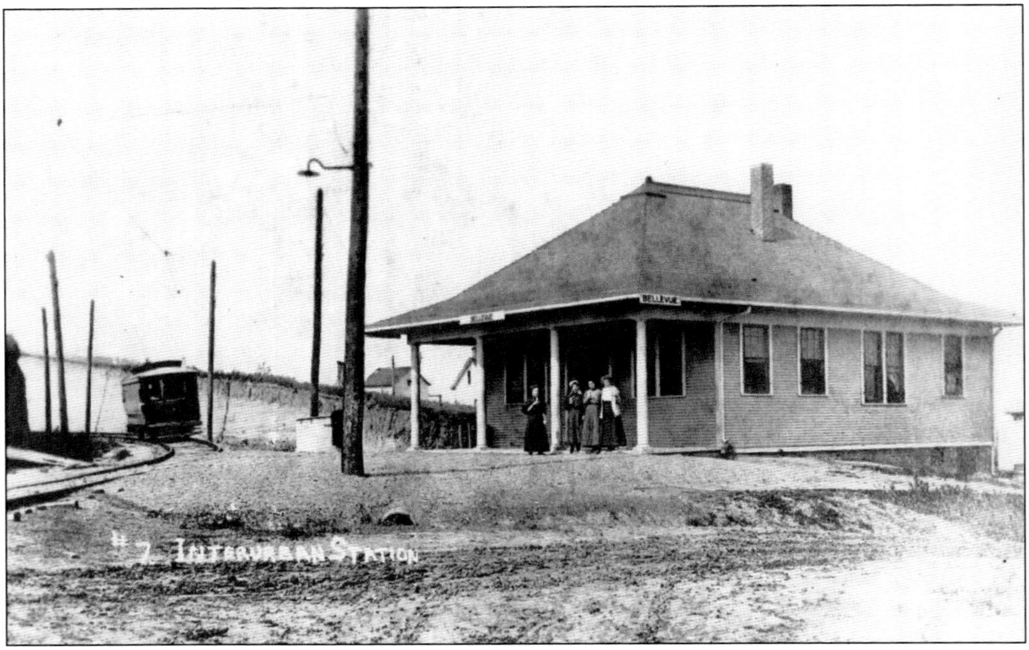

Built in 1906, the Omaha & Southern Interurban Railway line connected Bellevue and Fort Crook with South Omaha. At a time when horses were still the common method of transportation, the street car would have been a very efficient way of getting to the city, especially for students at Bellevue College, which the women in this photograph likely were. After years of low to no profits, the streetcars were replaced with buses in 1931.

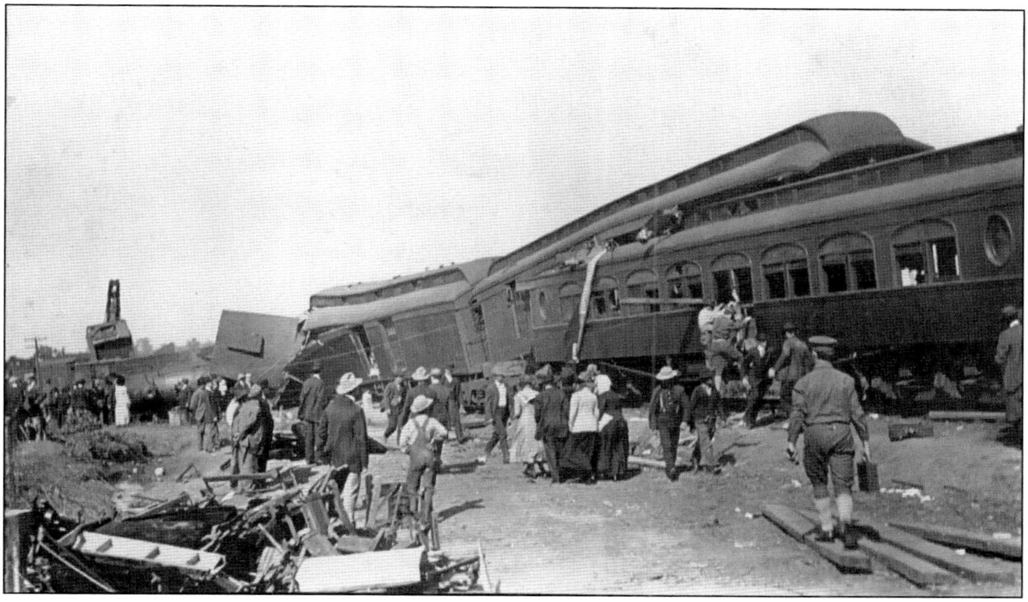

Unfortunately, this Omaha-bound train took a slight detour, terminating at Fort Crook on October 15, 1911. The Missouri Pacific passenger train collided with a fast-moving freight train, resulting in the deaths of eight with scores more injured. The disaster could have been worse if not for nearby soldiers who raced to the scene to put out the smoldering wreckage. The injured included Bellevue resident Edward Collins, as well as the governor of Florida, who was traveling at the time. Both dead and wounded were taken to the Fort Crook hospital. It was officially determined that the crew of the freight train had failed to inquire if there were any trains in their vicinity. Unofficially, lack of proper communication contributed to the accident, and not long after, a block signal was installed.

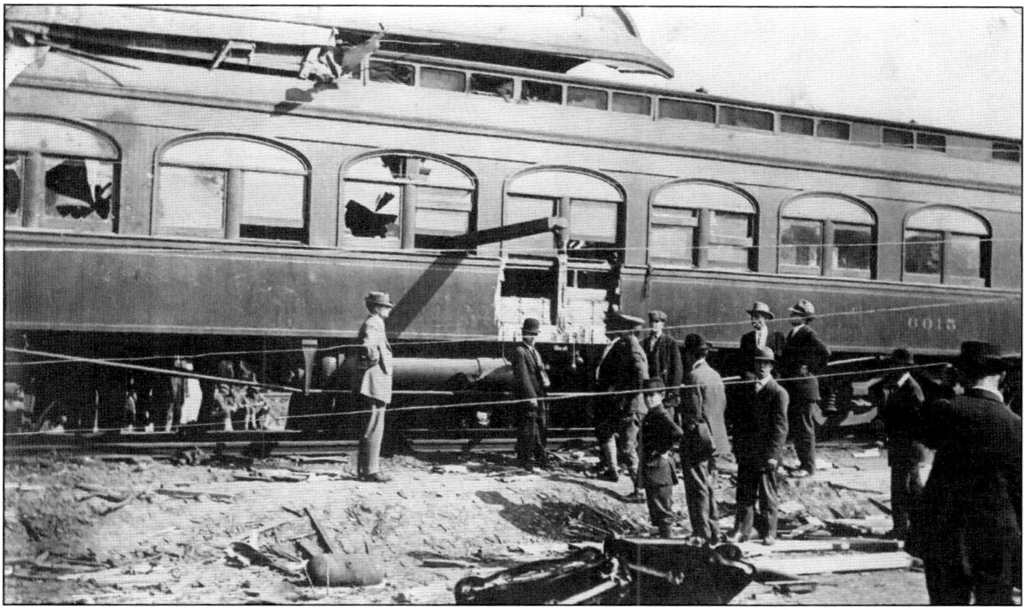

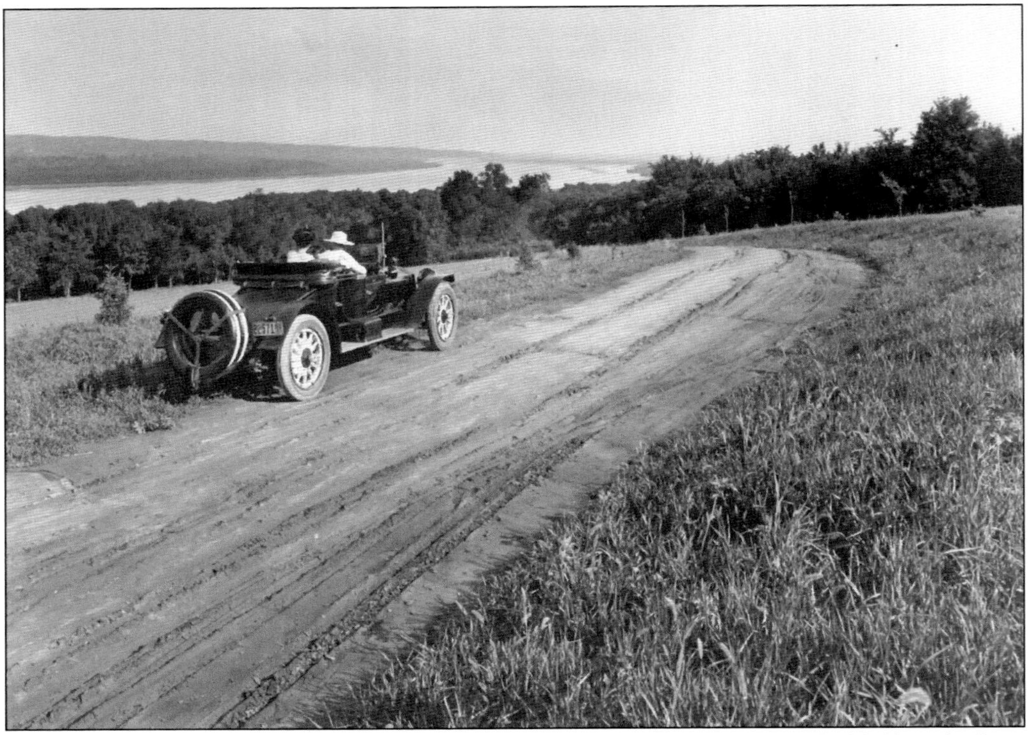

In 1917, Bellevue Boulevard was little more than a dirt road that twisted around a bluff overlooking the Missouri River. Despite the scenic view, the road could frequently become a mess of mud that had to be shared with the still-common horse and carriage. As early as the 1920s, homes did begin to appear along this beautiful piece of property. (Courtesy FNA.)

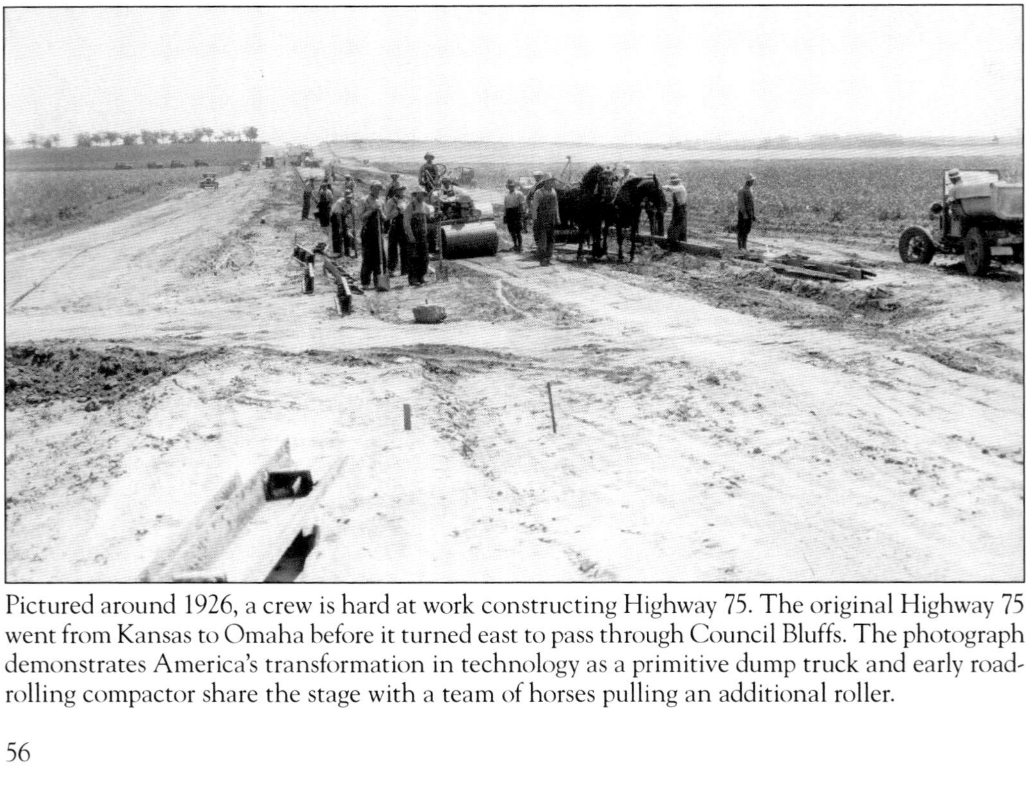

Pictured around 1926, a crew is hard at work constructing Highway 75. The original Highway 75 went from Kansas to Omaha before it turned east to pass through Council Bluffs. The photograph demonstrates America's transformation in technology as a primitive dump truck and early road-rolling compactor share the stage with a team of horses pulling an additional roller.

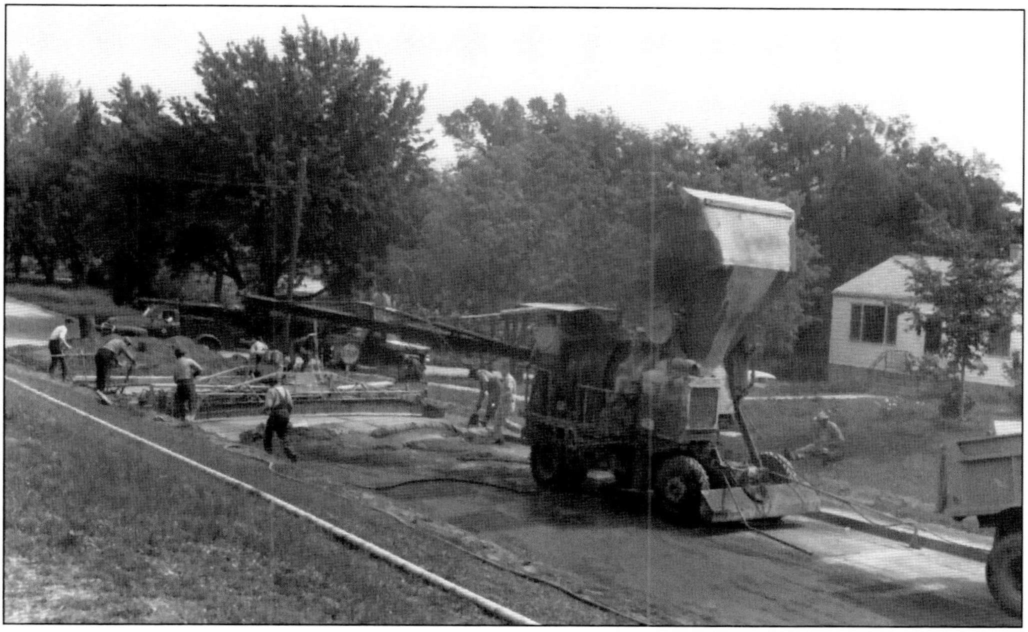

All it took was one rainfall before Bellevue could quickly turn into a mud hole. This changed in 1953 when local roads began to receive paving, including the intersection of 27th Avenue and Van Buren Street. As a precaution, there were repeated warnings posted in the *Bellevue Press* not to drive on the fresh concrete until it had fully hardened.

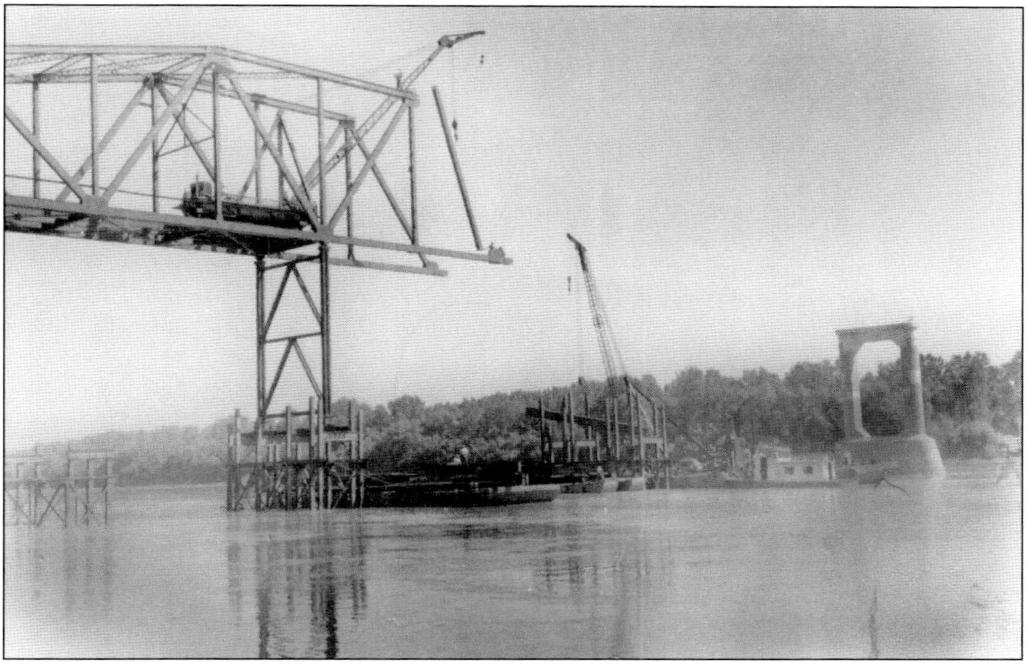

In this 1950 photograph, work is clearly under way for the half-finished Bellevue Bridge. Completed in 1952 after several years of discussion and preparation, the bridge was later christened the Grand Army of the Republic Bridge in 1954. William J. Howard Inc. of Chicago built the traditional two-lane truss bridge, while Kirkham, Michael, and Associates of Omaha served as the consulting engineer firm.

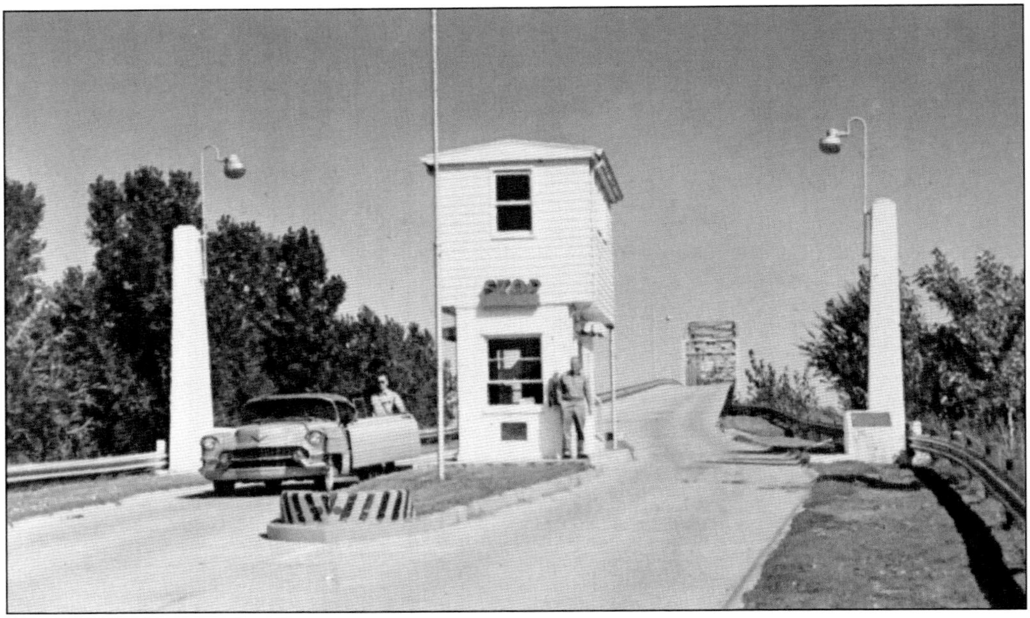

The 1,975-foot bridge connected Bellevue with Mills County, Iowa, and was advertised as a great way to circumvent Omaha if one wanted to head east. However, until the roads were fully completed and paved on the nearby Iowa side, traveling over the Missouri River via the Bellevue Bridge could only take one so far. Without fanfare or celebration, the driver of the first car paid toll man Ruben Ballard to cross the $3 million bridge on December 9, 1952.

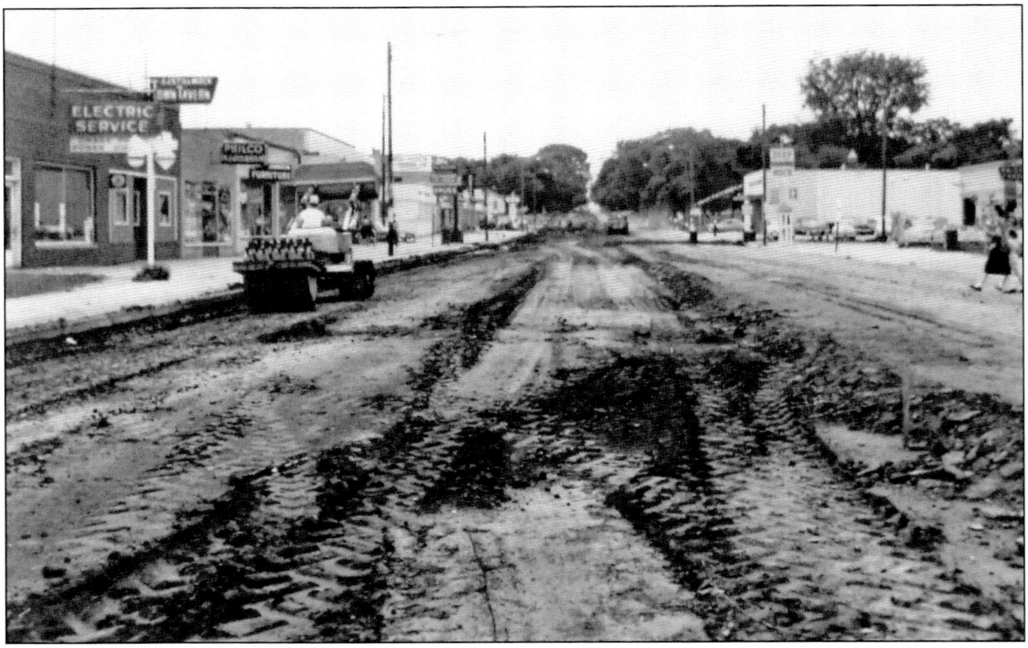

Proclaimed the "Festival of Progress," a two-day celebration was held September 19–20, 1954, in honor of the Bellevue Bridge and the newly modernized roads (shown here undergoing their transformation from dirt to smoothly paved streets). Monday, September 20 was declared a holiday for all school children and adults from ages 5 to 105 by Mayor Joe Morgan. The event coincided with Vice President Richard Nixon's visit to Bellevue and Offutt Air Force Base.

Upon first glimpse, the Bellevue Queen may have looked like a giant riverboat, but it was actually a large mock-up building that sat not far from the Missouri River at 2401 River Drive. Captain and proprietor Harold Stevens ensured that the restaurant and banquet hall had a nautical motif where one could partake in the Captain's Buffet or enjoy a drink in the Crow's Nest.

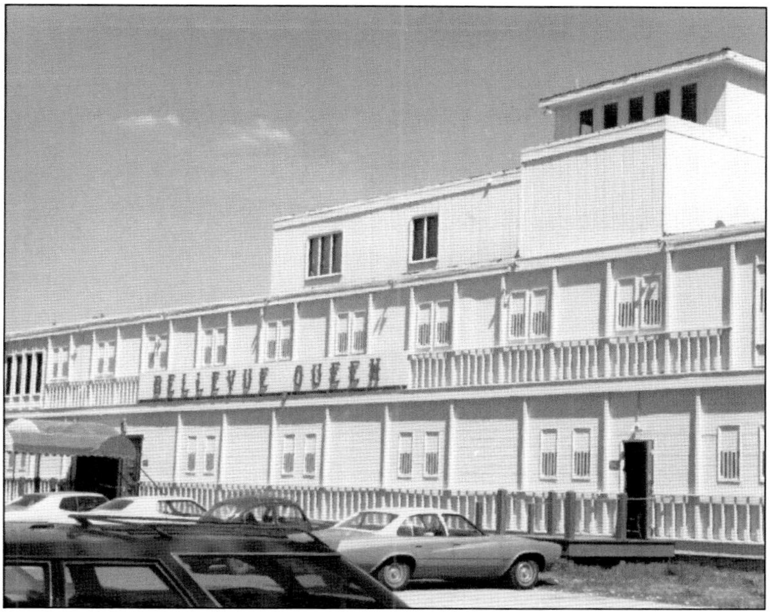

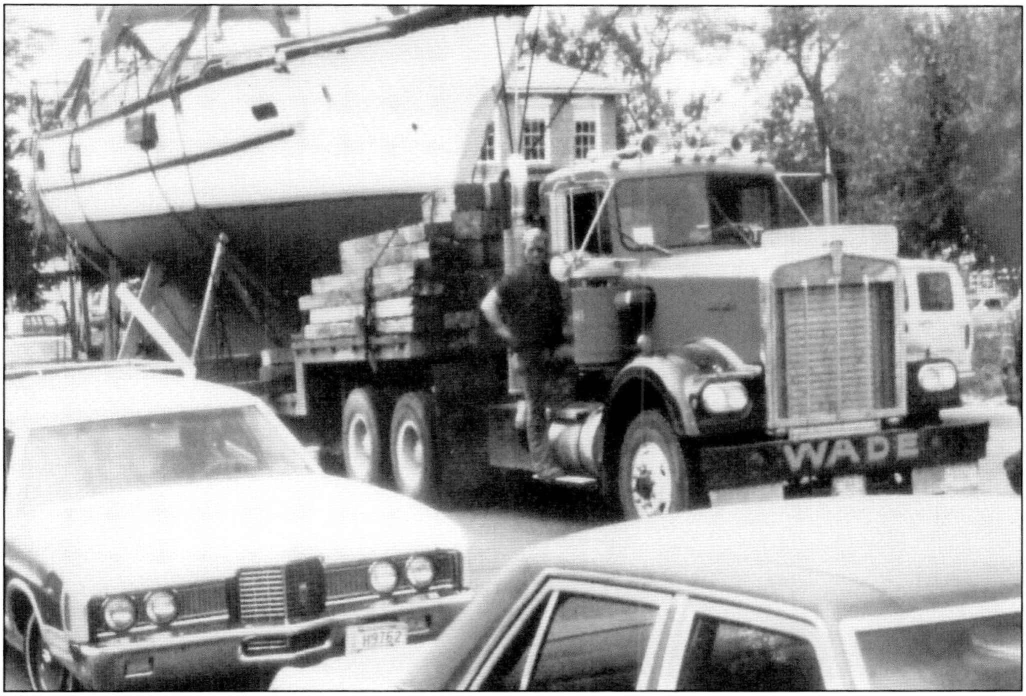

The *Ah Misty Green Go* sets off for the Missouri River on the back of a flatbed semitruck in 1979. What made the vessel unique was that it was constructed from concrete. The launching of Ben Green's boat was so popular, it was the first time the police department had to issue press passes. Instead of sinking, the boat floated downriver into the sunset.

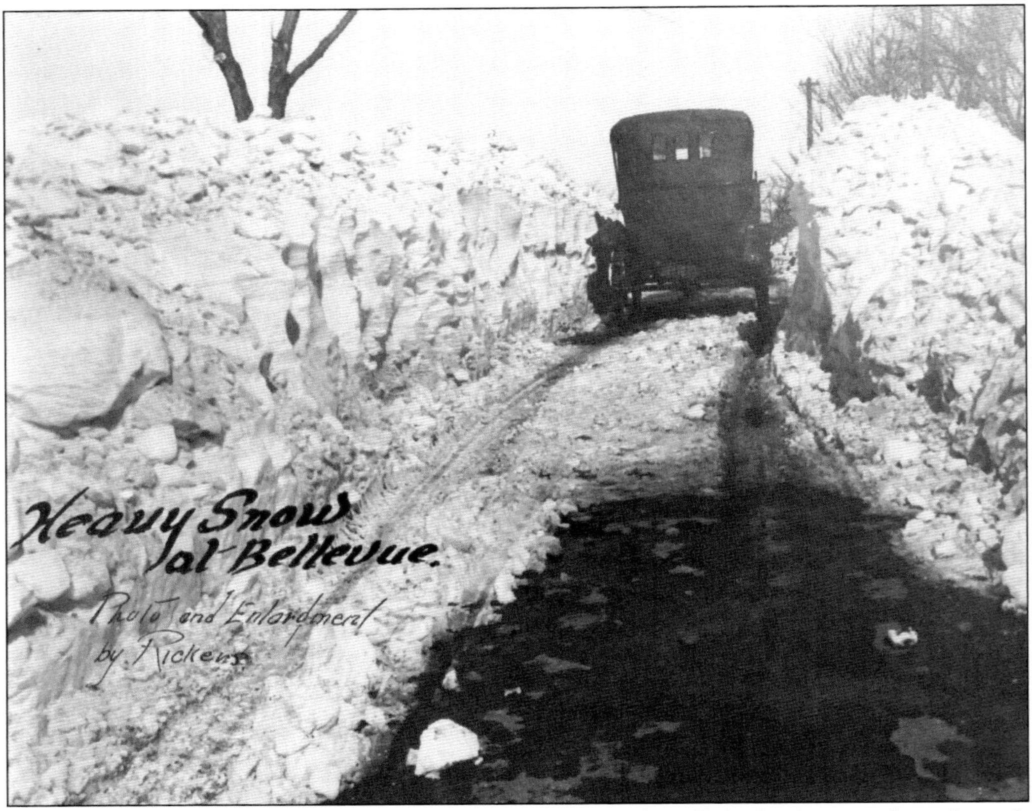

Extreme weather is no stranger to Bellevue. With roads that literally had to be carved out through the snow, travel would have been difficult, especially in Bellevue's hilly regions. The interurban would have had trouble if it rained at all. The street seen here was probably 20th Avenue, which would have gone up to the old Bellevue College.

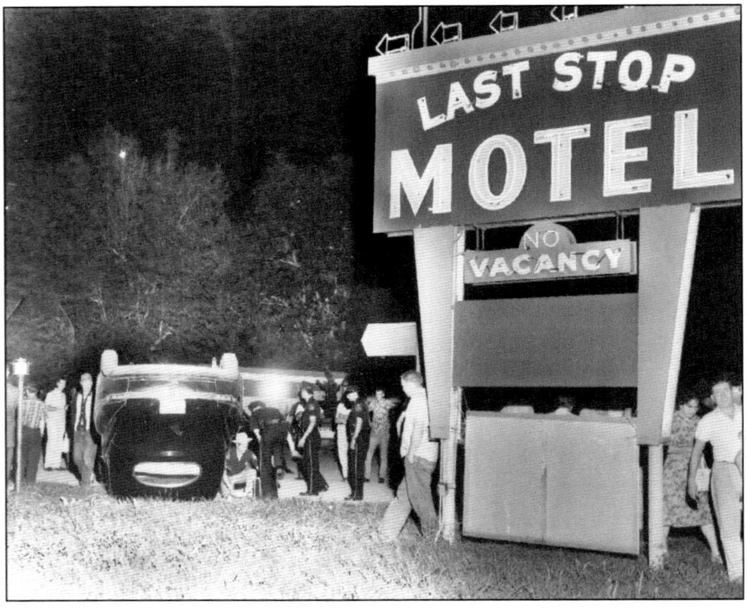

It truly was the last stop for this car that overturned outside the Last Stop Motel and Trailer Court, located at 8231 Ft. Crook Road. At the time, Howard Crane was the proprietor of the motel. Photographer and newspaperman John Gebbie would frequently be able to capture scenes such as these because his volunteer service with the fire department kept him near the action.

Four

Bellevue at Work

Bellevue is a city that works. Without the strong work ethic its people have put forward, the community would never have been able to dig itself out of its early difficult years to become a prosperous metropolis. A community is only as strong as the effort its people put into it. Bellevue residents have put their bodies, hearts, and souls into their work, and it is historically evident. It is important to not take for granted what is considered everyday life. Providing goods and services and doing it well has contributed to this corner of the world's successes. Local medical practices, area shops, and even the supermarket have been important contributors to our society.

The municipal services of police, medical, and fire have long been vigilant, providing a high level of quality emergency services to citizens and visitors of Bellevue. Like others, these men and women work to identify and solve problems within the community, albeit with the added difficulty of having to respond to an emergency in both the depths of winter and the heat of summer, depending on Nebraska's versatile climate.

Nothing ventured is nothing gained, and Bellevue at work does not come without risk. There is risk for the Bellevue banker, just as there has been risk for the Bellevue serviceman. One carries financial dangers; the other the simple threat of no longer existing. Both play a game of chance and without this personal jeopardy, Bellevue as a whole would not be the better place it is today. Businesses and stores have come and gone, but hard work has remained. It has driven this community and will continue to do so.

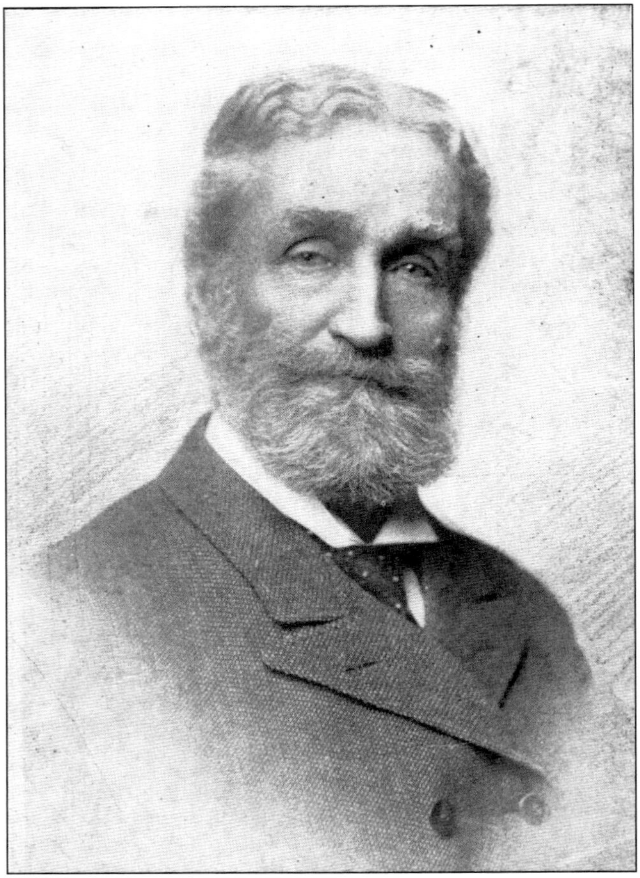

The Clarke Brothers were two of Bellevue's early entrepreneurs. Arriving in Bellevue in the mid-1850s, Henry Tefft Clarke (left) and his brother, Augustus W., established a general merchandise store. In 1856, they expanded with a steamboat service, and in 1862, they secured a contract with the federal government for supplies to Fort Kearney. Even as it was determined that the transcontinental railroad would not be coming to Bellevue, the brothers were running an ox-driven commercial freight venue between Bellevue and Denver. However, once it was clear that the railroad would not be passing through, Henry sold his interest to his brother and got into the bridge-making business. Augustus would stay in Bellevue until 1877 before moving to Papillion and expanding the business, as well as opening a bank there in 1880.

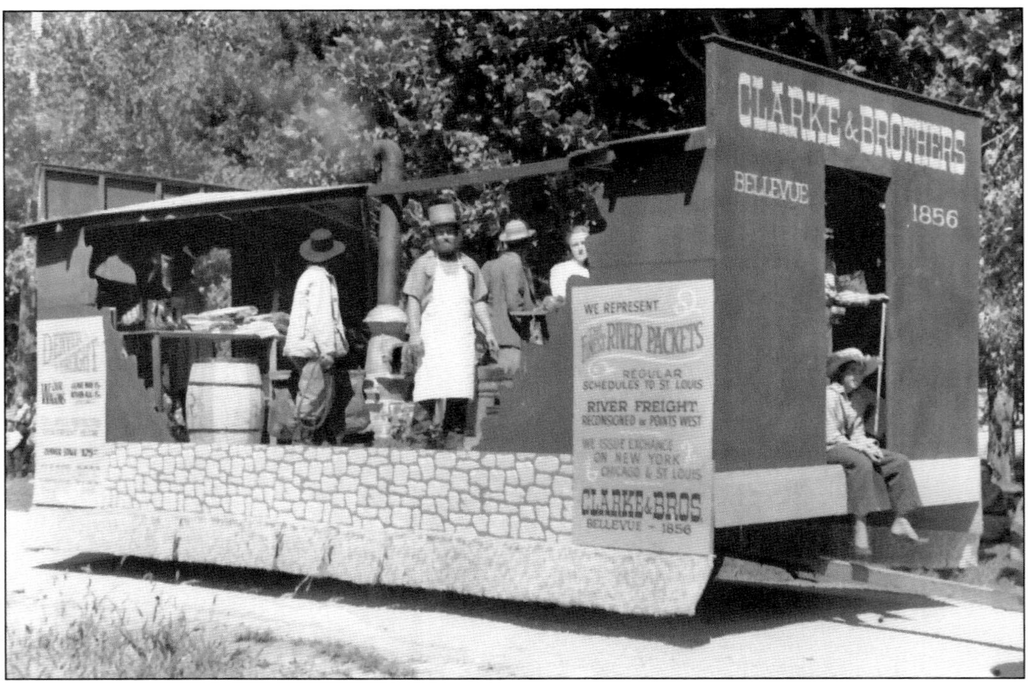

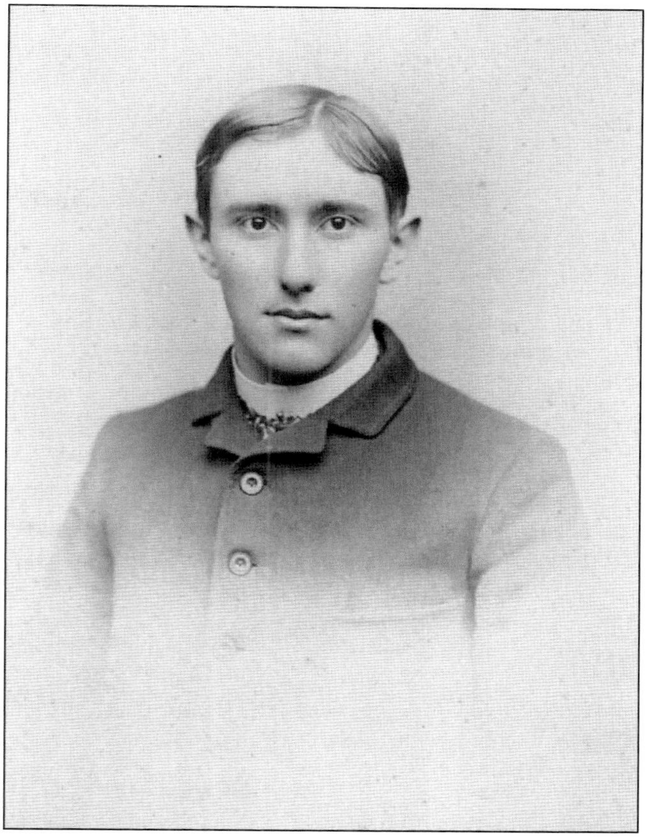

Many seeking medical help visited the residence and office of Dr. William H. Betz. The town doctor also commonly made house calls. Betz practiced medicine in the area for 50 years, becoming a staple in the community. During World War I, Betz served as the chief of surgeons at Fort Omaha. In 1937, he opened the Bellevue Clinic, the groundwork for the first school nurse program in the state. At the start of World War II, he tried to reenlist, but at 74 years old, he was turned away. Betz has both a road and an elementary school named after him.

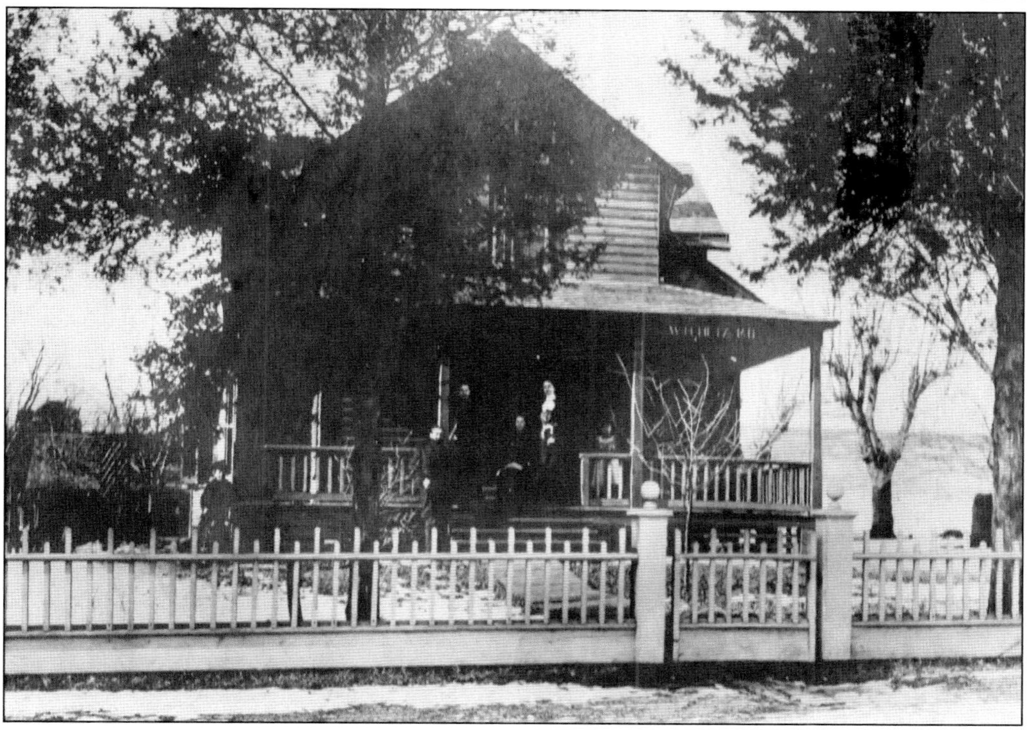

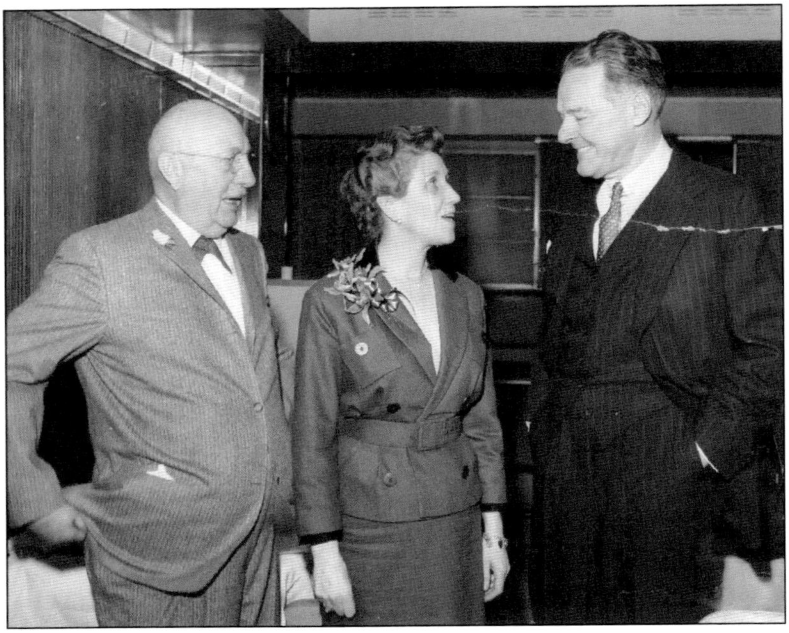

Charles Reed (left), president of Bank of Bellevue, was an individual often at the forefront of the action. Reed is pictured here with senator and later US ambassador to the United Nations, Henry Cabot Lodge Jr. In addition to providing banking and loan services to those in the community, Reed was also an attorney, author, and World War I veteran.

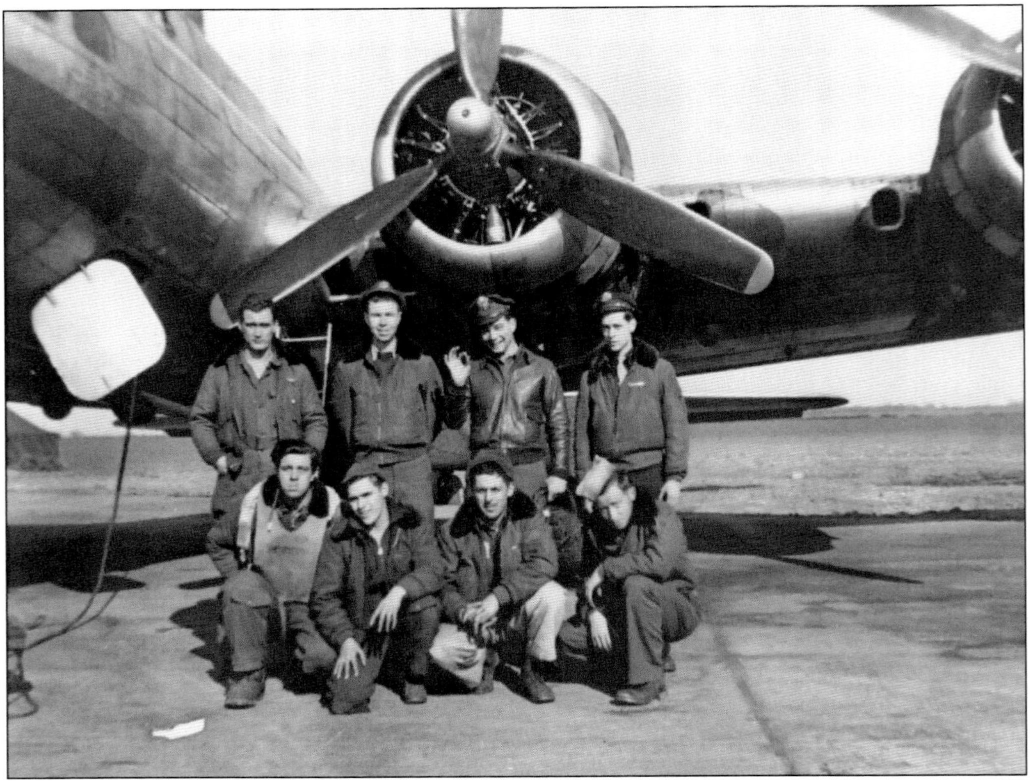

Some positions required travel. In the case of Bellevue resident Gail Farrell, his profession frequently required him to go to Germany. Pictured in the front row, far right with a cocked hat, Farrell was a tail gunner on a B-17 with the 379th Bombardment Group. After the war, he was stationed at Offutt Air Force Bace and served as the associate editor of the Strategic Air Command magazine *Combat Crew*.

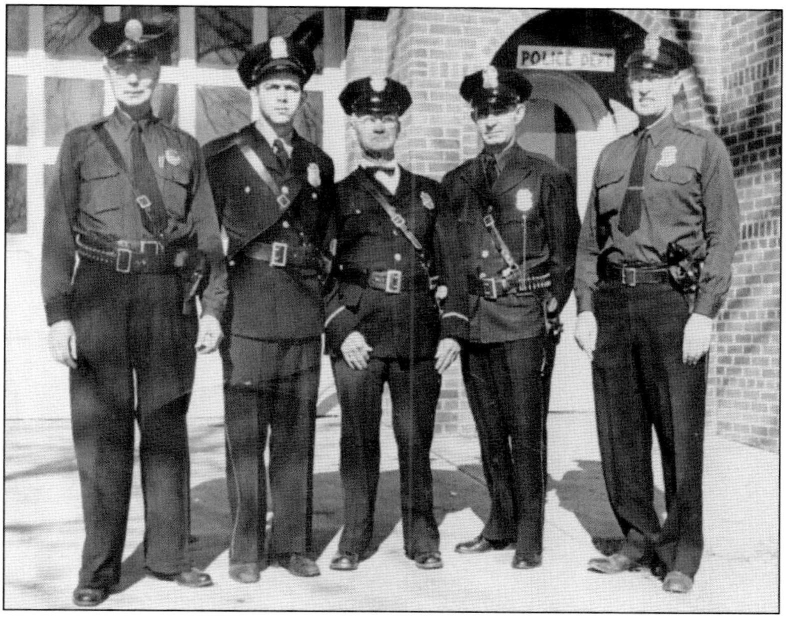

Adorned with pistol and Sam Browne belts, the Bellevue Police Department carry a sense of professionalism with them, even when this photograph was taken sometime in the late 1940s or early 1950s. Included in the image are chief of police Frank Maxey, Kenny Beaman, and Joe Gow, grandson of Judge James Gow.

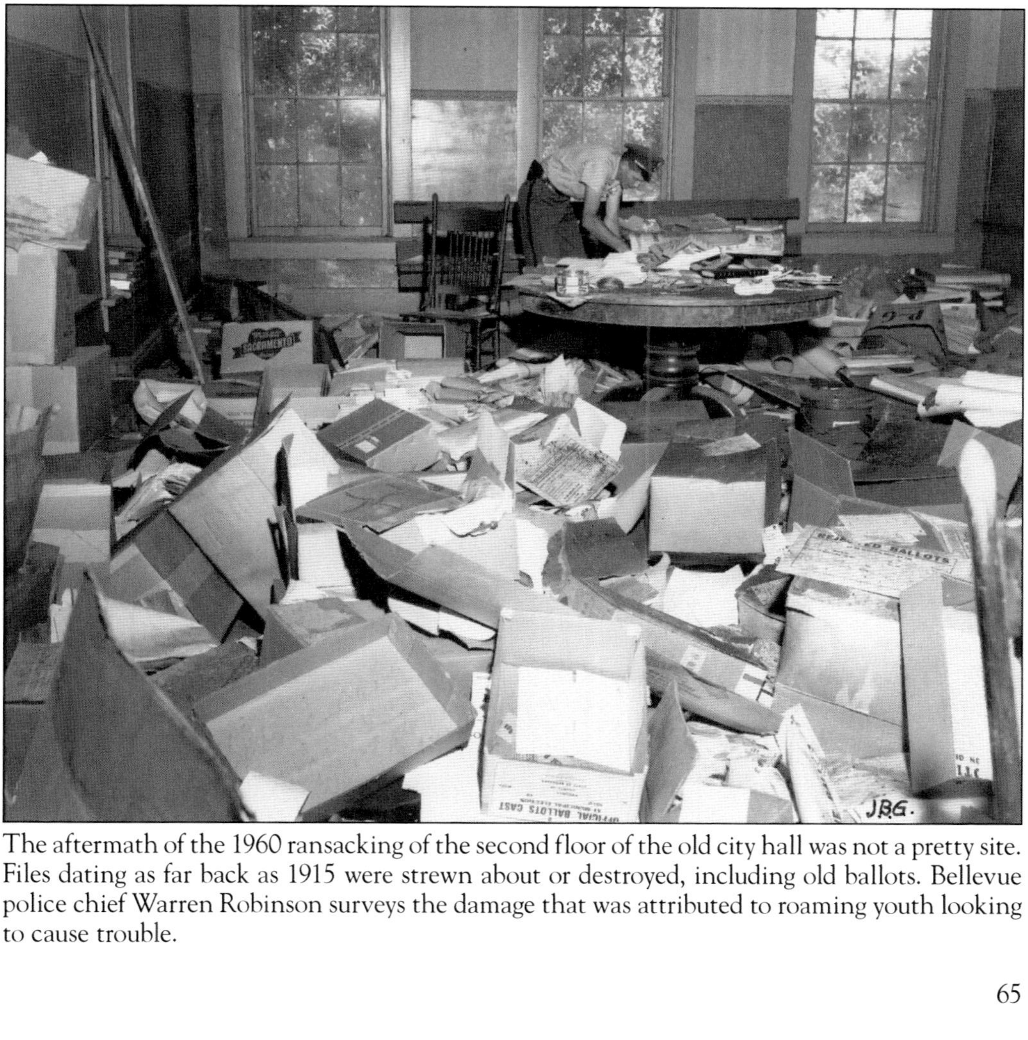

The aftermath of the 1960 ransacking of the second floor of the old city hall was not a pretty site. Files dating as far back as 1915 were strewn about or destroyed, including old ballots. Bellevue police chief Warren Robinson surveys the damage that was attributed to roaming youth looking to cause trouble.

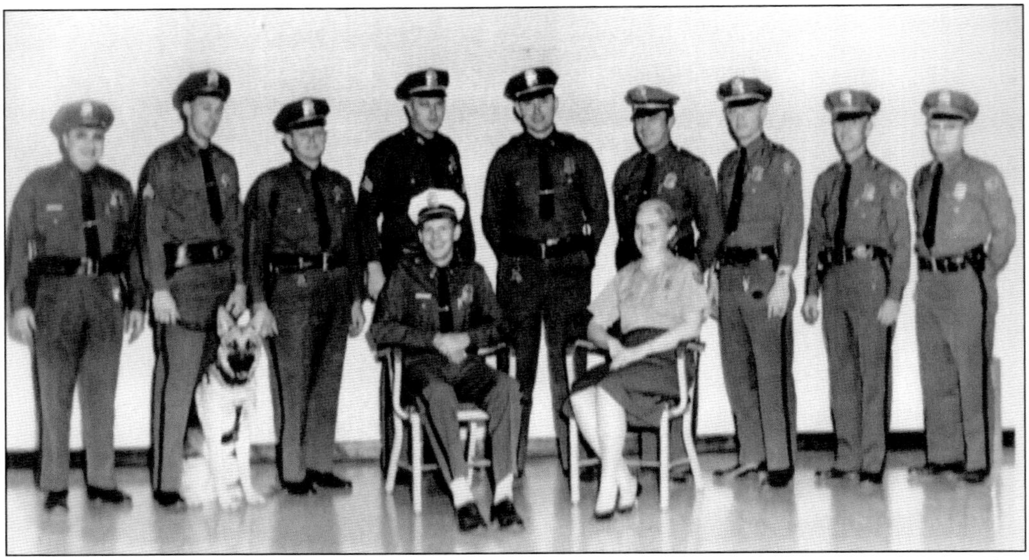

In 1954, the Bellevue police force consisted of four patrolmen, a deputy chief, and the chief. This 1962 group photograph features nine officers standing behind K-9 Officer Ray, Chief Robinson, and police matron Jean Westcott. In 1966, the force increased to 21 men. As chief of police from 1958 to 1986, Robinson oversaw much of the department expansion, including the first female officer and the first motorcycle. (Courtesy Sergeant Dave Rech.)

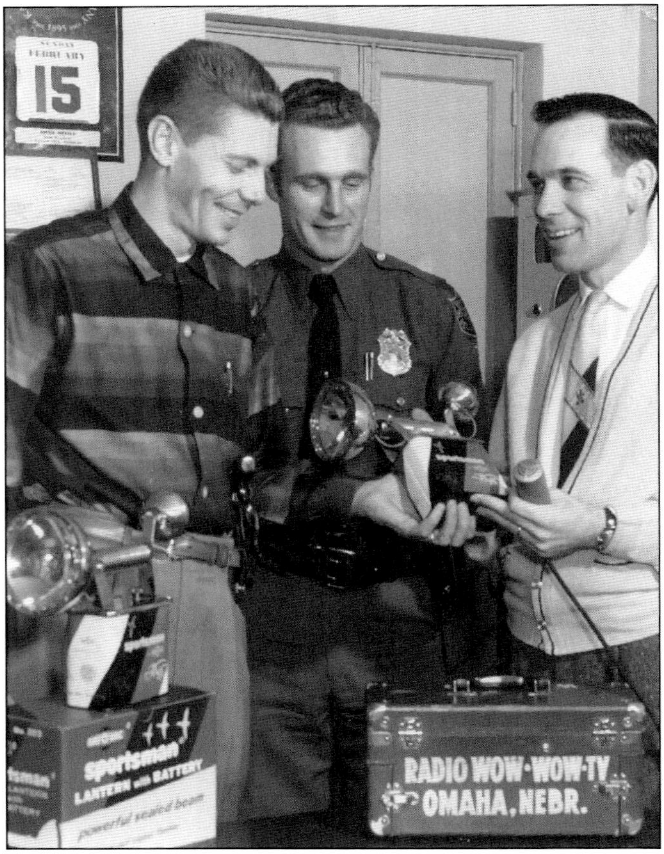

Jolly Joe Martin (right) of WOW Radio presents two Ray-O-Vac lanterns to police chief Warren Robinson (left) on behalf of the Ray-O-Vac Company, while patrolman Bernard Danowski watches. One light would be installed in a police cruiser, while the other would be used where needed. The addition of two flashlights was lauded as a big deal at the time of the presentation on February 15, 1959.

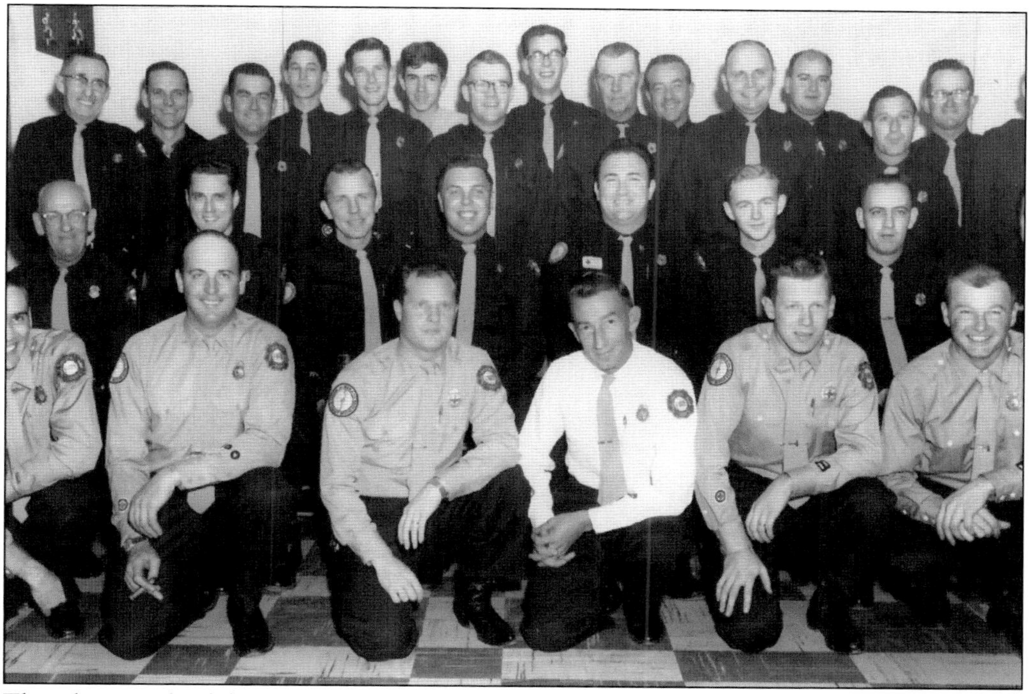

This photograph of the Bellevue Volunteer Fire Department was taken during December 1965. Mainly identified by their last names, they are, from left to right (first row) Hoschar, Wootton, Friend, Jack Westcott, McClemons, and Nelson; (second row) Reicks, Gebbie, Timme, Harnish, Stacey, Jim Westcott, and Goolsby; (third row) Neale, Bland, McCaw, Schneider, McRoberts, John Westcott, Hess, Watson, Godberson, Shaw, Citta, Rugl, Vandell, and Albers. (Courtesy Ed Wootton.)

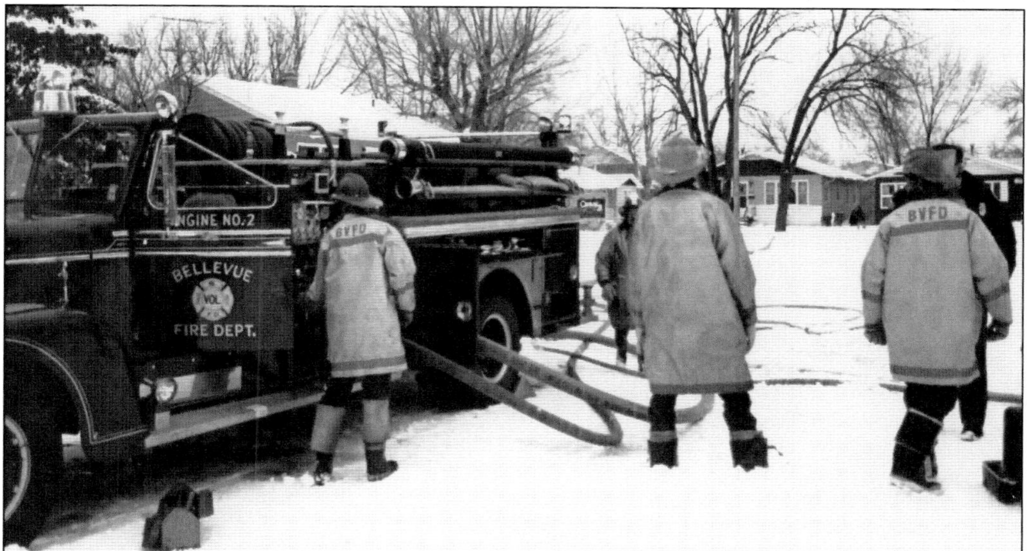

Engine no. 2 of the Bellevue Volunteer Fire Department responds to a blaze during the winter. As if fighting a fire in frigid temperatures was not enough, they had to commute to the fire exposed to the elements, as the open cabin on the water pumper clearly shows. With their backs turned, the firefighters are clearly more interested in fighting the flames than receiving credit. (Courtesy Ed Wootton.)

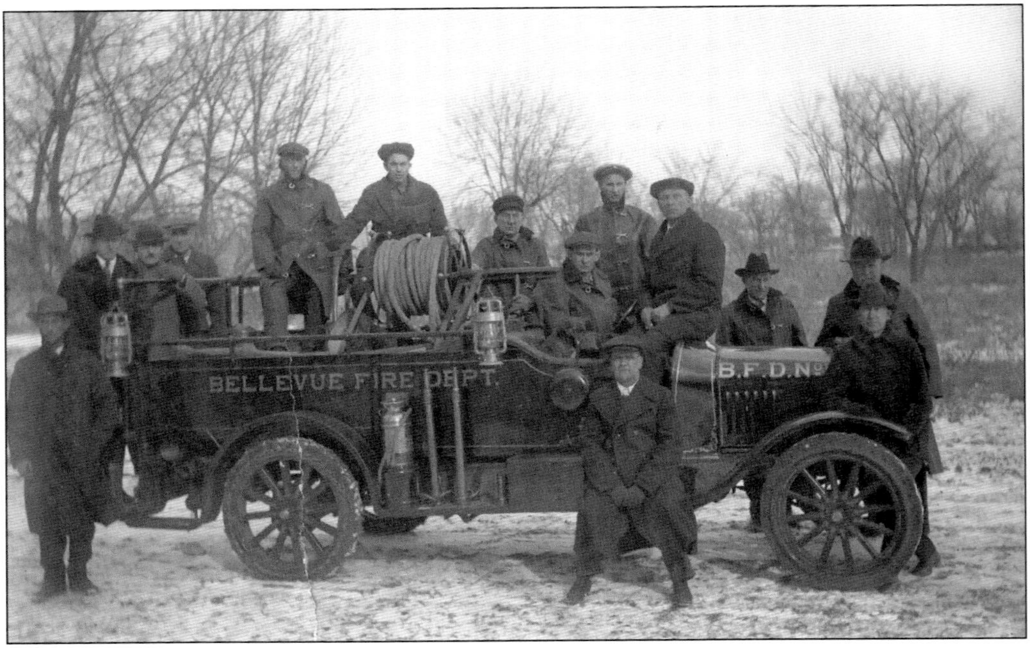

For a community of its size in 1903, the Bellevue Volunteer Fire Department was fortunate to have a mechanized rig in operation. Among the firefighters of the day featured are Wilbur Kast, William Gow, Art Balid, Jim Short, John Olsen, Howard Collins, Chris Jansen, Fred Stevens, Lou Burnes, Dick Margarum, and B. Sterba.

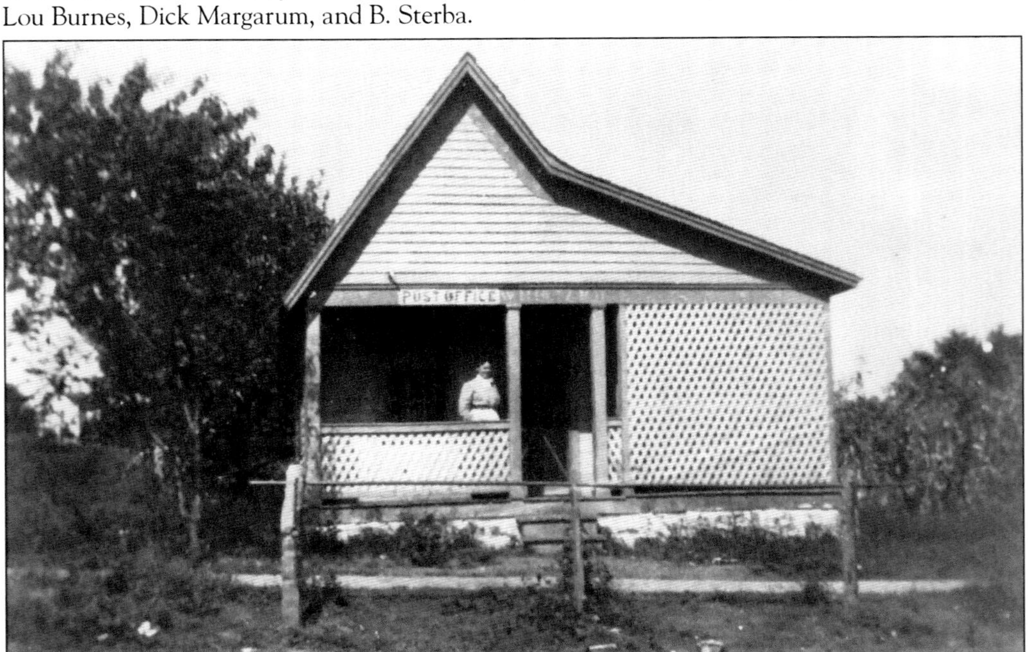

In this image, postmaster Helen (Fletcher) Zimmerman stands out front of the Bellevue Post Office in 1912. Established as the territorial post office in 1855, the post office has been held within numerous buildings as the town changed in size. During the early days, it was located where the local postmaster wanted it. For Zimmerman, it was at Franklin Street and 19th Avenue, across from Washington Park. (Courtesy Nebraska State Historical Society.)

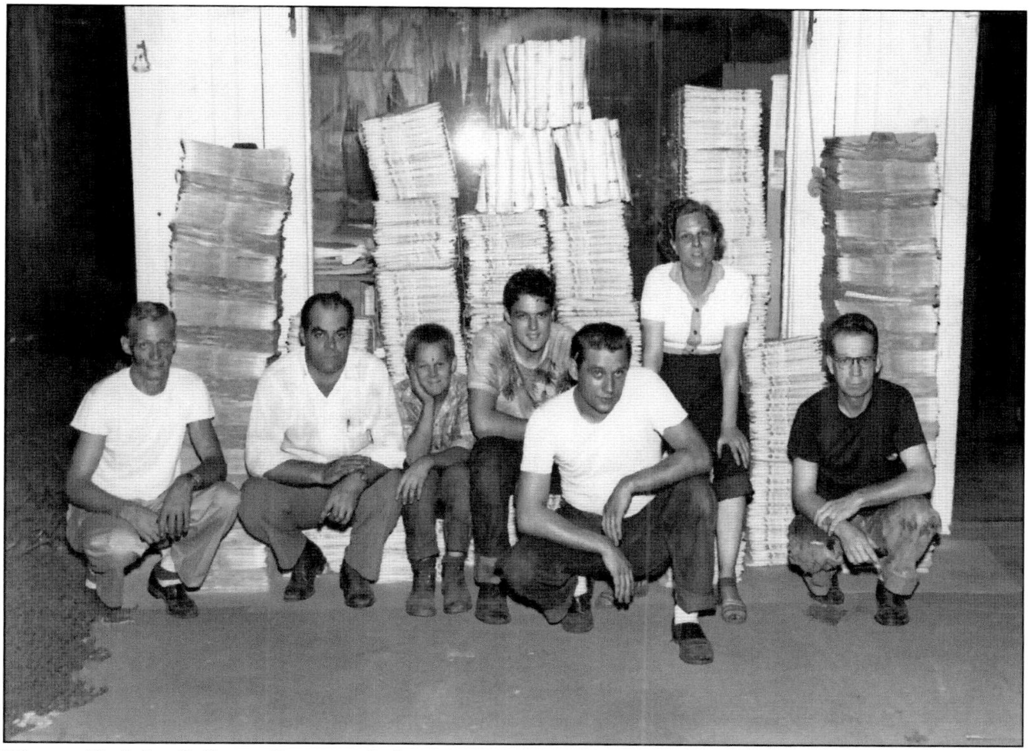

The staff of the *Bellevue Press,* including members of the Gebbie family, takes a break from their work to pose for a picture outside their storefront offices. Beginning on December 7, 1945, the paper offered the best in news, views, and happenings in and around the Bellevue-Offutt community. The paper's initial temporary headquarters was out of a home at 1504 Washington Street.

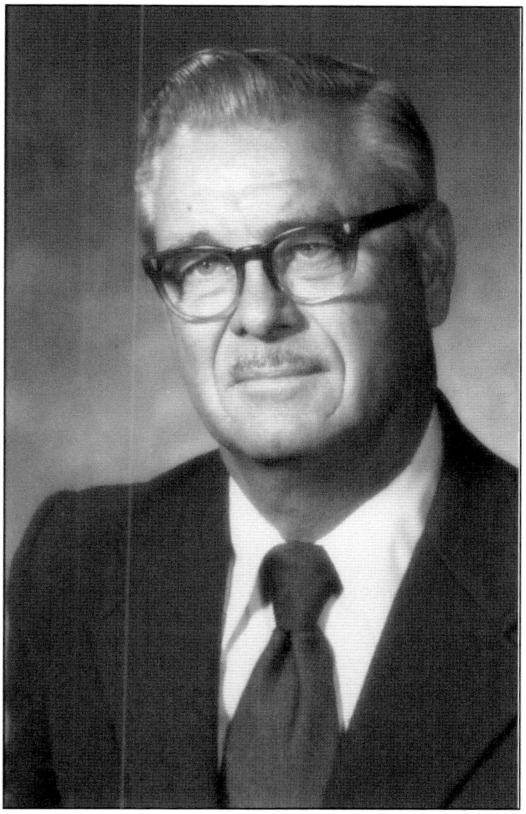

Active in his community, Ray Lind served in several elected offices, including as a member of the board of school district No. 5 from 1950 to 1953, the Bellevue City Council from 1968 to 1976, and as Sarpy County commissioner from 1976 until 1988. A champion of the community, Lind was a familiar face.

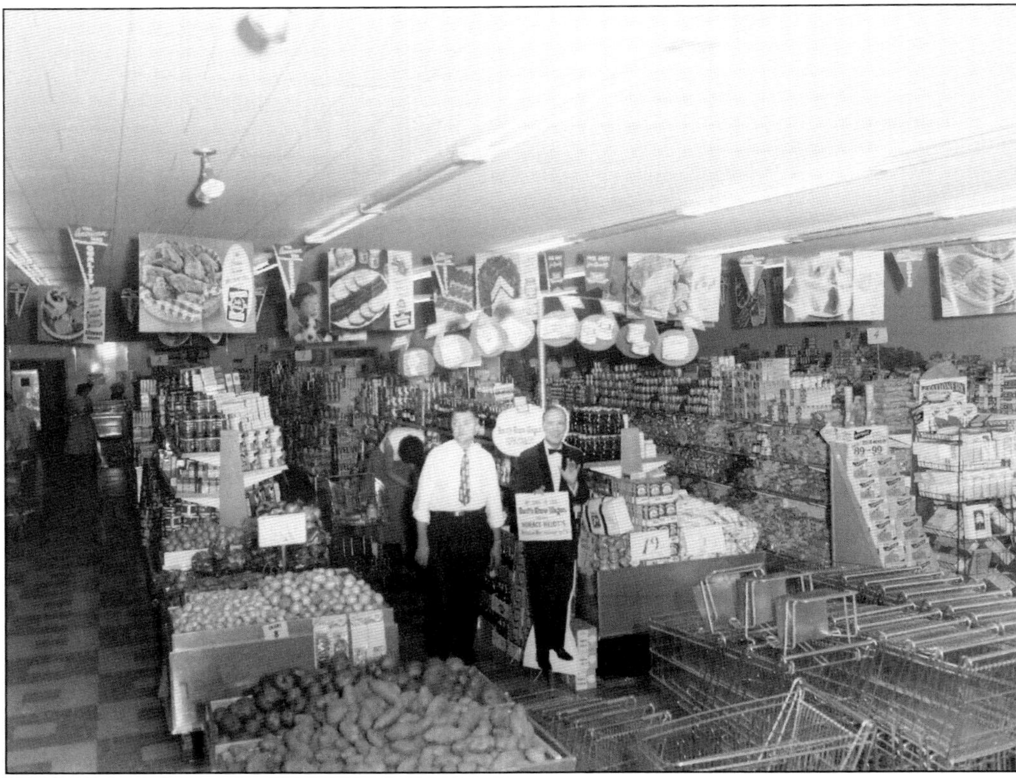

In 1953, Kousgaard's Super Market replaced a smaller previous incarnation. The new building had all the modern features, including brand new lighting and fixtures in order to create a pleasurable shopping experience. Hjalmer Kousgaard stands in his grocery store next to a cardboard cutout promoting the 1955 television program *Swift Show Wagon* with bandleader Horce Heidt. (Courtesy Joyce Ritche.)

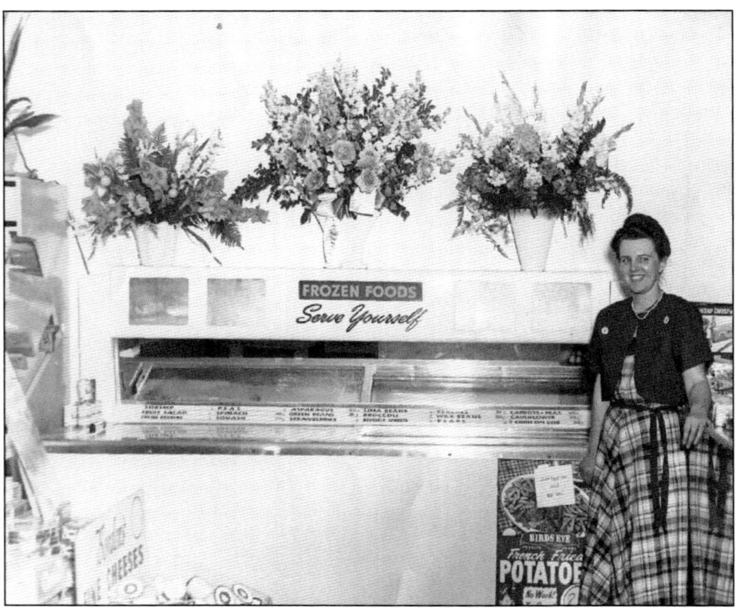

Vivian Kousgaard stands next to the fine frozen food section at Kousgaard's Super Market. The 1953 prices from their grand opening advertisement were much more reasonable than their competitor's listings, and in some instances, they were almost half the cost. Prices included ground beef at 29¢ a pound, a dozen eggs for 45¢, and bananas at 10¢ per pound. (Courtesy Joyce Ritche.)

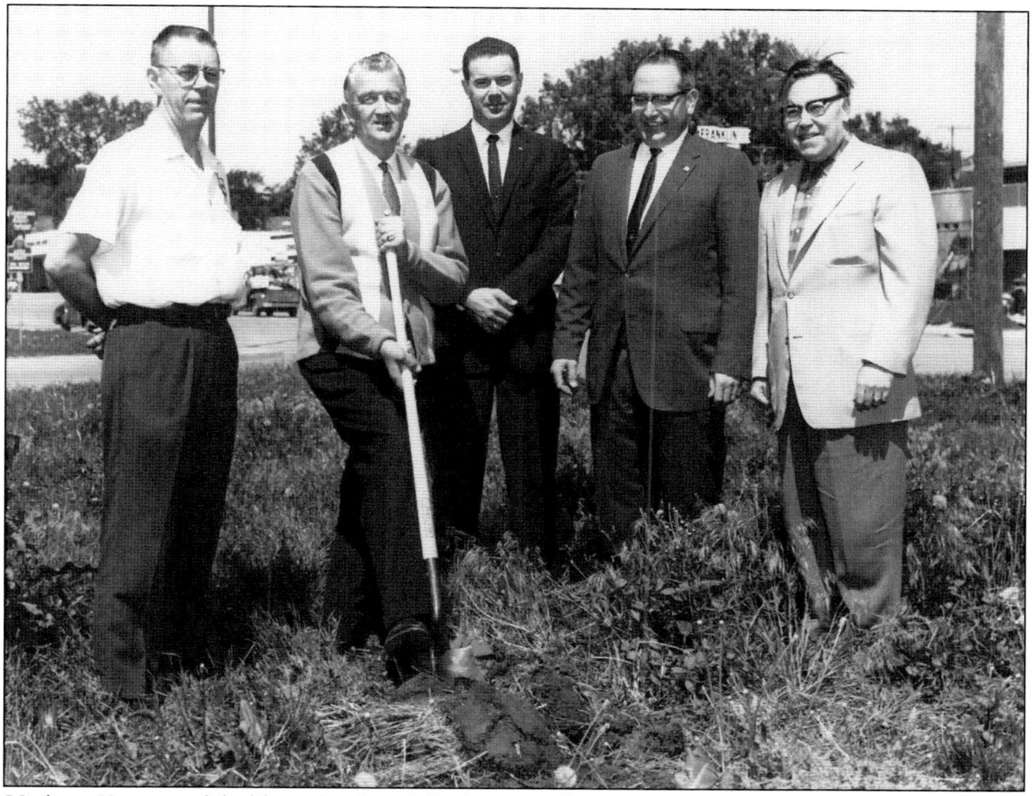

Hjalmer Kousgaard, holding the shovel, broke ground on May 16, 1963, for Kousgaard's Shopping Center at Mission Avenue and Franklin Street. Pictured with him are, from left to right, Charles Jones of Western Auto, John Long of Nebraska Savings, John Johnson of Johnson's Pharmacy, and L.H. Freeman of Freeman Furniture. Once the shopping center was built, Jones, Johnson, and Freeman's businesses would occupy the space. (Courtesy Joyce Ritche.)

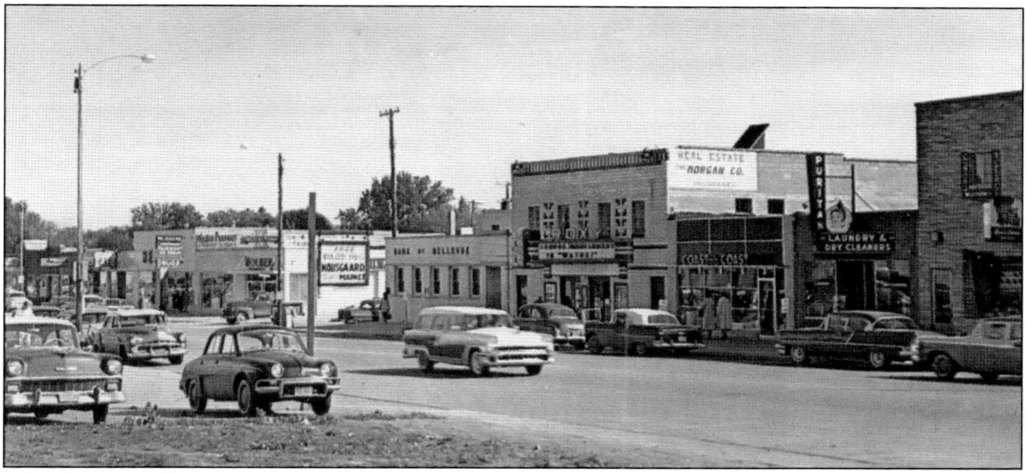

The closest Bellevue has come to a centralized commercial district is the Olde Towne area along Mission Avenue. City Hall, Johnson's Pharmacy, Bellevue Appliance, Kousgaard's Super Market, Bank of Bellevue, Dobbs Cleaners, and the Roxy Theater were all located in this general vicinity. With the sudden tremendous growth Bellevue encountered, this area soon became dwarfed as the city's borders expanded outward.

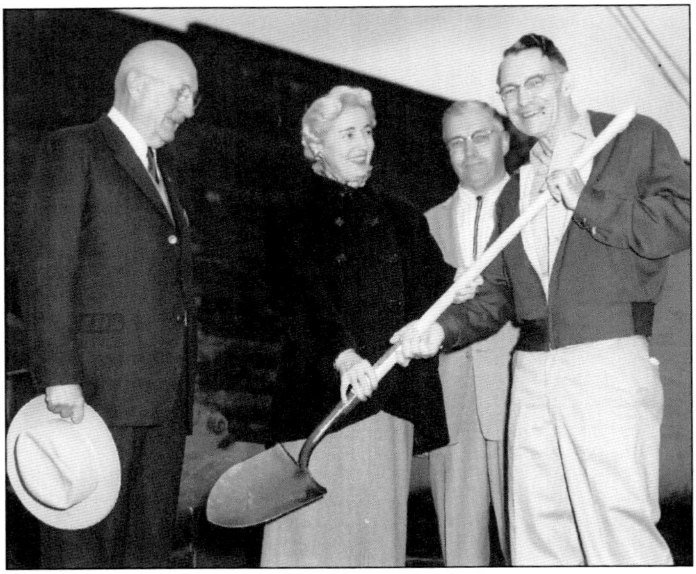

Mae Power, wife of Gen. Thomas S. Power, commander of Strategic Air Command, is seen at the ground breaking for the Bellevue Bank with, from left to right, Charlie Reed, builder Harold Jinings, and Mayor Vernon Woodle. Although Reed was the bank president, vice president Hugh Campbell performed daily operations. Campbell personally waited on the first customer, Jeffrey Lynn Campbell (no relation). When the bank opened in March 1951, it had been 95 years since Bellevue had a bank. (Courtesy Ron Woodle.)

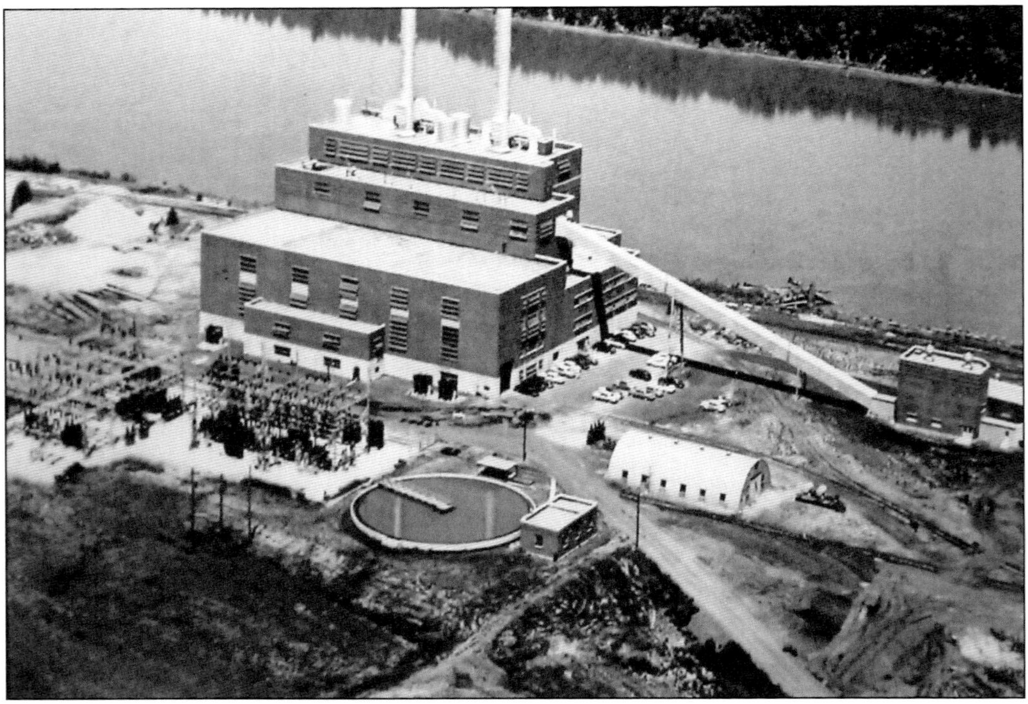

Sitting on the Missouri River waterfront, the coal-fired Kramer Power Plant was demolished in 2004. All that currently remains of the 10-story building is a small section of the cooling station concrete with empty window frames gazing upon the roaring river. When built in 1949, the Kramer Power Plant quite literally powered Bellevue into the modern age until retired in 1987.

Five

A Community at Play

Bellevue has worked hard, but it also historically has shown it knows how to enjoy itself. Arts, entertainment, and escapism have been key components for Bellevue.

A considerable sum of this can be tied to the rich forested land that consists of Fontenelle Forest and the surrounding area. Akin to an enchanted forest within a fairy tale, the wooded area near Bellevue Boulevard has served as home to a country club, Boy Scout camp, and Young Women's Christian Association retreat. Great talent and character have emerged from the memorable experiences for those who have patronized this unique topography of Nebraska.

Athletics including baseball, America's national pastime, have long been a part of Bellevue. Iowa might be baseball heaven for players of the past, but at one time, they ran the bases in Bellevue, Nebraska. Summer after summer, the local town team would be locked in combat on the field against nearby community teams for a victory, a conquest that most definitely came with bragging rights.

Still, other amusements have been popular in Bellevue, including both community and movie theaters. At one time, there were three places to see a film: the air-conditioned indoor Roxy Theater and the two separate drive-in theaters. Not bad, considering people had congregated to watch films on a white sheet in a back alley yard at one time. Today, the movie megaplex has replaced the theater experience from a bygone era.

Community events and parades have bonded the population together. Everyone from mayors to elephants has been involved at some point. For the last 43 years, the Arrows to Aerospace Celebration has been a diversion for young and old alike. Prior to that, the Bellevue Days community events did much of the same. The great outdoors and fresh air that the heartland offers continue to be enjoyed by the people of Bellevue. Most importantly, these events have offered community members the ability to relax, come together, and just have a good time. The message is happiness because we're all in it together.

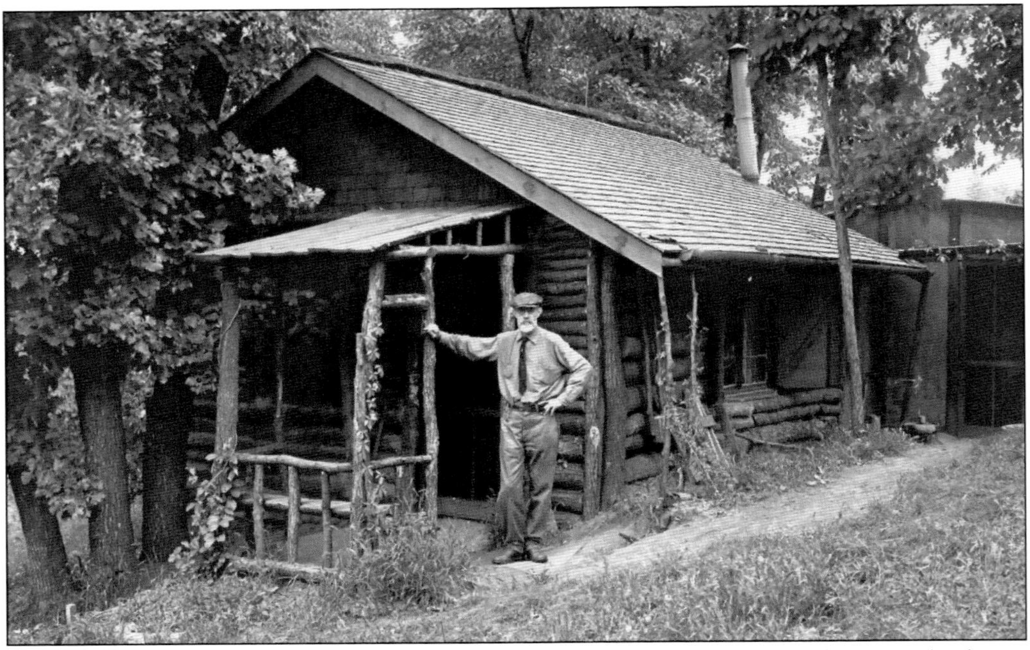

Accomplished artist Robert Gilder painted numerous seasonal Nebraska landscapes at his home studio, Wake Robin. Built in 1916 and located in Fontenelle Forest, the cabin served as a tranquil retirement home for Gilder. Also an archeologist, Gilder took part in the discovery of what was considered at the time to be the oldest human remains in North America.

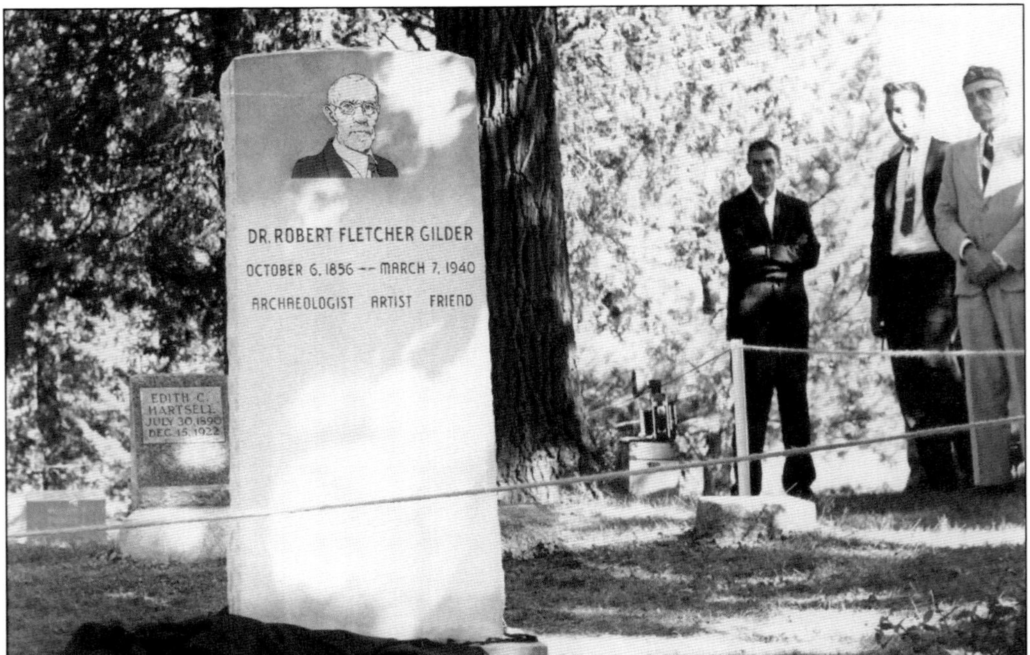

Robert Gilder died after a short battle with pneumonia in 1940. He was 83 at the time of his death, but he was still a very active and sharp man in his golden years. In 1961, to commemorate the archeologist, artist, and friend, the Bellevue American Legion and the Omaha World Herald raised funds to place a special marker next to the original simple headstone in Bellevue Cemetery.

Held at Camp Gifford, the Boy Scout sacred society known as Nani Ba Zhu involved much Indian lore, including elaborate Native American costumes. The name itself came from the supreme being of the Chippeway tribes. The group actively met at Camp Gifford from 1919 until it ceased to function in 1939. Nani Ba Zhu, however, has seen a revival elsewhere in recent years, continuing the Boy Scout tradition founded in Bellevue.

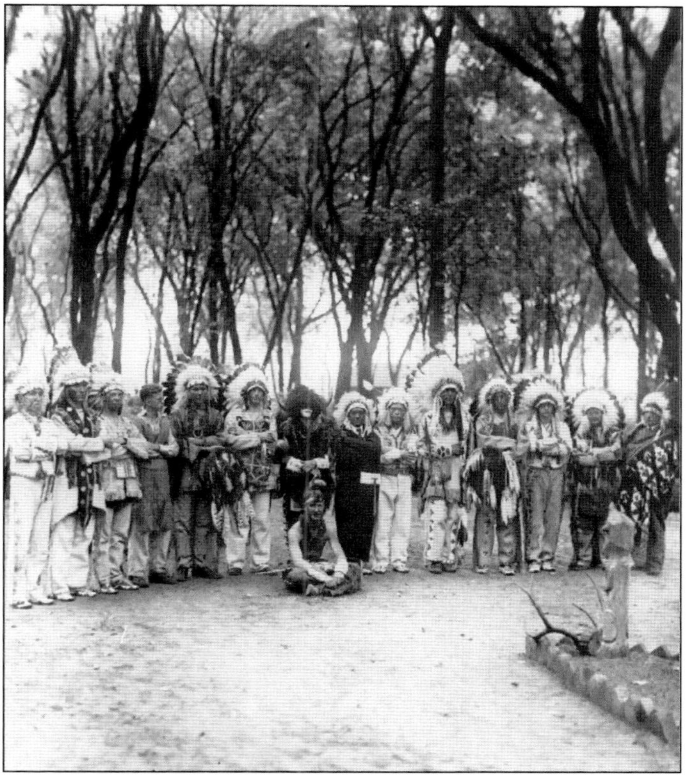

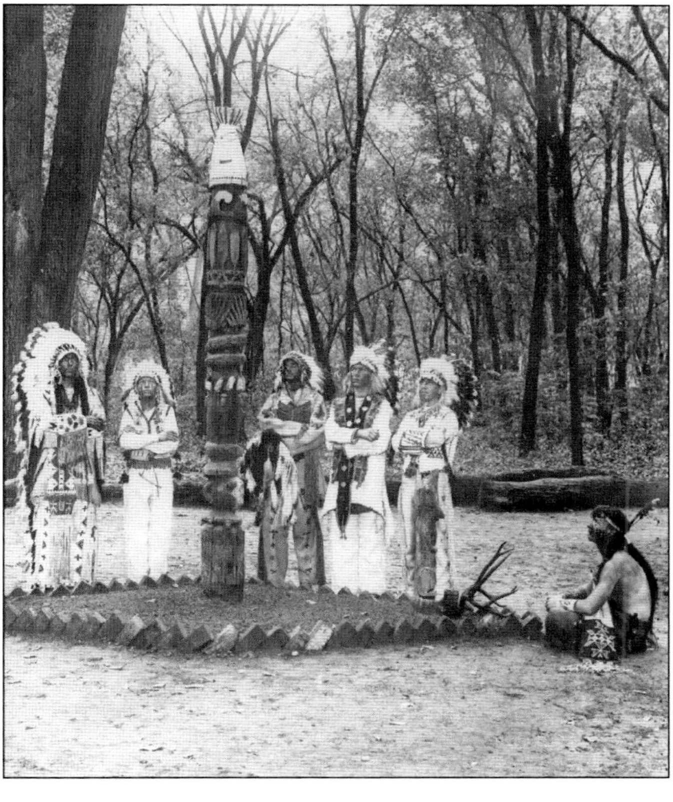

Each year, the Nani Ba Zhu members would carve a portion of the totem pole. Bellevue resident Ed Sterba, sitting on the ground in this 1928 meeting, took part in the carving. Only the top one percent of Boy Scouts were permitted to join the organization. A number of Bellevue boys were involved in Nani Ba Zhu, as was the actor Henry Fonda.

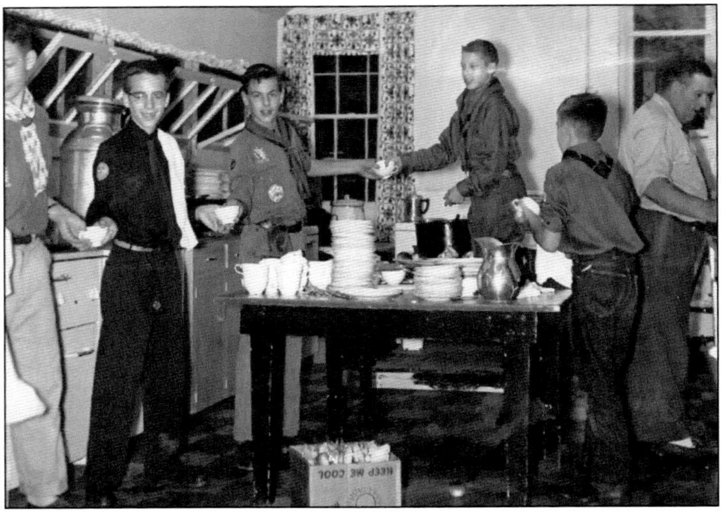

Local Boy Scouts have been doing their best to help other people in Bellevue, dating back to Camp Gifford. During a 1953 event, Boy Scout Troop 53 helped with fundraising efforts for their sponsor, the First Presbyterian Church, by working in the kitchen and serving dinner. Still active in the community, they continue to work on service projects, including sending flags to armed forces members.

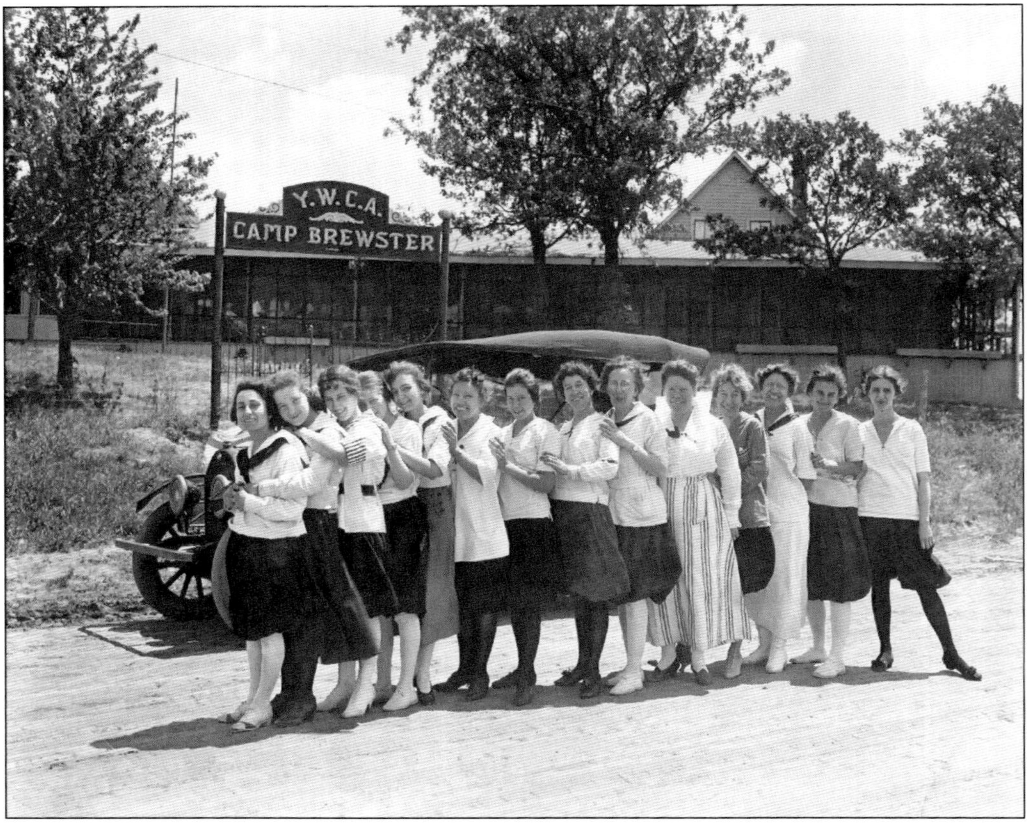

For more than 40 years, young women enjoyed the beautiful landscape of Bellevue at Camp Brewster, YWCA Camp. Originally a country club and later the YWCA campsite, the grounds were forced to close in 1968. In the 1970s, the clubhouse seen in the background was used for a practice fire for the Bellevue Volunteer Fire Department. An occasional fragment of blue concrete from the swimming pool can still be found.

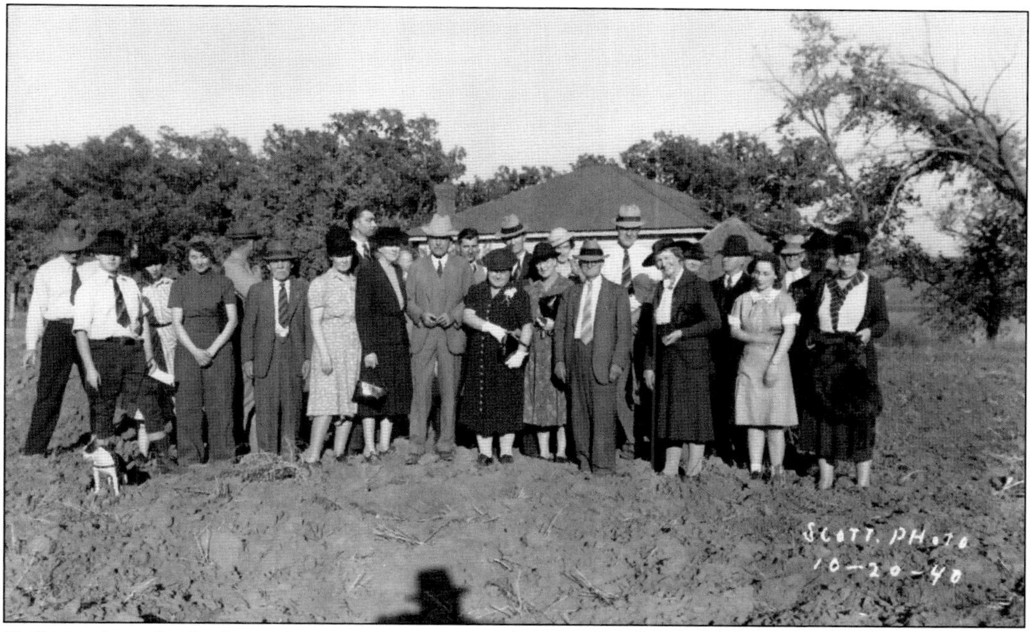

Bellevue has also had people interested in its prehistory. Evidence of this period was still apparent in the mid 20th century. Groups were frequently organized, as was this one through the Fontenelle Nature Club on October 20, 1940, to search for evidence of the effects of the ice age on the Great Plains. On the same day, they also visited the present site of Twin Creek Shopping Center at 36th Street and Highway 370. During their visit, a farm belonging to Amos Gates occupied the space. Before that, an Omaha Indian village solely inhabited this intersection that sits near the Papio Creek. (Courtesy FNA.)

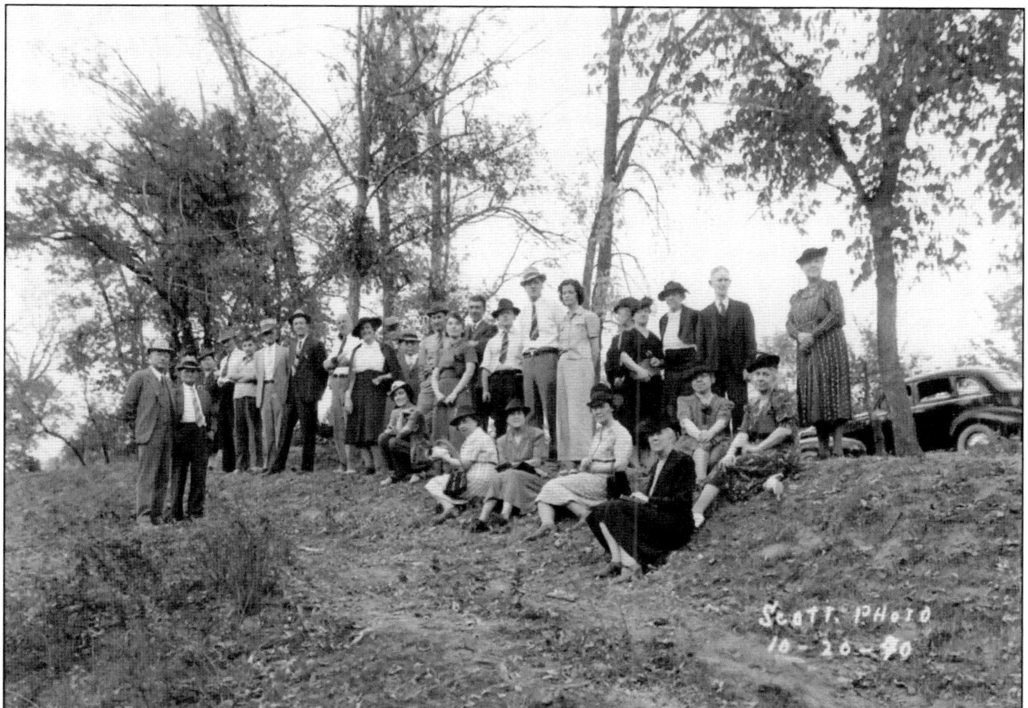

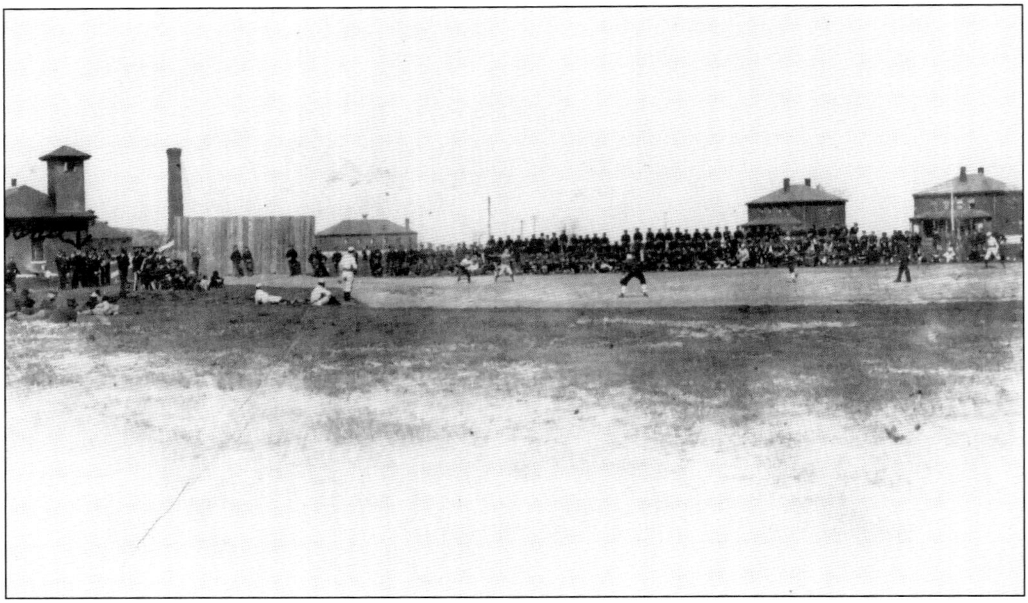

Men of the 30th Infantry Regiment at Fort Crook take a break from soldiering to enjoy a game of baseball. Fort Crook had a dedicated baseball diamond, and the games were a popular draw that included the accompanying music of the regimental band. Several buildings from NCO's Row are visible in the background.

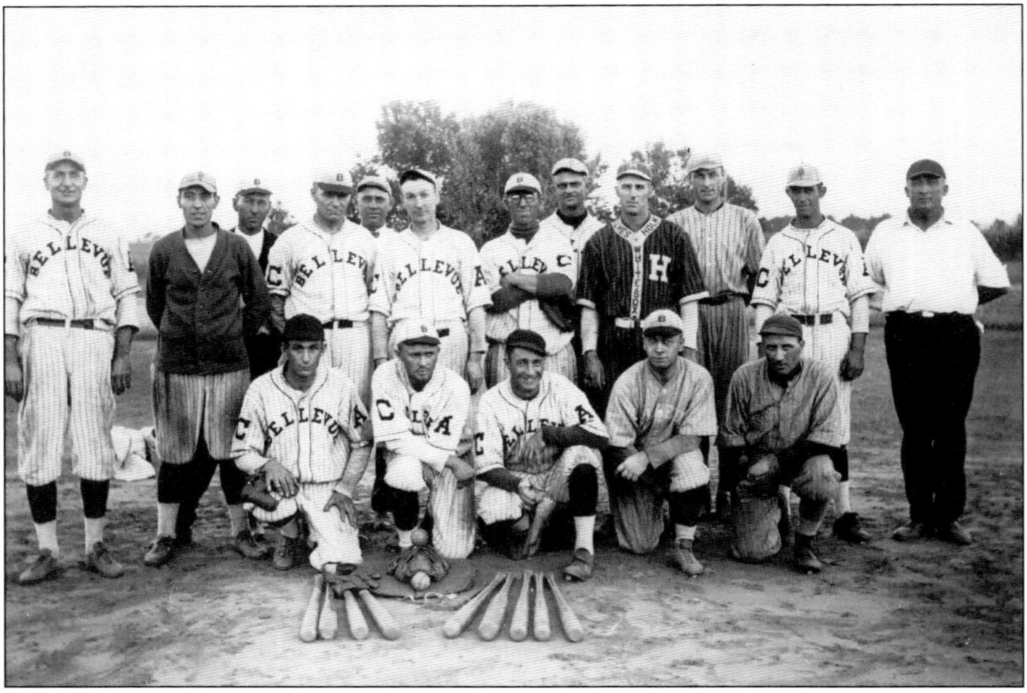

The Bellevue town team would play other area teams, such as the Papillion Colts, and later, the Cardinals. Occasionally, exhibition matches would be held where games would be played against traveling barnstorming teams. These were often popular with both fans and curiosity seekers alike who would come out to watch the home team play the Nebraska Indians, an all–Native American team.

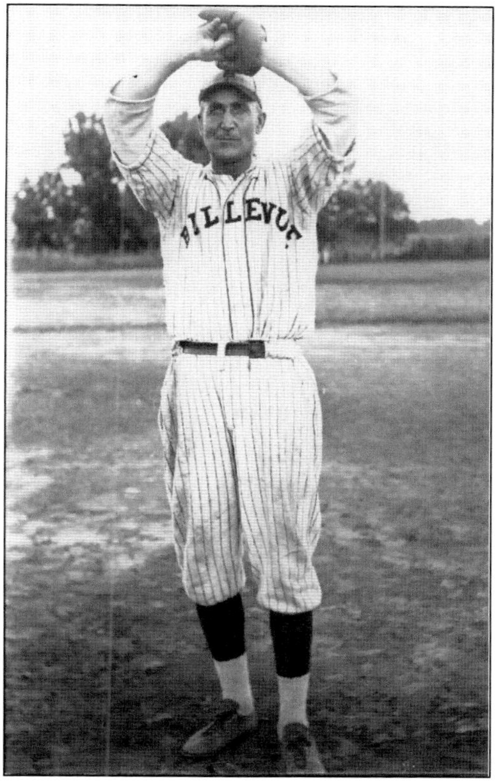

Shown in 1925, Andy Graves winds up while centerfielder Earl Olsen appears ready for a catch. The two were members of Bellevue's town baseball team. On June 18, 1925, the Bellevue Athletics broke the Papio Colts winning streak, defeating them 8 to 5. Olsen went 1 for 2 at bat. With seven errors, the Colts essentially fell victim to themselves. In a rematch in mid-September, the Athletics again defeated the Colts 7 to 5. Although heavy-hitting Athletics right fielder "Red" Hindman batted a .444 average that year, he only went 1 for 5 that day. The Athletics closed out their successful season with another win the following week.

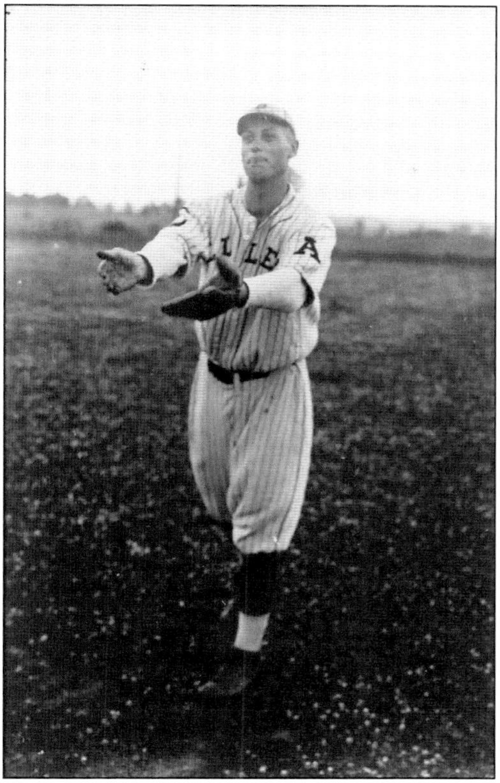

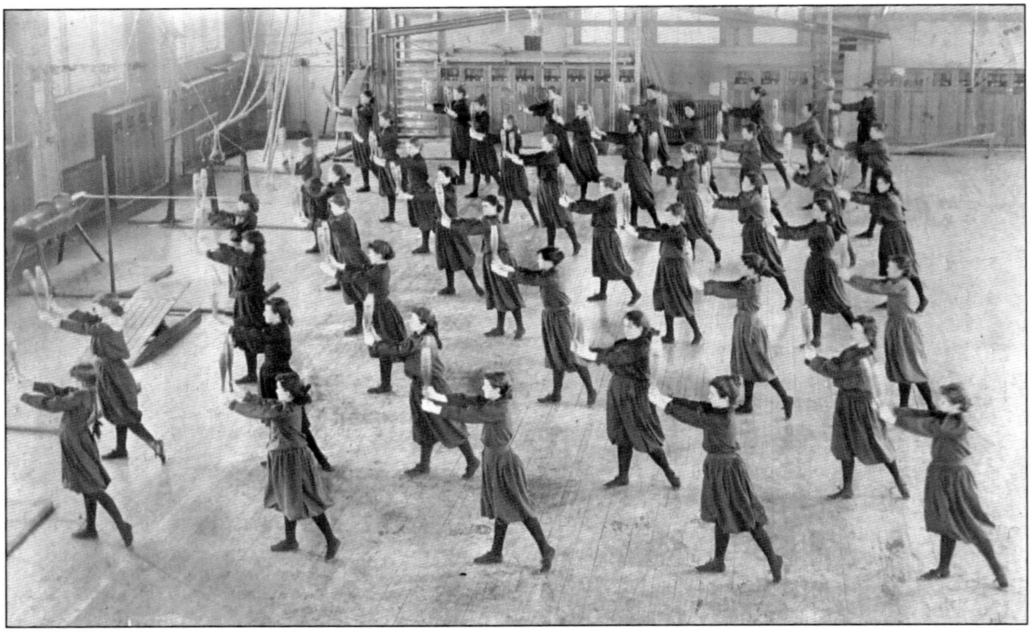

The women of Bellevue College partake in their customary vigorous workout with Indian club weights. Athletics were in high demand at Bellevue College for both men and women. The popularity led to winning state championships for several years in football, baseball, and track. The college received a new dedicated gymnasium in 1916, but this photograph taken in 1904 or 1905 would have been in the older multipurpose facility.

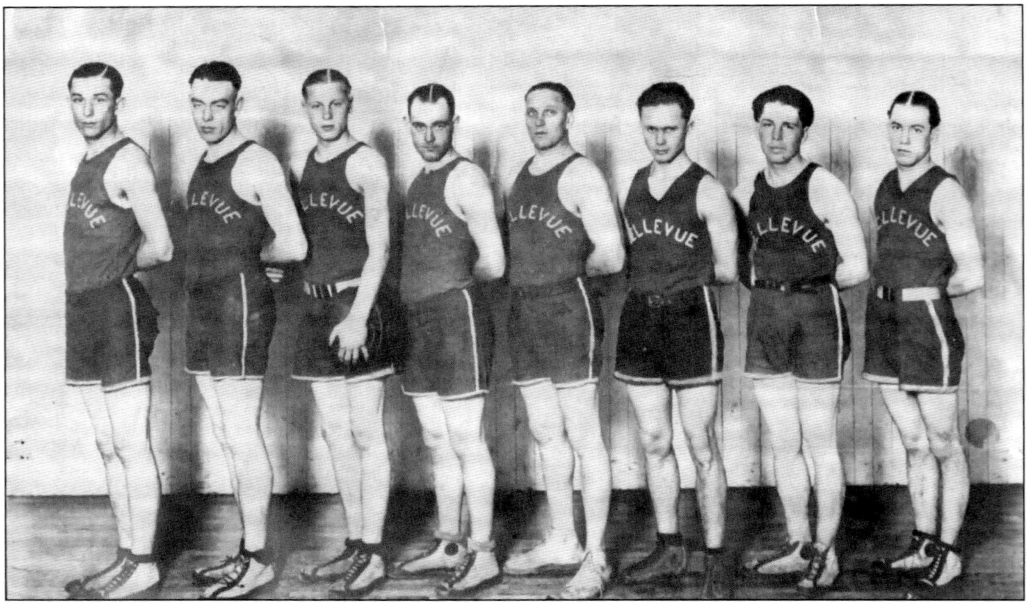

In the 1923–1924 season, Bellevue took home the Nebraska state basketball championship. These eight tore up the court with a record of 17 wins and just one loss. Because shirts were in short supply, being on the team at that time did not necessarily give you the right to wear a jersey.

Born in Bellevue in August 1875, Henry Tefft Clarke Jr. went on to play major-league baseball for two teams that have since become extinct. The first of these was widely considered one of the worst teams in the history of professional baseball, the Cleveland Spiders. The other team Clarke played for was the Chicago Orphans, predecessor to the Chicago Cubs. After hanging up his spikes, Clarke Jr. served in the Nebraska House of Representatives.

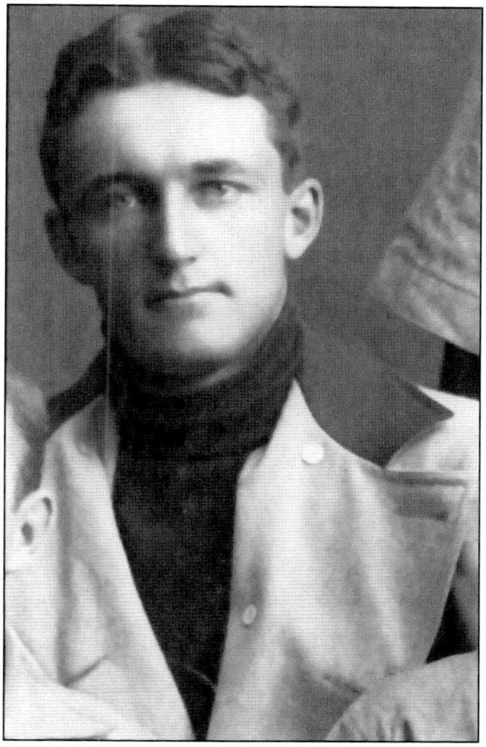

The Merryland, which later became the Black Kat and even later the New Modern Night Club, was a gin joint and roadhouse notorious as a gambling hall, resulting in frequent police raids. A 1935 post-Prohibition raid turned up roulette, dice, and craps games. Also found were $85 in marked bills and an elaborate buzzer system to warn that John Q. Law was approaching.

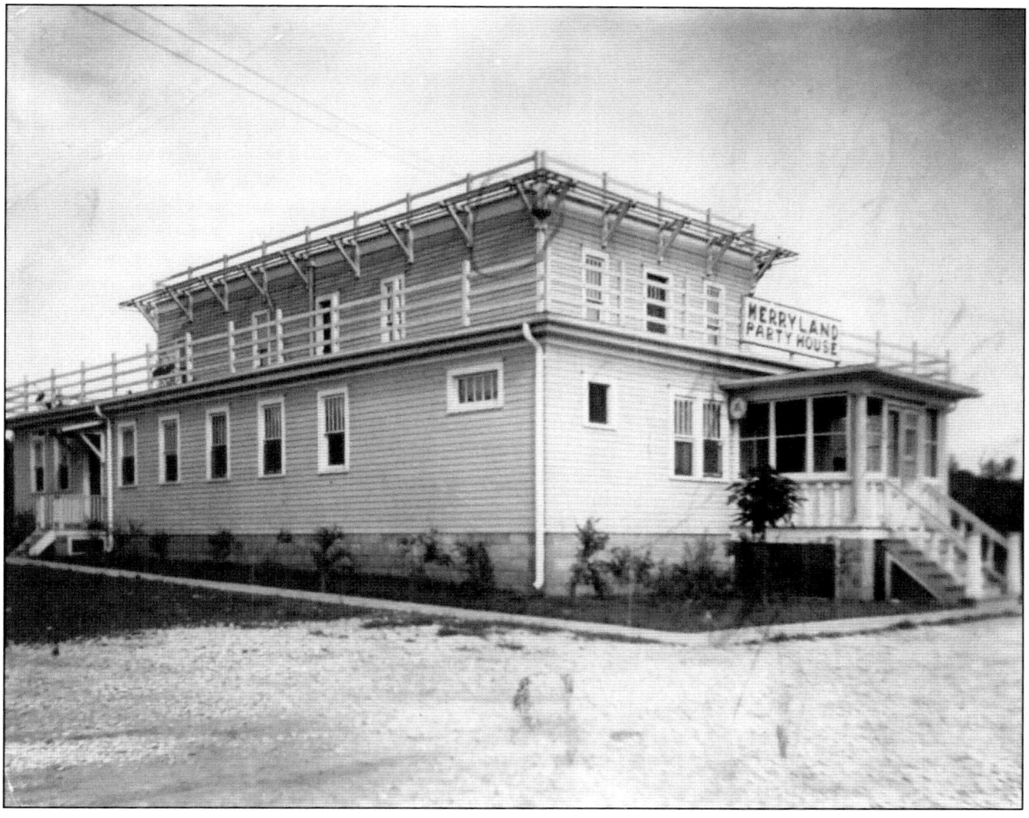

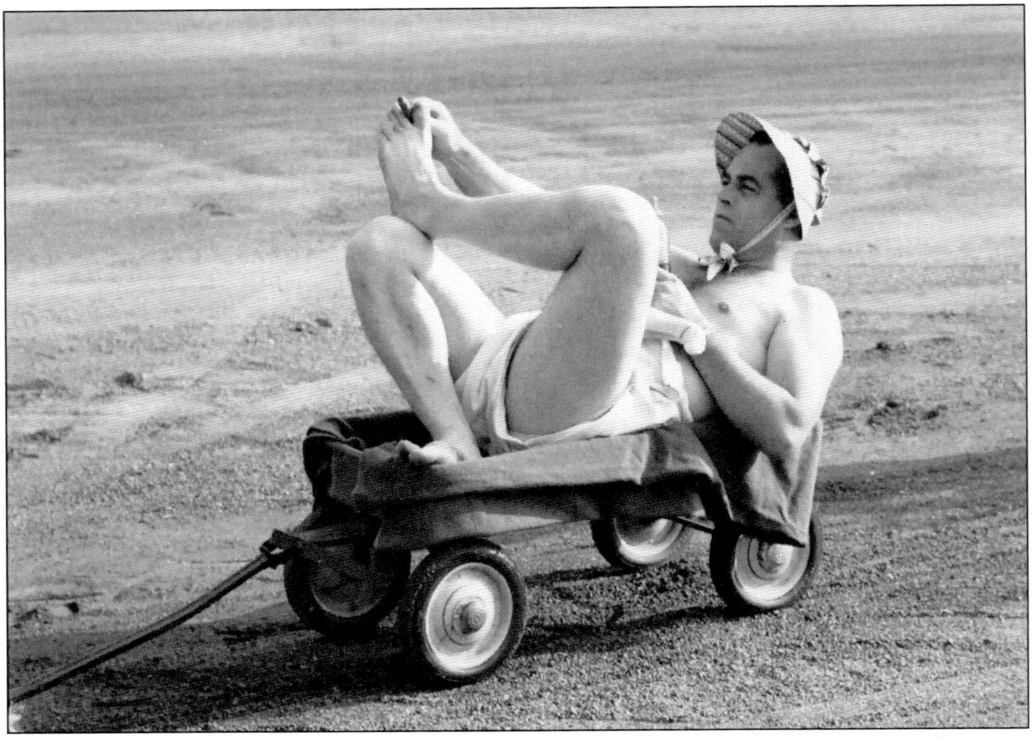

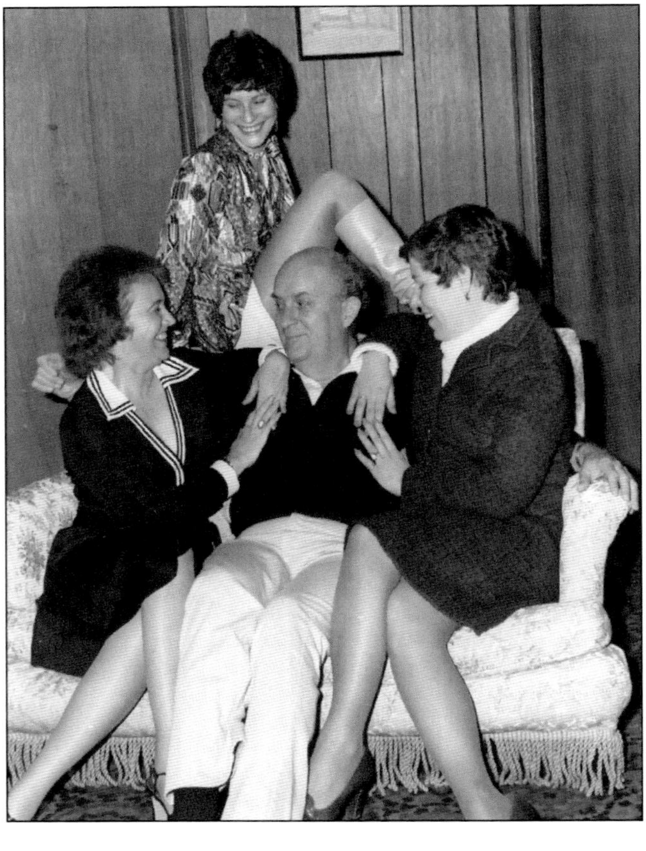

All work and no play makes John Gebbie a dull boy. Many of the photographs within this book stem from his collection. With a cigar in his toes and a baby bottle reportedly full of bourbon, he clearly also knew how to enjoy himself, as seen in this 1947 image from the VFW Parade.

Founded in 1968, the Bellevue Little Theater is Sarpy County's only performing arts center. In 1977, they were able to purchase the 244-seat vintage Roxy Theater. From left to right, Sandy Thompson, Vicki Davis, Ed Swanson, and Paula Siegel perform during the production of *Last of the Red Hot Lovers*. (Courtesy Bette Swanson.)

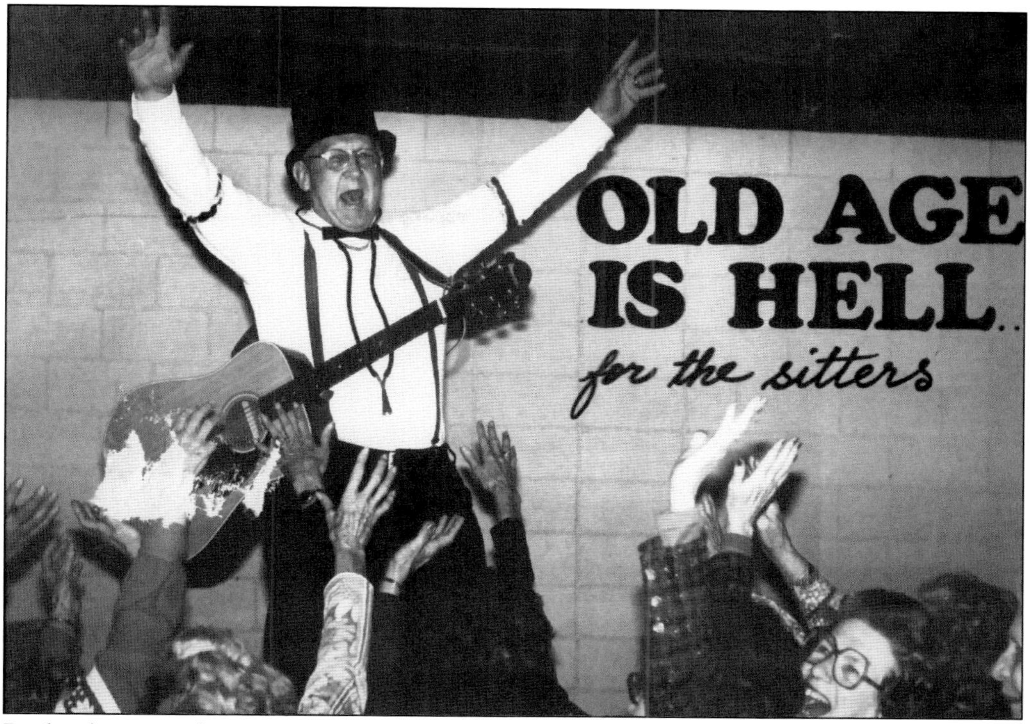

By day, he was a doctor, and a good one at that. By night, he was a doctor who played guitar. Mobbed by fans, Dr. Francis was a prolific singer of novelty songs that can be found on 33 and 45 rpm records. His album *Old Age is Hell for the Sitters*, coproduced by Senior Citizen Records, featured such songs as "Senior Citizen Girl" and "Prescription for a Divorce."

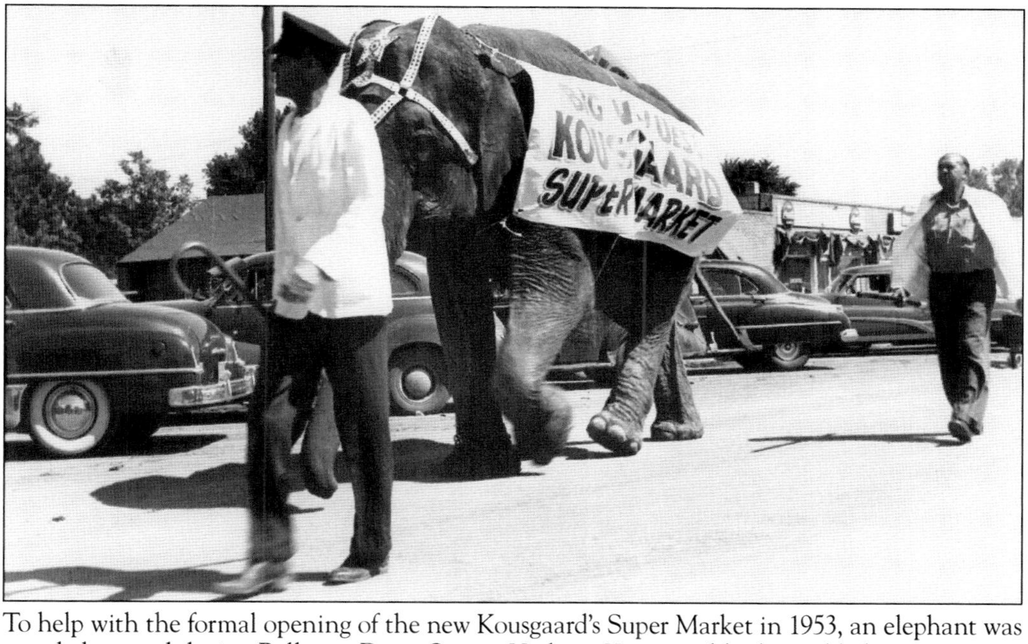

To help with the formal opening of the new Kousgaard's Super Market in 1953, an elephant was paraded around during Bellevue Days. Owner Hjalmer Kousgaard had stumbled upon a circus troupe stranded at the local drive-in theater. It was not long after that he acquired a new attraction for the local parade. (Courtesy Joyce Ritche.)

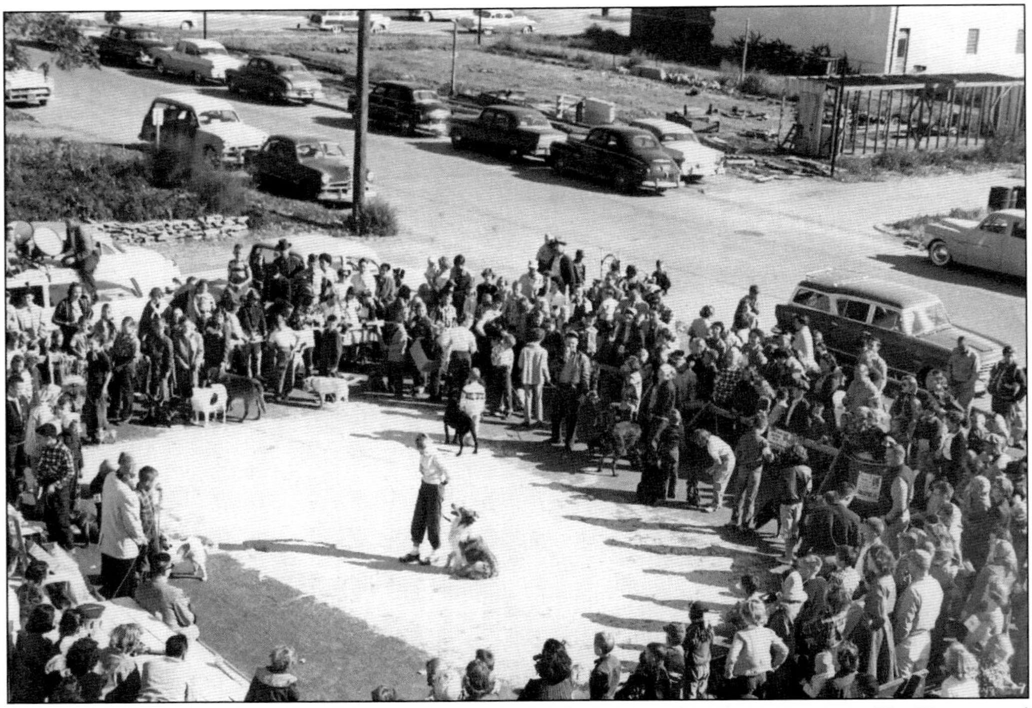

Dogs and children alike flocked to the second annual amateur dog show sponsored by Kousgaard Super Market and Quaker Oats on October 6, 1956. Dixie Clamp, co-owner of Bellevue Upholstering, served as master of ceremonies for the 200 dogs and 1,000 people in attendance. First place went to Bobby Lane, but additional awards went to smallest dog, shaggiest dog, and dog with the longest tail. The dogs that attended Bellevue's dog show were each treated to two free cans of Ken-L Ration dog food. Children received the nearly as good an incentive of free ice cream. (Courtesy Joyce Ritchie)

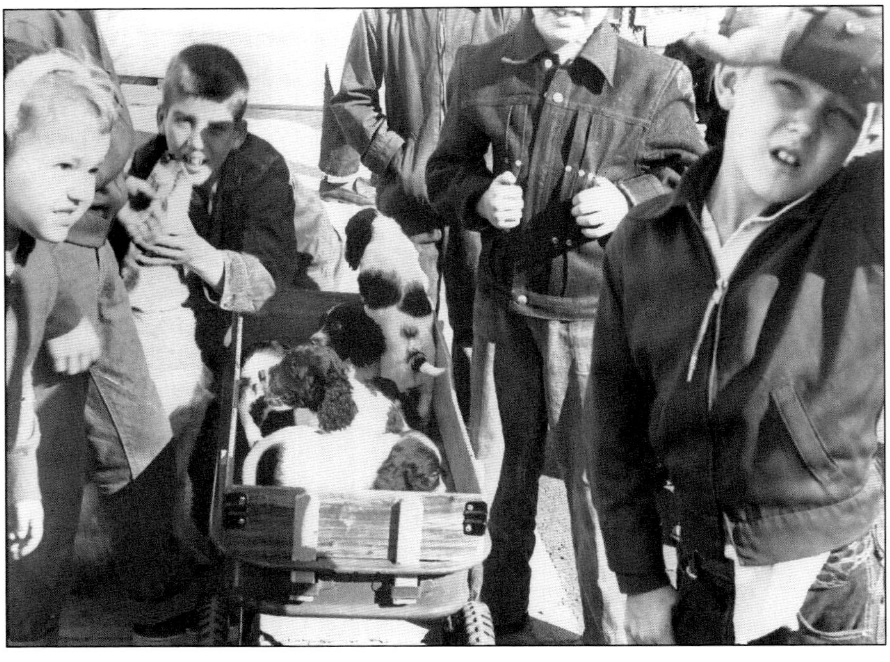

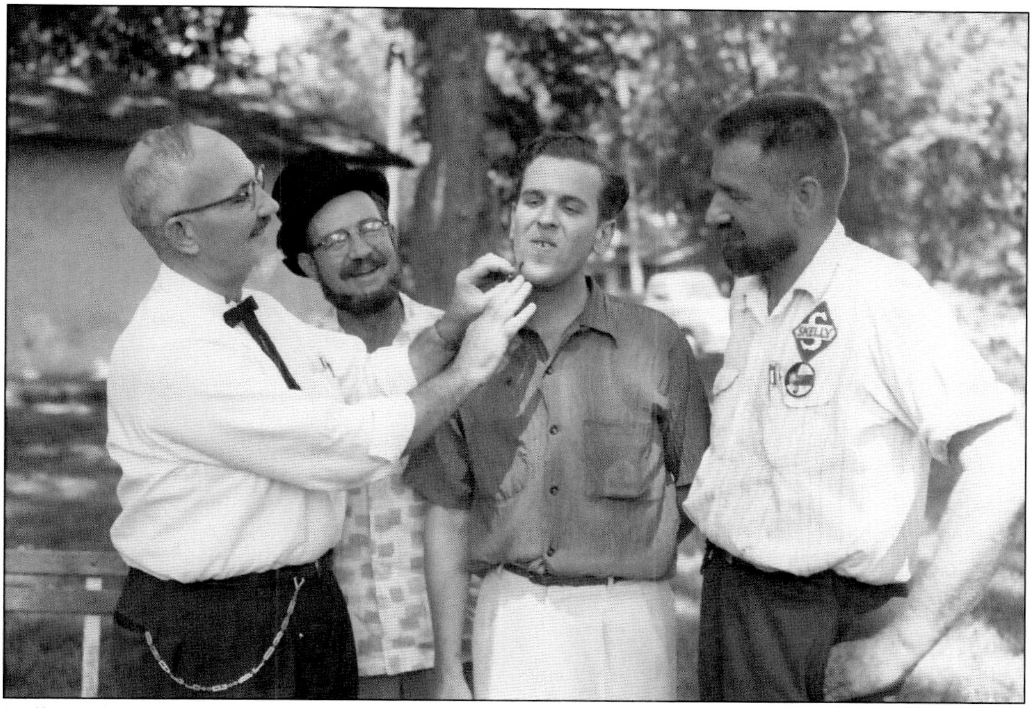

Bellevue began as just another community in Douglas County. The Nebraska Territory Legislative Act of February 7, 1857, altered the county boundaries, thus creating the need for Sarpy County. In 1957, a major centennial celebration was held in honor of the event to mark both the history and progress made within Bellevue and Sarpy County. In the process of getting dressed in period wear, residents pose above for a group shot during the celebration of their independence. Below, Lyle DeMoss of WOW Radio conducts an interview with others, including Harlan Lewis, during a 24-hour continuous salute named Bellevue Day.

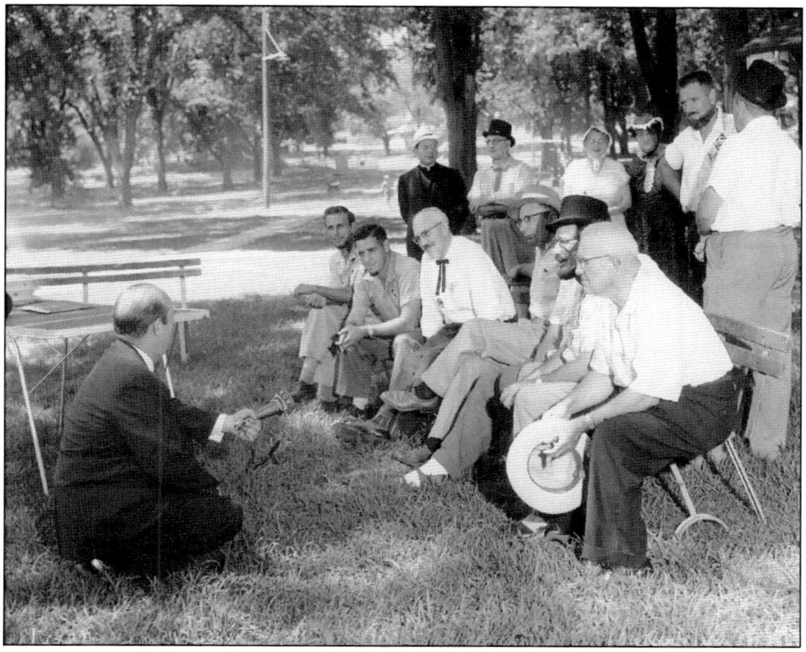

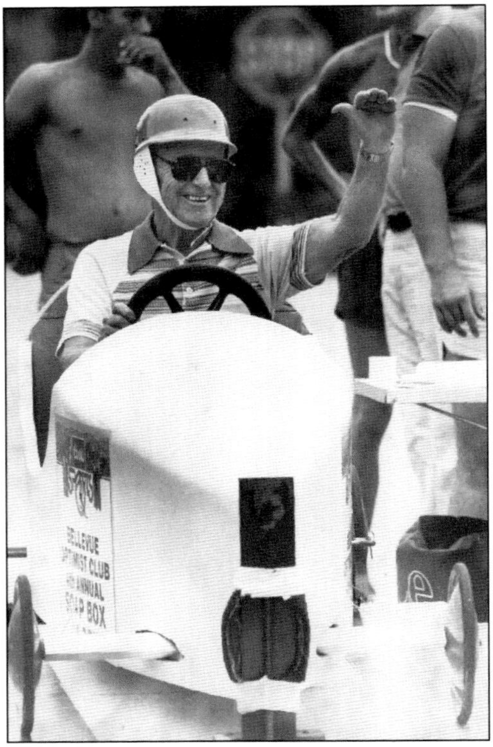

Former mayor Robert Haworth was not one to be exclusively found at his desk. Instead, he could commonly be found out in the community, as was the case during the annual Bellevue Optimist Soapbox Derby. Haworth would commonly offer his support to a variety of organizations and causes, including the Knights of Columbus Tootsie Roll Drive, VFW Poppy Program, and the Bellevue Jaycees and Lions Club. (City of Bellevue.)

Bellevue mayor Joe Baldwin offers a hitchhiking gorilla a ride in his convertible. The gorilla was in town along with Lee Simmons, director of Omaha's Henry Doorly Zoo. The city of Bellevue donated a heavy tractor implement to the zoo. Today, Simmons has several lemurs named after him, while Baldwin has several baseball diamonds that serve little league teams named in his honor.

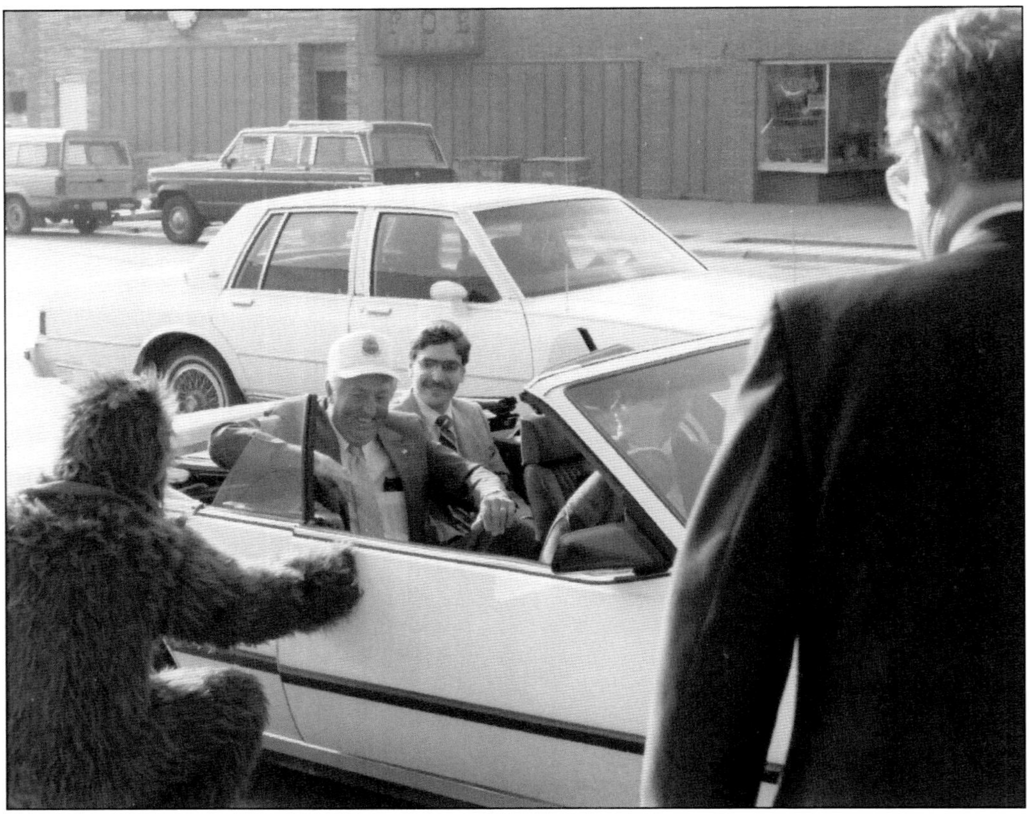

Six

EDUCATION

Education has always taken precedence in Bellevue. Since the first days of settlers in the area, missionaries not only brought their religion, but also their efforts to provide a Western education to the Native American population. Once the community filled in beyond the initial missionaries, explorers, trappers, and traders, it was necessary to build two schools to accommodate the local children. In 1860, sixty-eight children attended school within the community. Yet with the city in deep decline by the 1880s, Bellevue lacked a public high school. This meant teenagers attended school in nearby Papillion, or in some instances, did not attend at all.

The establishment of Bellevue College is one of the two happenings that saved the community from extinction. This would not have been possible without a significant philanthropic undertaking by both locals and individuals out east that put their faith and finances into Bellevue. Even if the outcome of the first Bellevue College ended in disappointment, it served as the stimulus to aid in Bellevue's survival.

By the time Bellevue entered the postwar era, the Bellevue Public School System was scrambling in order to meet the demands of an ever-growing community. The now old, crowded schools built to accommodate the trickle of growth were closed, and new and additional ones sprang up in their place.

To add to the surge in the education field, a new Bellevue College was established in the mid-1960s. In a community once lacking a high school, there are now three public high schools and one private high school within Bellevue's borders. Education in Bellevue has not prospered just because of money or leadership. It has prevailed due to the dedication and commitment to lifelong learning.

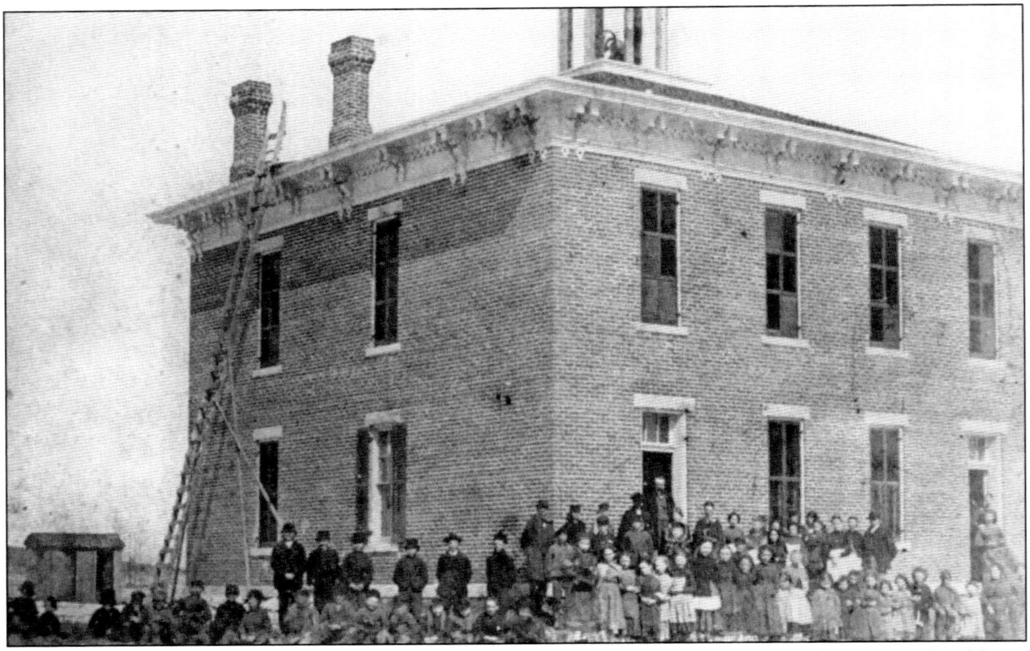

Built in 1869, this school was the first in Bellevue to combine all eight grades in one building. Simply known as Bellevue School District 1, it became Main School in 1911 and later, Bellevue Junior/Senior High. Throughout these years, numerous additions were made to improve the scope and size of the original building, leading up to 1966 when it would become Mission Junior High, now a middle school.

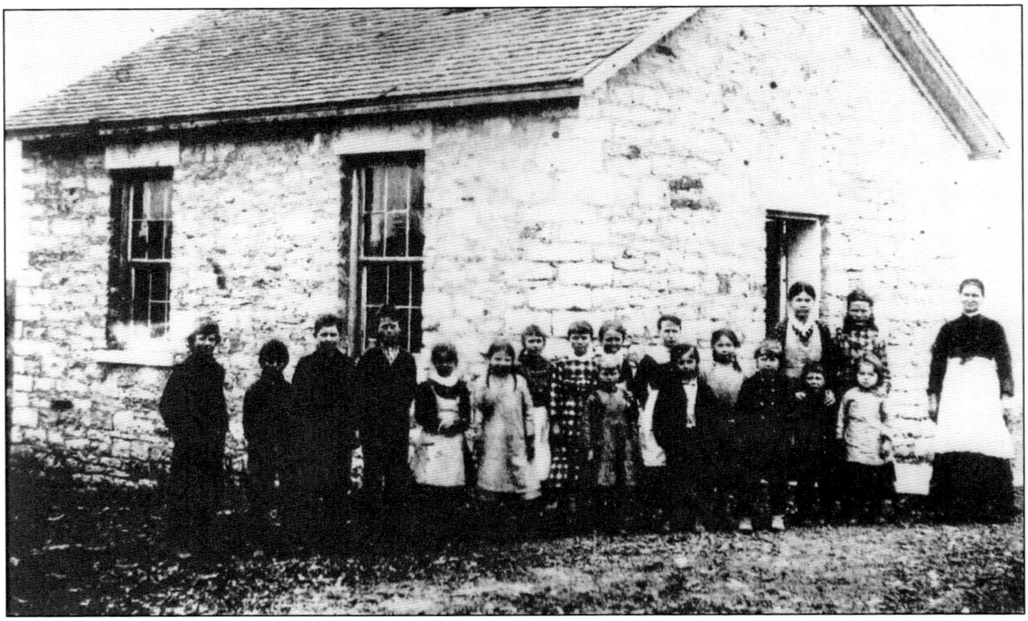

Located on the Gates property, the old stone schoolhouse was eventually destroyed in a fire. In 1885 when this class photograph was taken, Samantha Gates taught at least 18 students, including Dell McCarty, Pat Mulligan, Clarence McCarty, Archie Bishop, Susie McCarty, Marion McCarty, Nellie McCarty, Mary Key, Sarah McCarty, Nettie Wold, Susie Key, Lucy and Emma Bishop, and Mary McCarty.

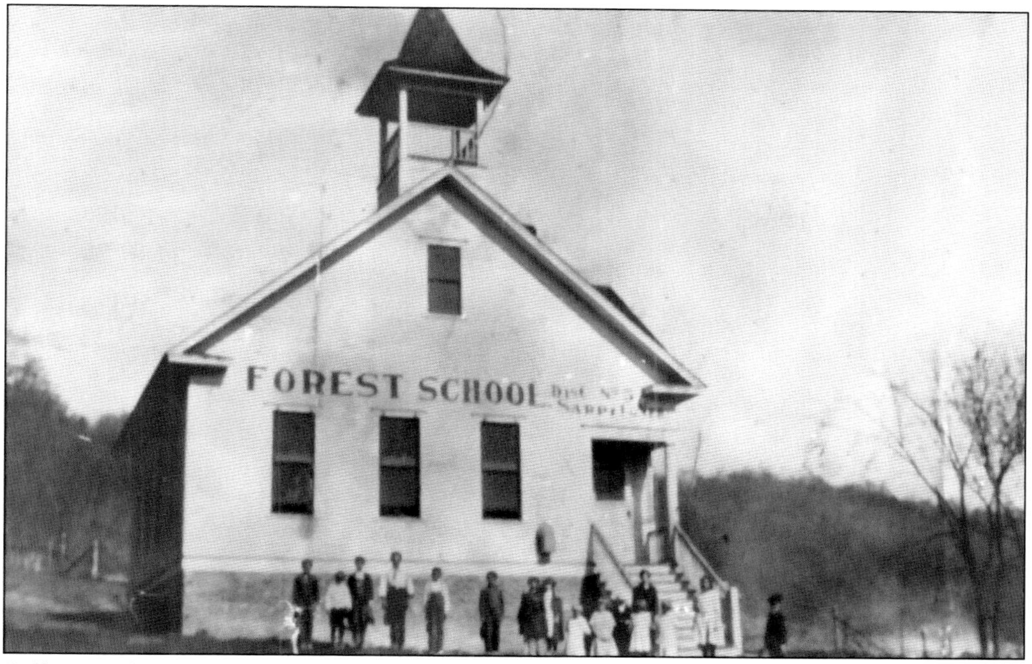

Bellevue School District 5, otherwise known as Forest School, was set back off Bellevue Boulevard, halfway between the street and the CB&Q line. In 1870, there were 20 independent school districts operating in Sarpy County. Through the years, many of them would be consolidated into the Bellevue Public Schools. By 1921, the four schools in the fifth district were run out of dilapidated buildings that were even then not up to fire code. In 1976, the Fontenelle Natural Association tore down the school, as seen below with, from left to right, naturalist Art Dee, chief ranger Charlie Grant, and director Bob Fluchel. (Courtesy FNA)

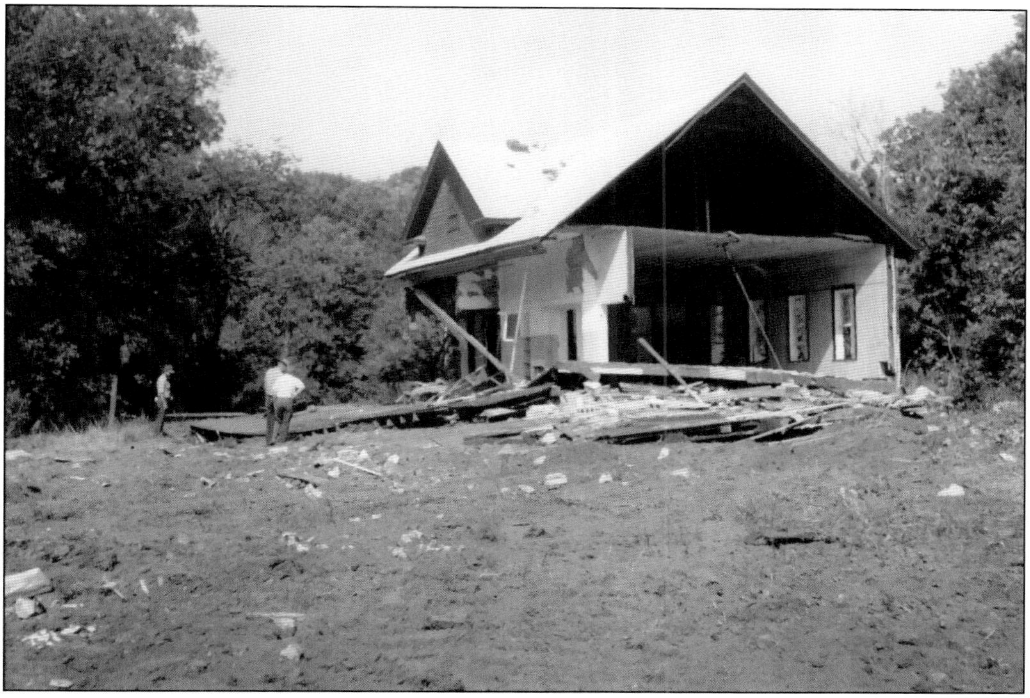

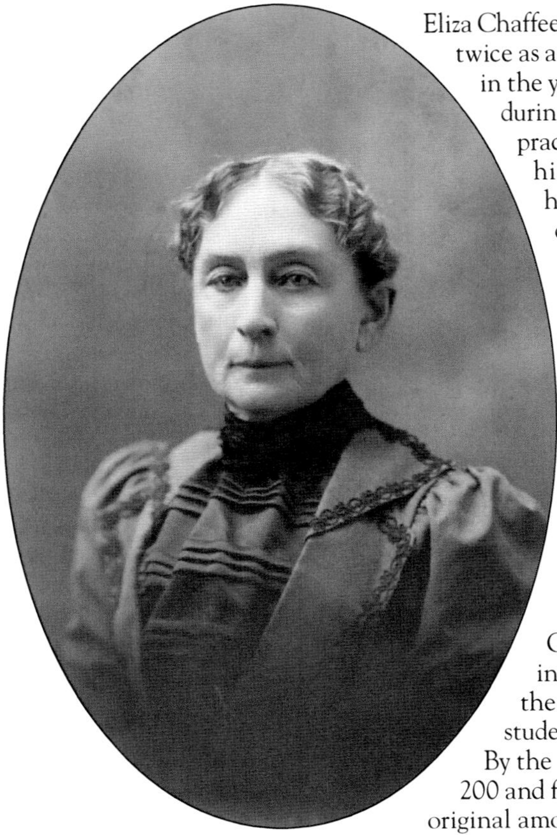

Eliza Chaffee, the widow of Dr. Horace H. Chaffee, served twice as a member of the Bellevue Board of Education in the years following the couple's move to Bellevue during September 1859. The doctor was a successful practitioner in the area for nearly 30 years until his death in 1893. In 1969, their large 1880 home was burned to the ground in a training drill for firefighters.

The Reverend Dr. David R. Kerr, seen here with his wife, was the president of Bellevue College. Kerr first came to Bellevue College in 1889 and supervised the transformation of the school from a two-building campus with 30 students to a respected higher-learning institution. By the time he left in 1903, enrollment was nearing 200 and funding had increased over six times from its original amount.

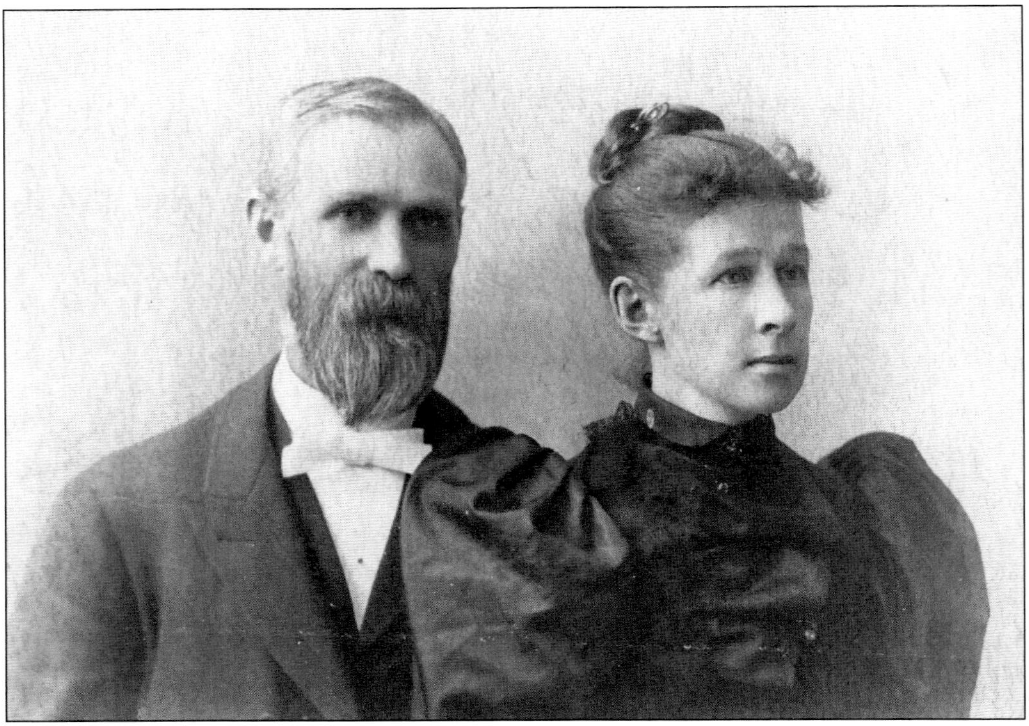

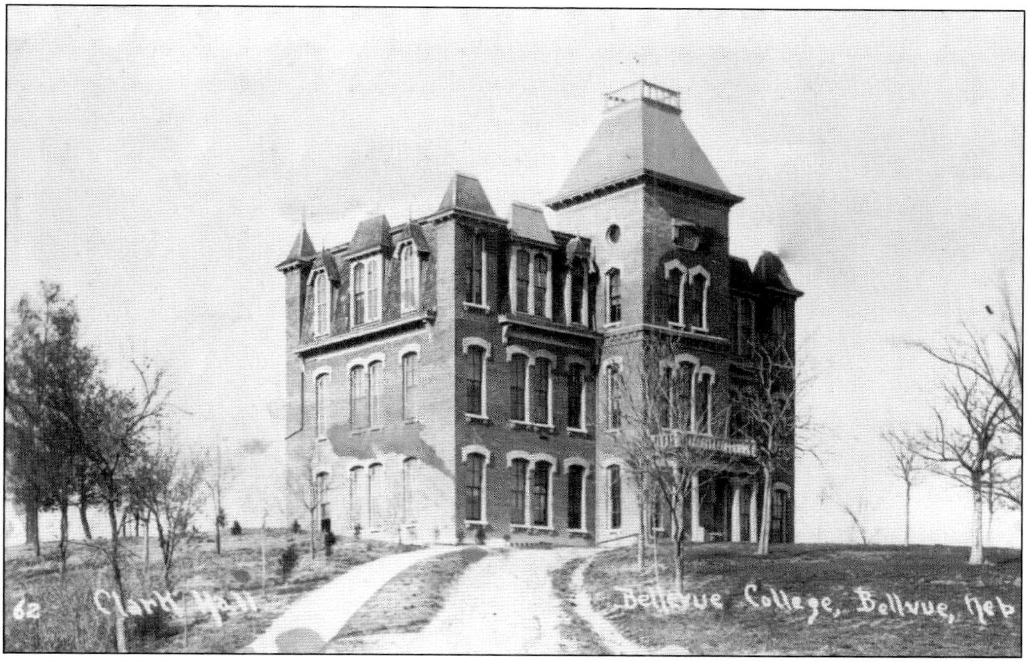

On July 4, 1883, the cornerstone was laid for Clarke Hall, the first building on the campus of Bellevue College. Presbyterian elder Henry T. Clarke donated more than $20,000 to construct the building, so naturally, it was named after him. Essential to the foundation of the college, the building housed classrooms, the library, and a chapel. During the 1908 tornado, the tower was torn off.

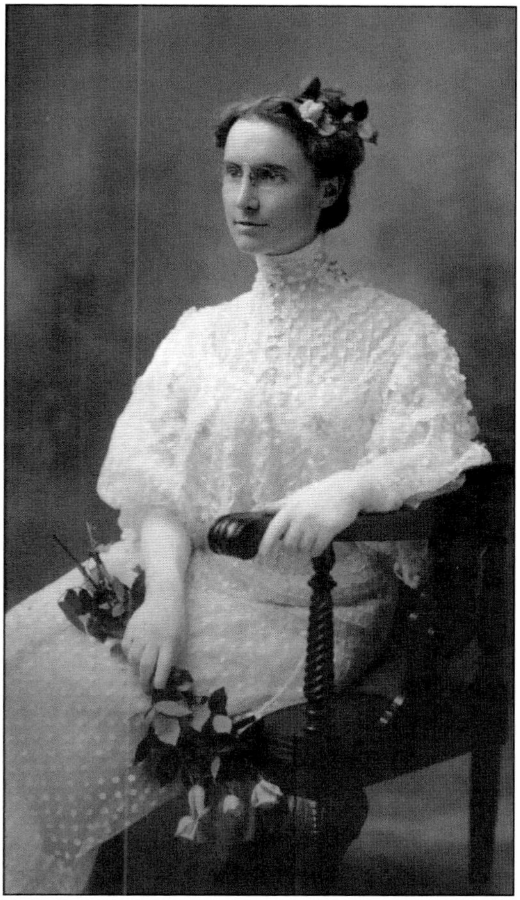

Delta Pearl Jones, a Bellevue graduate, returned to teach Latin from 1897 to 1908. Seen here in her wedding dress, she married Dr. James Sterenberg on June 14, 1905. Sterenberg taught Greek at Bellevue College from 1902 to 1909 and later served as dean and acting president once Reverend Kerr left. Dr. James Sterenberg's curriculum vitae included a master of arts from Harvard, and a PhD obtained in Munich.

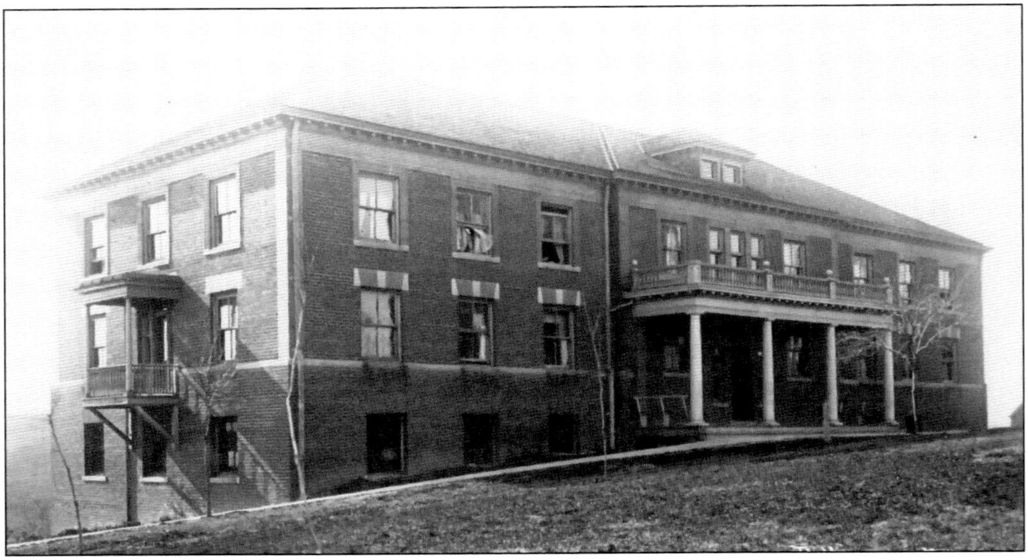

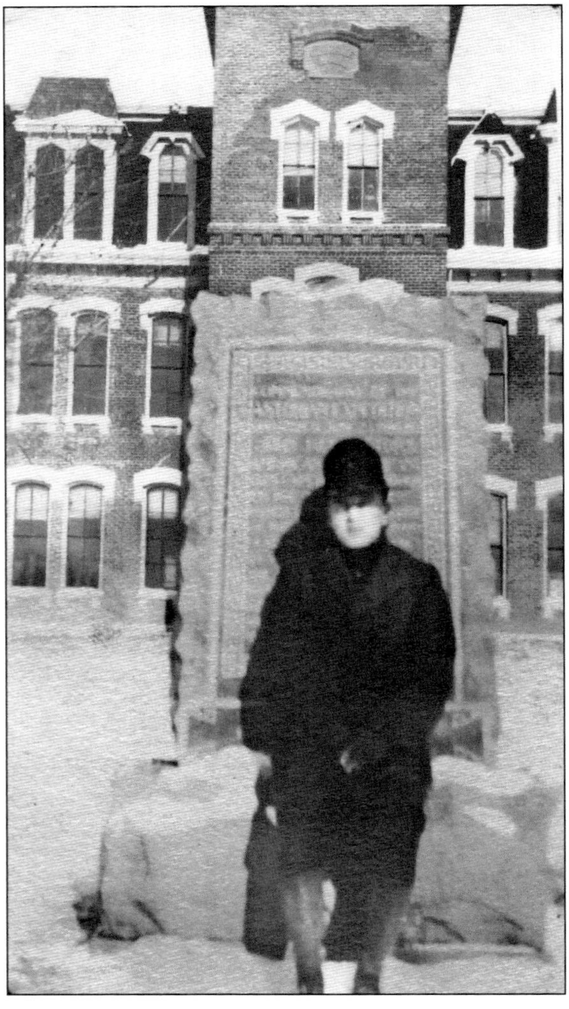

Fontenelle Hall, completed in 1903, housed much of the female student body on campus. As customary on any college campus in any era, youthful pranks could occur. One of these resulted in the girls being confined to their dorm and without the permission to date. In an act of defiance, they proceeded to make as much cacophonous noise as they could with band instruments.

Clarence Zurcher, seen here in uniform in front of Clarke Hall and the 1910 Astorian Monument, almost signifies the end of Bellevue College. By World War I, enrollment was drastically down, the school was insolvent, and support from the Presbyterian synod was dwindling. The campus hobbled along as a vocational school, among other uses, until it officially closed in 1934, transferring all remaining resources to Hastings College. (Courtesy Harriet Sullivan.)

The Charles S. Reed Community Center, named after the Bellevue banker, is the original location of the early Bellevue High School, known as Pioneer, but more commonly known as the "sheep shed" because of its shabby accommodations. It served the community for 15 years until the new high school was built in 1937. The new high school became Mission Middle School.

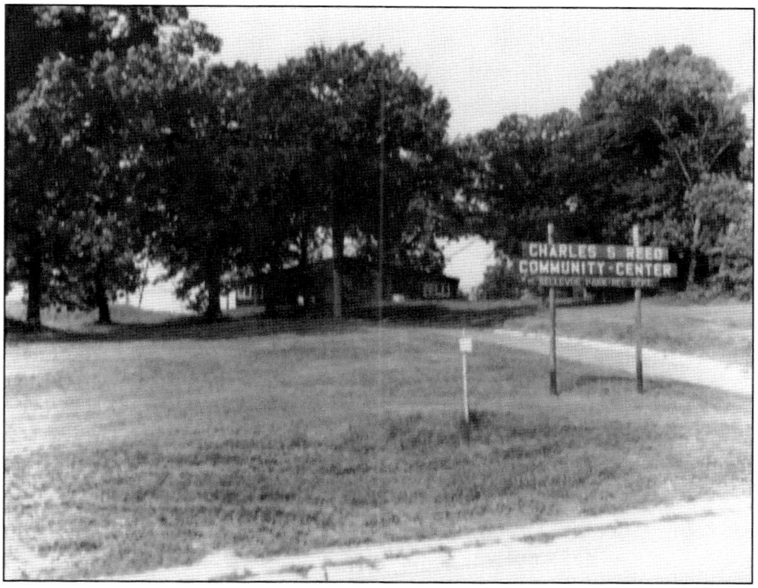

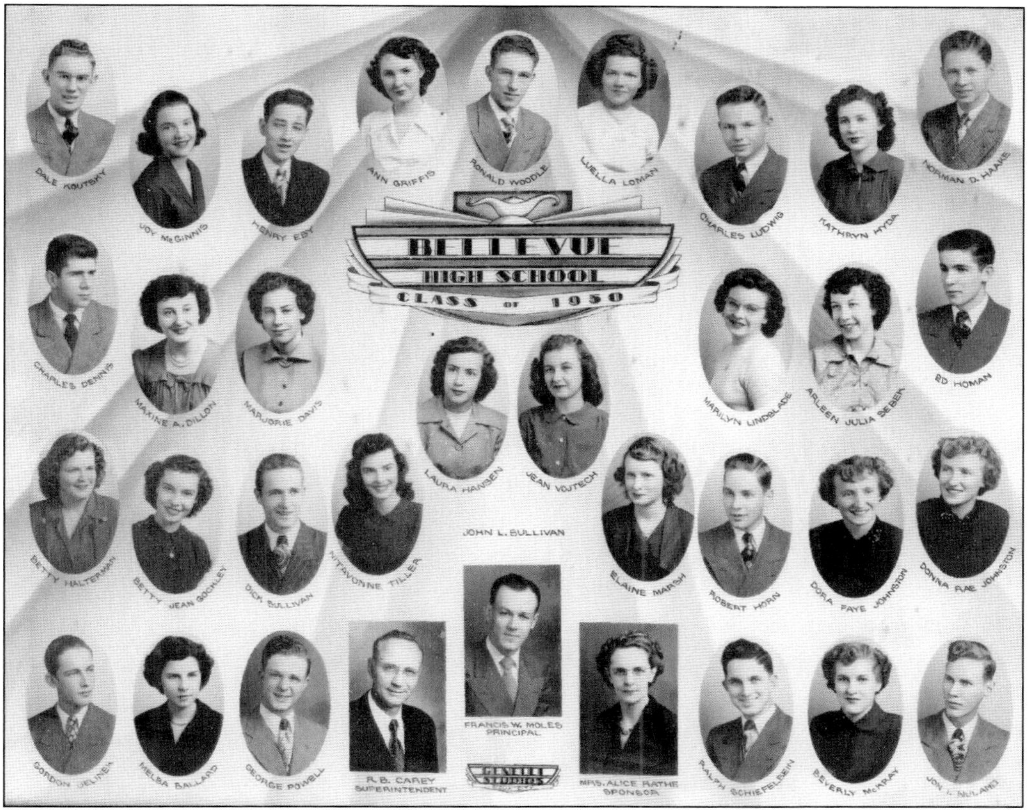

The 1950 graduating class of Bellevue High School could barely fill a single classroom today. As Bellevue and Offutt Air Force Base grew, the number of graduates would increase dramatically, so much so that it was necessary to build a new high school in 1962. In 1977, another high school opened, creating a crosstown rivalry of Bellevue East versus Bellevue West.

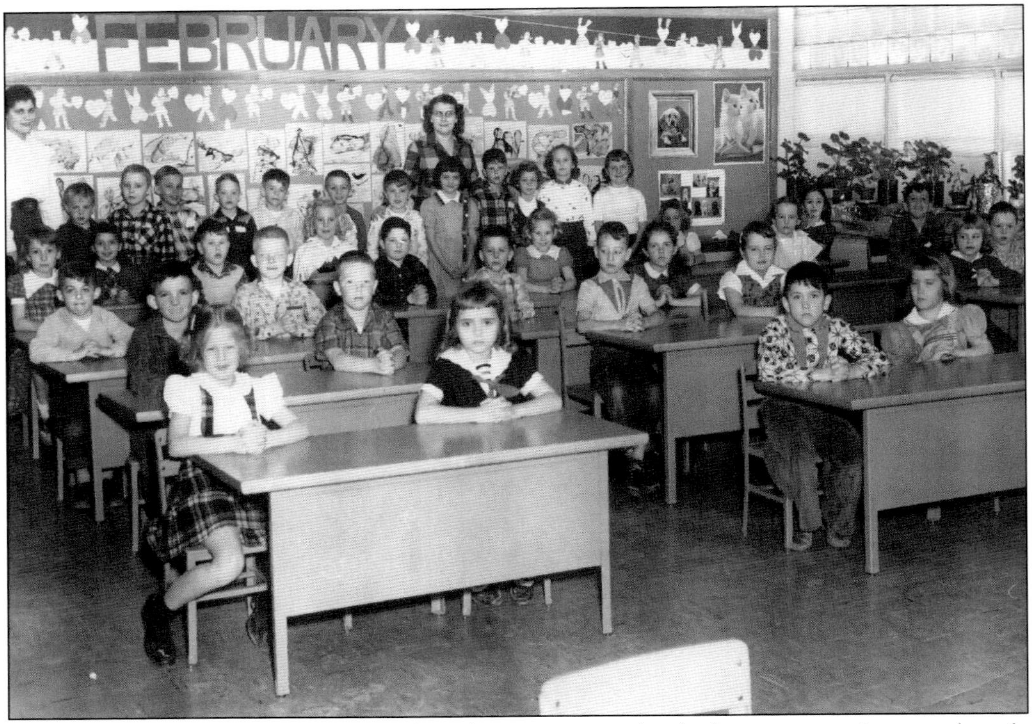

In all probability, puppies and kittens have been a perpetual sight for some time in second-grade classrooms throughout Bellevue. This 1955–1956 second-grade class at Belleaire Elementary School was no exception. The public selected the name of the school via a naming contest. The school was built in 1952 with its sister school, Betz Elementary, as a response to 700 new children moving to Offutt Air Force base with their parents. Seventeen new faculty members were added to the school district to handle the increased influx of students. Seen below, not long after its completion, one cannot help but notice how dwarfed Belleaire is by the surrounding barren landscape. Foliage, as well as building expansions, have since filled out the immediate area.

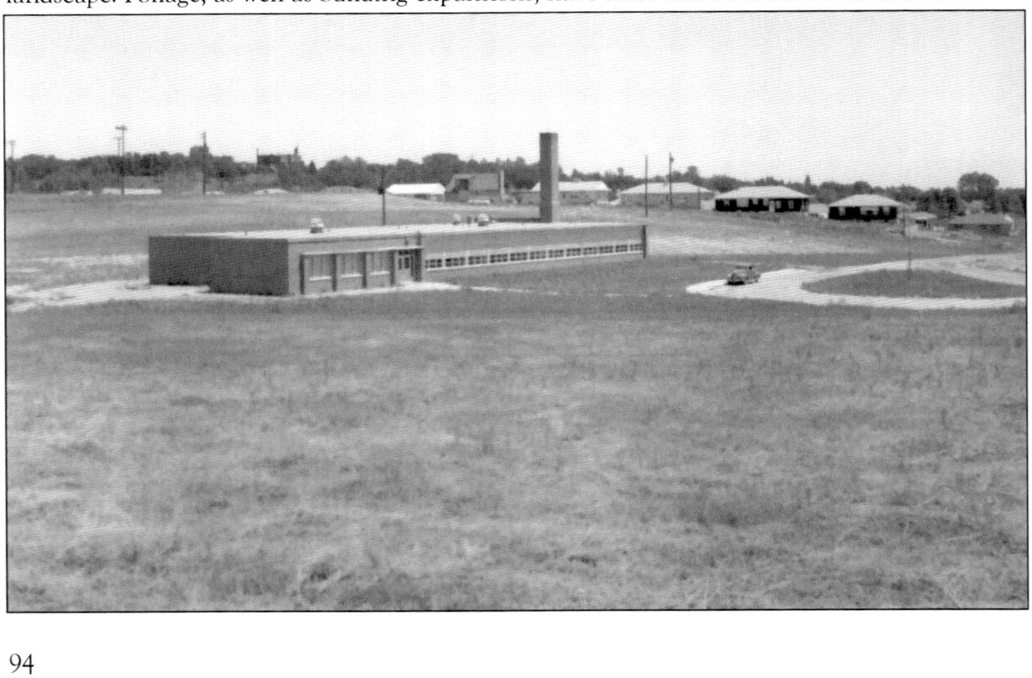

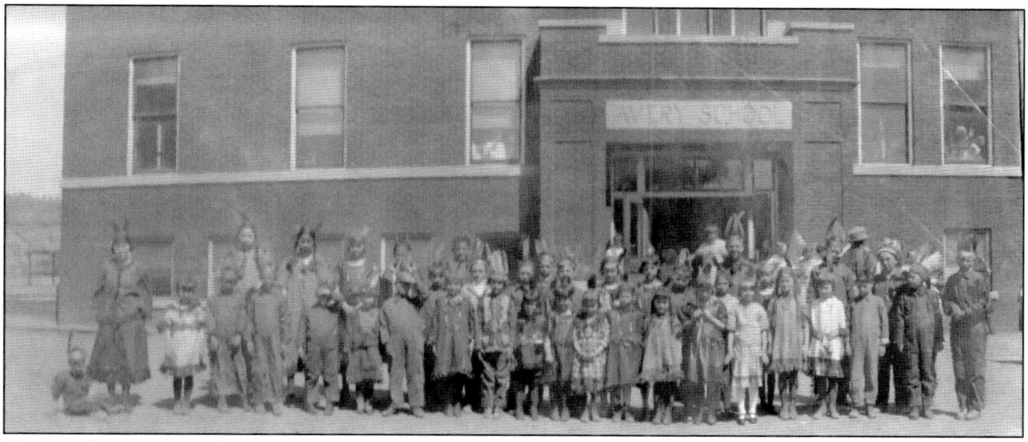

Originally part of School District no. 5, Avery School went through several transformations until a brick structure was erected in 1916. Similar to the town of Fort Crook, Avery was a separate community that has since been incorporated into Bellevue. In 1953, seventy-seven percent of the patrons successfully petitioned to have District no. 5 divided and Avery became District no. 44. In 1961, Avery voted to have its district join the Bellevue Public Schools. Part of the 1916 brick building is still in use today.

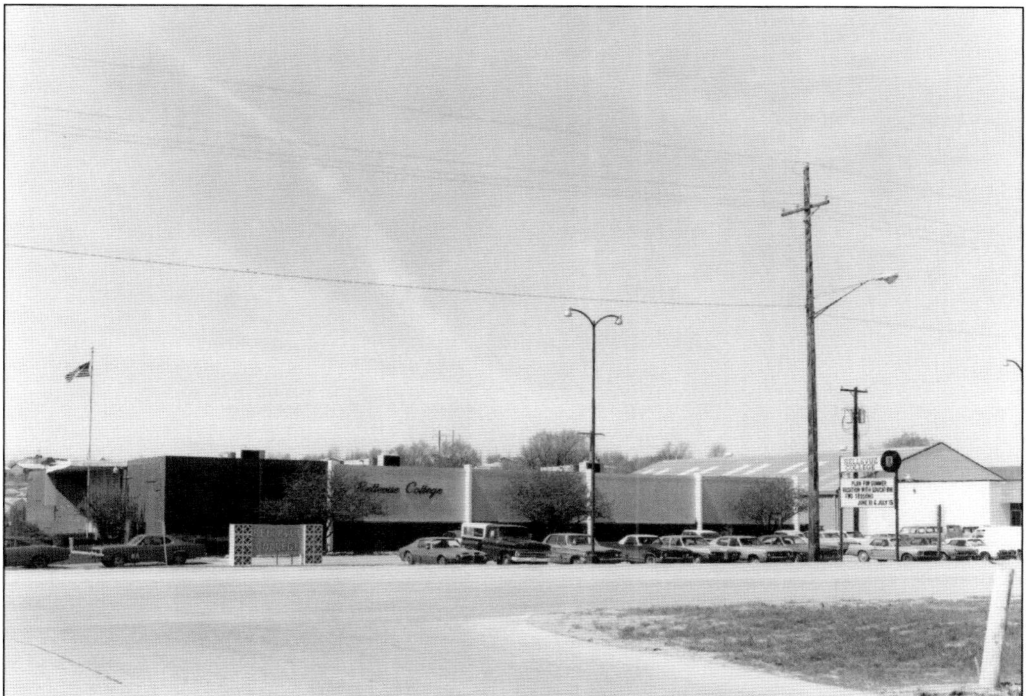

In June 1965, Bellevue College was reborn. Beginning as little more than an idea, the fledging school would grow to become a well-respected higher-learning institution in adult education. In 1994, the name was changed to Bellevue University to recognize its growing size and quality. What started with 37 graduates now has an enrollment of more 11,000 annually.

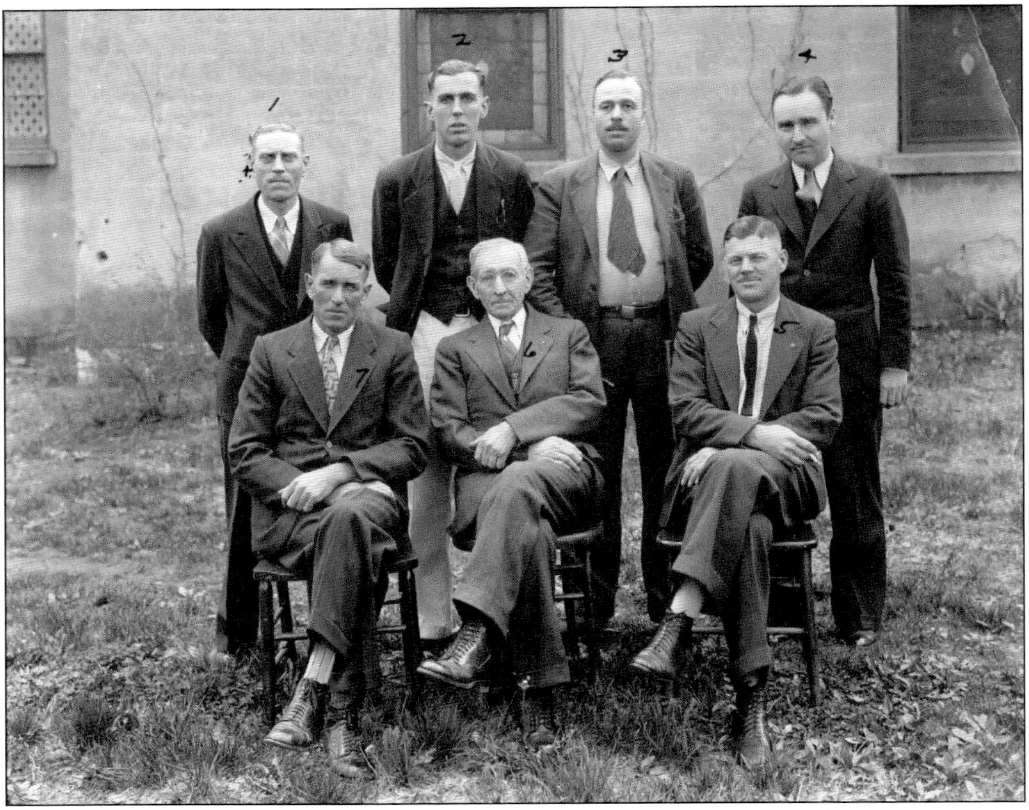

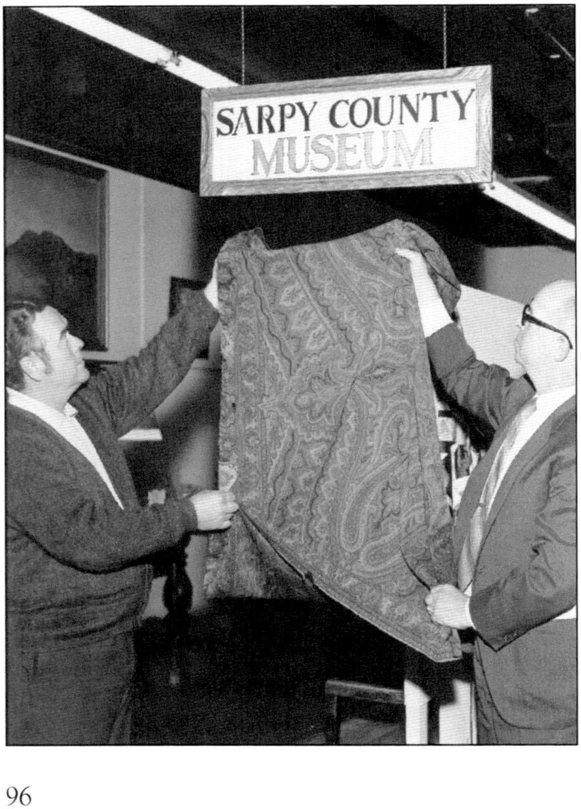

Acknowledging the historical importance of the area, the Sarpy County Historical Society made early efforts to preserve and share the history of Bellevue. Thanks to funds made possible by the Works Progress Administration, the historical society was able to publish a pamphlet in 1917 on the history of Bellevue. Both Harold B. Gates (3) and William Taylor (7) were Bellevue residents.

Originally a handful of display cases in the back of a store, the Sarpy County Museum grew to become a 7,500 square foot museum through the help of donors, the county commissioners, and a sizeable government grant in 1979. County commissioner Norm Magnusson, right, helps unveil a new sign at the museum.

Seven

From Arrows to Aerospace

The history of Offutt Air Force Base is an interesting one that has been nearly conjoined with the history of Bellevue since the inception of the military installation. With an act by the US Congress signed by Pres. Grover Cleveland, the future of Offutt Air Force Base was born. This took place July 23, 1888, 15 years before the Wright Brother's Kitty Hawk flight and four years prior to the birth of Offutt's namesake. Instead, the name of the new army fort was Fort Crook. Since then, the mission of Fort Crook has frequently changed and evolved. During the years marked by America's expanding role through the world, it served as a transfer center for personnel coming and going. During World War I, it served as a basic training center, and in the interwar years, it served as an airmail hub. Throughout World War II, the base churned out bombers for the allied war effort, leaving an impact on not only local history, but also world history.

With the Cold War heating up, Offutt Air Force Base became the host base for Strategic Air Command (SAC) in 1948. In 1966, host responsibilities shifted to the newly arrived 55th Wing. The unit has since been the backbone of Offutt. SAC faithfully performed its profession of peace until after the Soviet Union collapsed, whereupon they stood down. At that time, the US Strategic Command stood up with the mission of serving as command and control for the safeguard of global security of the United States. Today, Offutt is home to over two dozen units, and also serves as the headquarters of the Air Force Weather Agency, a more recent addition to the base's proud history. Through this long history, Bellevue has enjoyed a special relationship with Offutt, a relationship that will only continue to prosper in the future.

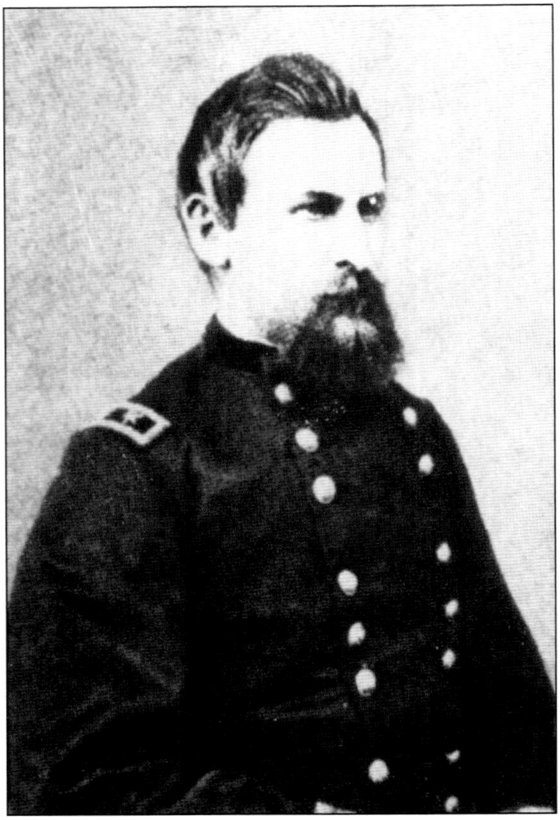

The namesake behind the fort, Gen. George Crook was a career soldier remembered for his participation in the Civil War and Indian Wars. A West Point graduate, General Crook twice served as the commander of the Department of the Platte, tasked with overseeing the safety and security of the Oregon Trail and the railroads. In 1890, at the age of 61, he died suddenly of a heart attack.

In this photograph taken in approximately 1896, Fort Crook appears as little more than a sparse collection of buildings. On one side sits a collection of homes that make up Officers' Row. On the other side are the barracks for enlisted men. The parade ground in the center separates the two, and while there were a few auxiliary buildings such as the blacksmith, this was virtually the entirety of the fledgling outpost in its early years.

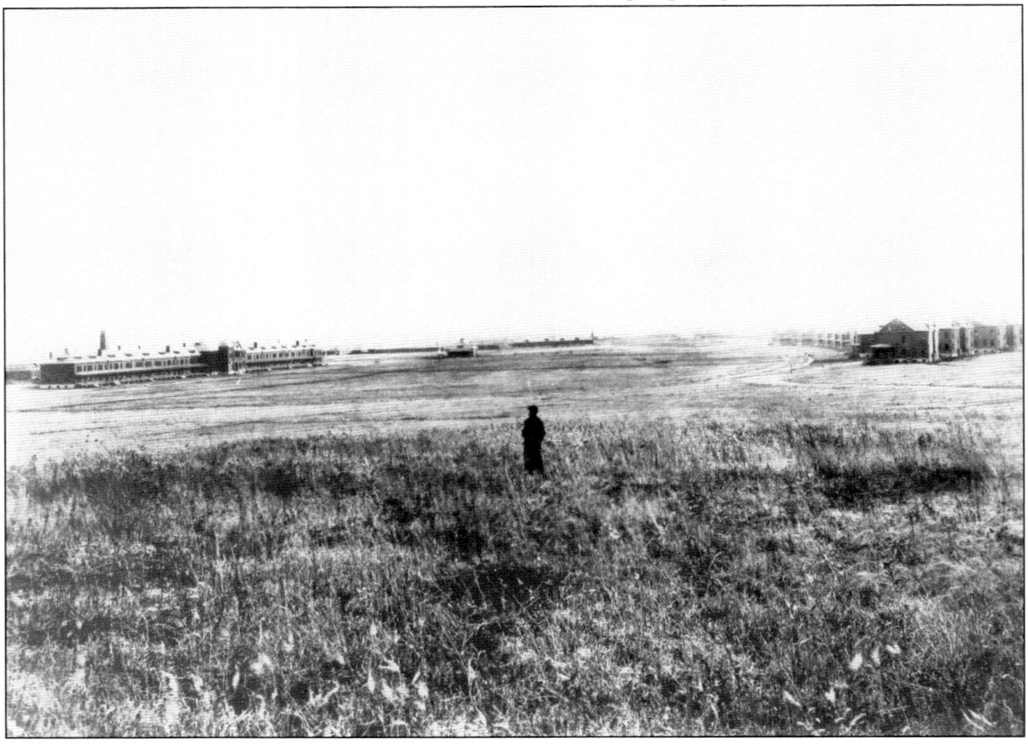

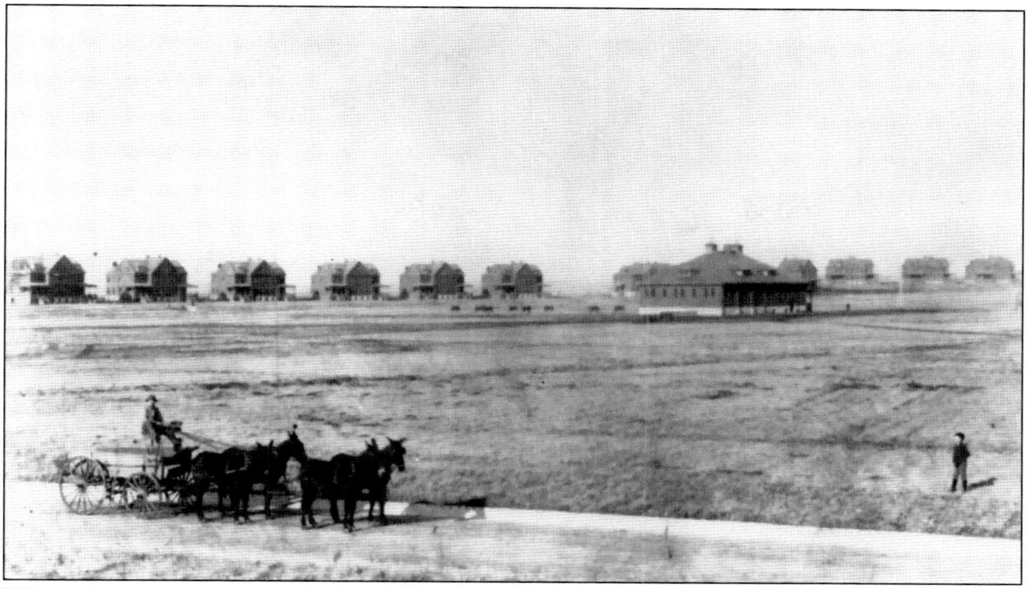

When the image above was captured in 1896, the fort was only 10 miles south from Omaha's post office, and yet, the landscape does not reflect even the remotest notion of being located near an urban center. All major buildings were completed and ready for occupancy on May 1. On June 20, the first army personnel of C Company, 22nd Infantry Regiment, arrived at the fort to assume command. This consisted of 10 enlisted men and their immediate officer, 2nd Lt. David S. Stanley. It would be another nine days after that before a senior officer would arrive at the fort. A more intimate view is offered below of the center parade ground nine years later in 1905 during a Fourth of July Patriotic Salute.

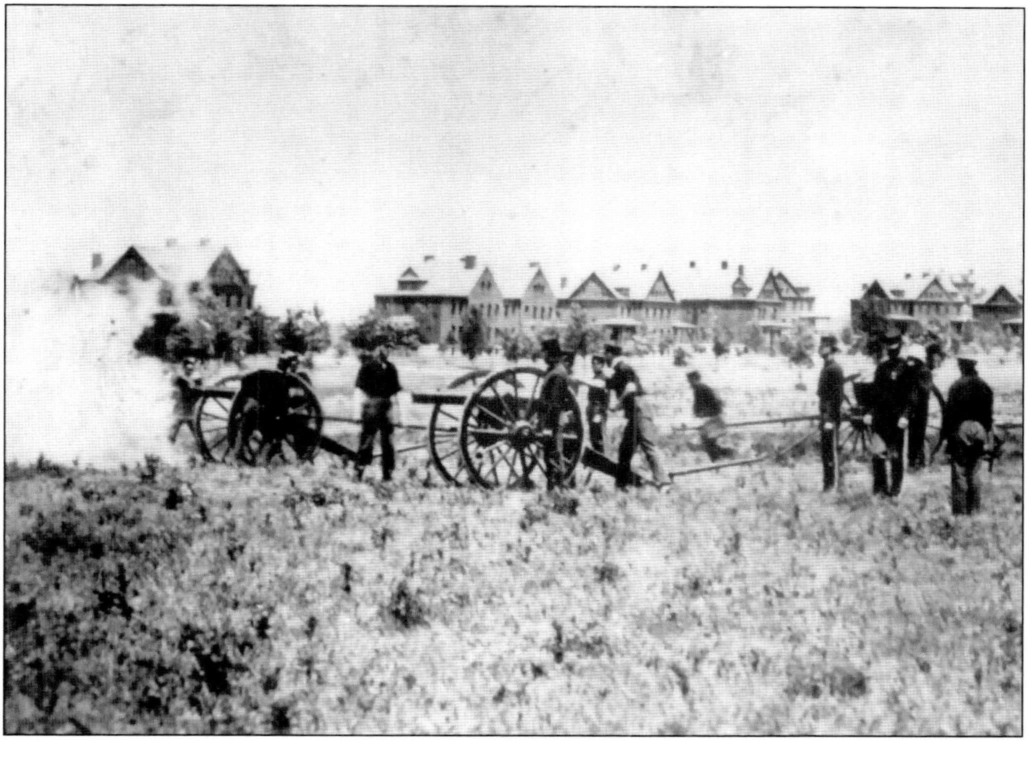

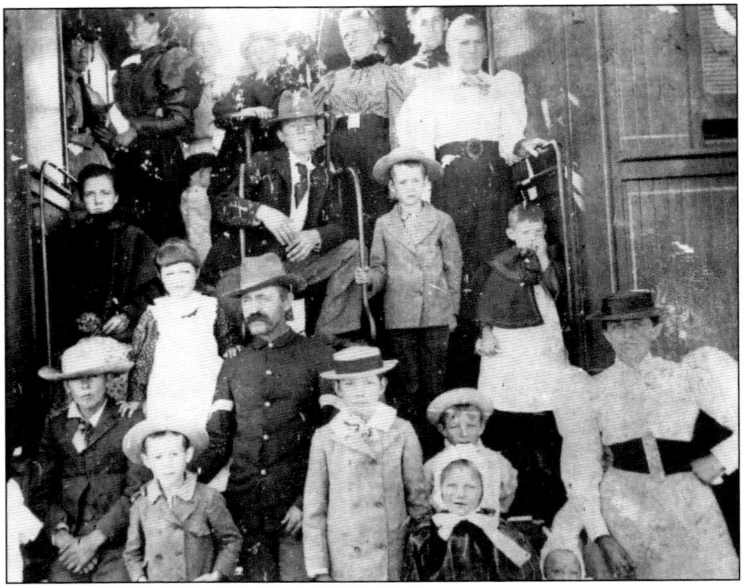

The 22nd Infantry arrived by train with their families in 1896. Once the Spanish-American War broke out in 1898, the 22nd would be deployed to Cuba and then the Philippines. During the 22nd's interim stay at Fort Crook between deployments, a number of soldiers suffered from tropical diseases. Six men were buried on the base cemetery from September to January 1899. Many more never returned to Nebraska.

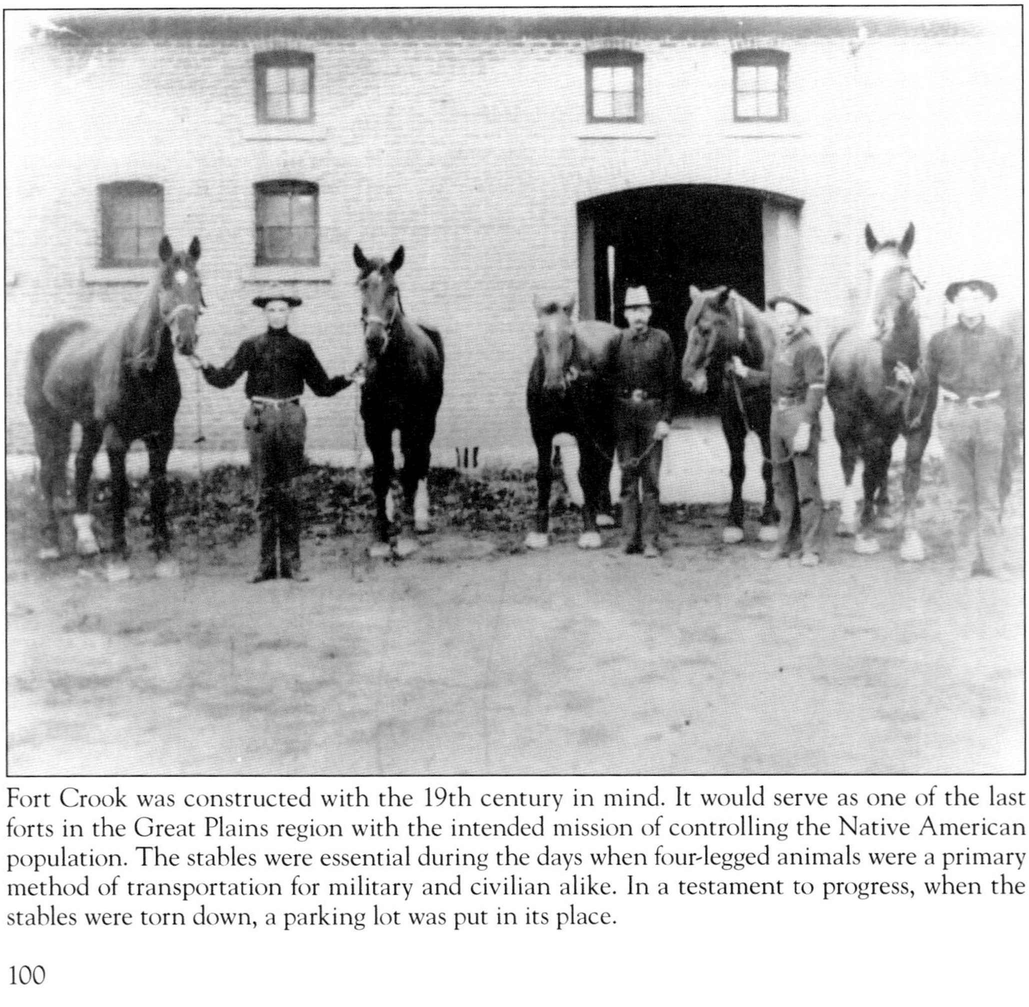

Fort Crook was constructed with the 19th century in mind. It would serve as one of the last forts in the Great Plains region with the intended mission of controlling the Native American population. The stables were essential during the days when four-legged animals were a primary method of transportation for military and civilian alike. In a testament to progress, when the stables were torn down, a parking lot was put in its place.

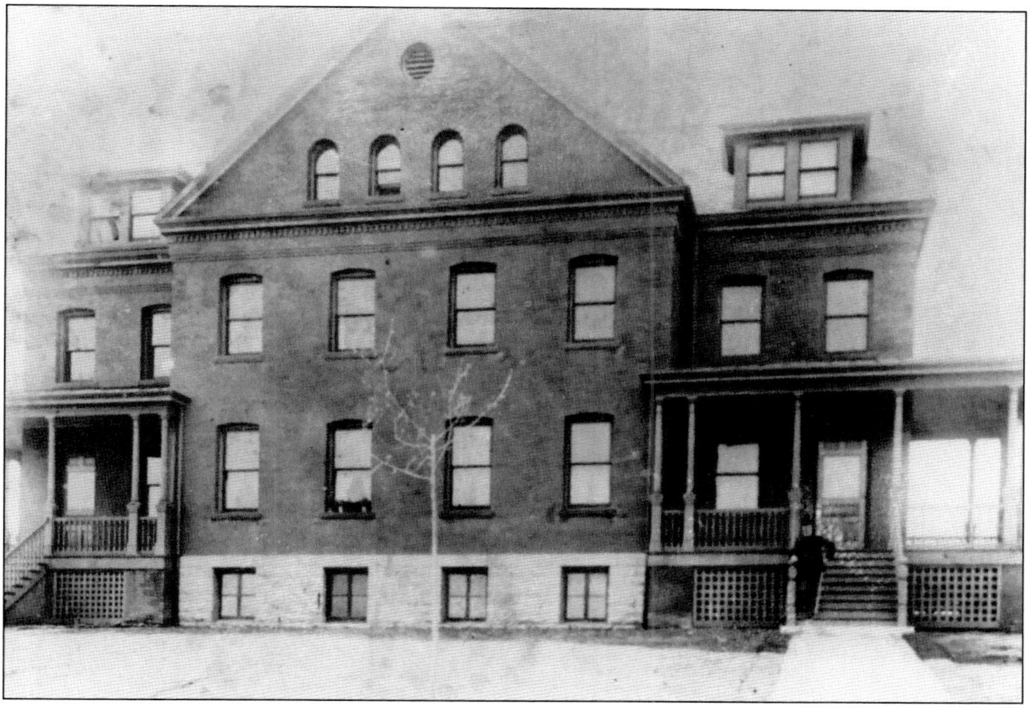

Construction of Officers' Row began in 1891 and was completed in 1896 at a cost of $8,750 per residence. Quarters 21 and 22, seen in the 1908 photograph above, were duplex units, as were all 28 quarters with the exception of Quarters 13, for a bachelor officer, and Quarters 16, a single occupancy dwelling for the commanding officer. Two duplex units were torn down in 1941 to make room for a new runway. As the significance of the fort grew, so too did Officers' Row. It was renamed Generals' Row to accommodate senior officers, including at one time Gen. Curtis LeMay. The buildings have been updated in many ways through the ages but their appearance and structure cannot be changed in order to preserve their historical nature.

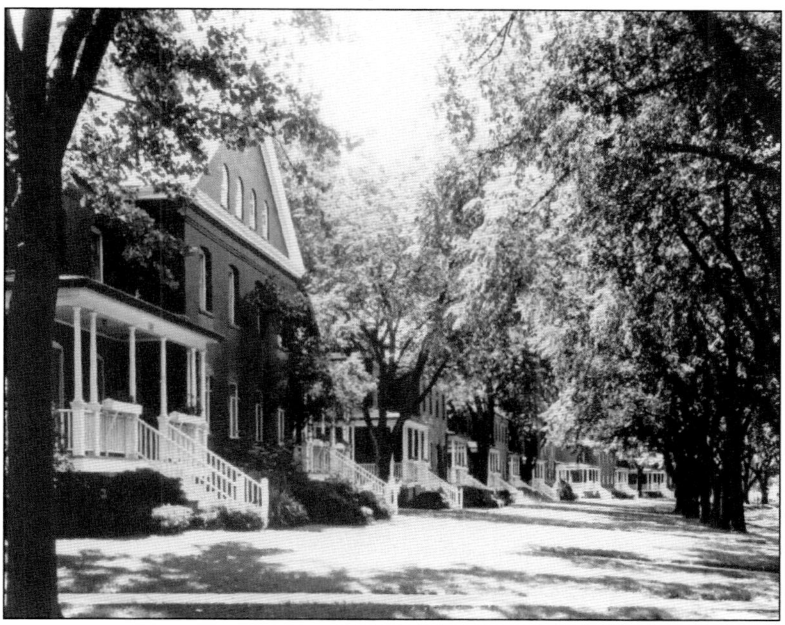

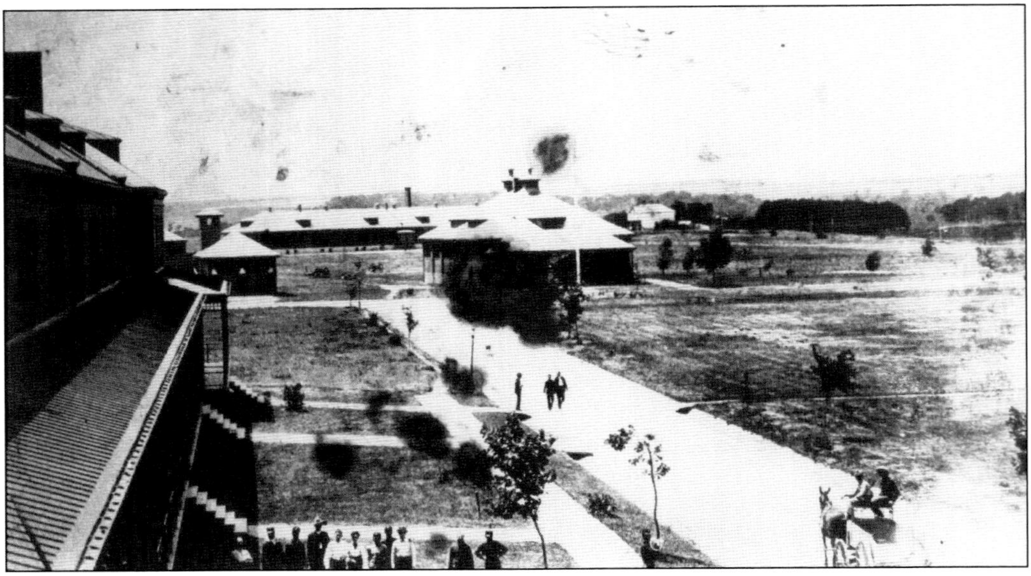

The barracks to house enlisted men were originally built as one long building with two residential wings, along with a central mess and recreational area. In December 1946, a fire broke out in a bowling alley that was in the central portion of the building. Base and Bellevue firefighters were needed to extinguish the blaze. Despite their efforts, the middle section was lost. However, they were able to prevent the fire from spreading, and the residential wings were saved. Today, the now two separate buildings are still in use and have been placed in the National Register of Historic Places.

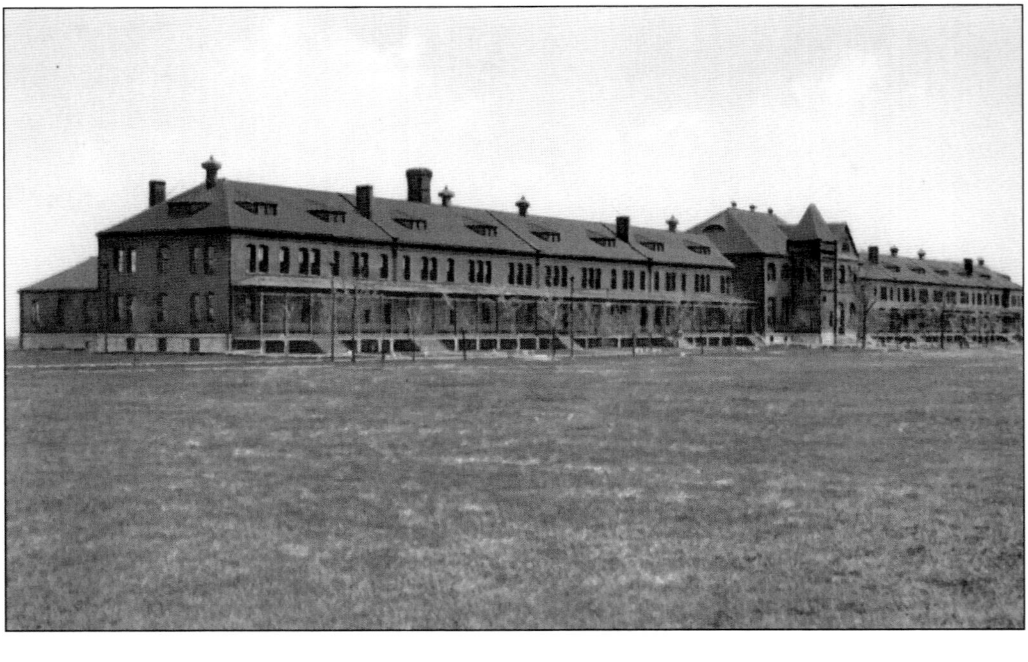

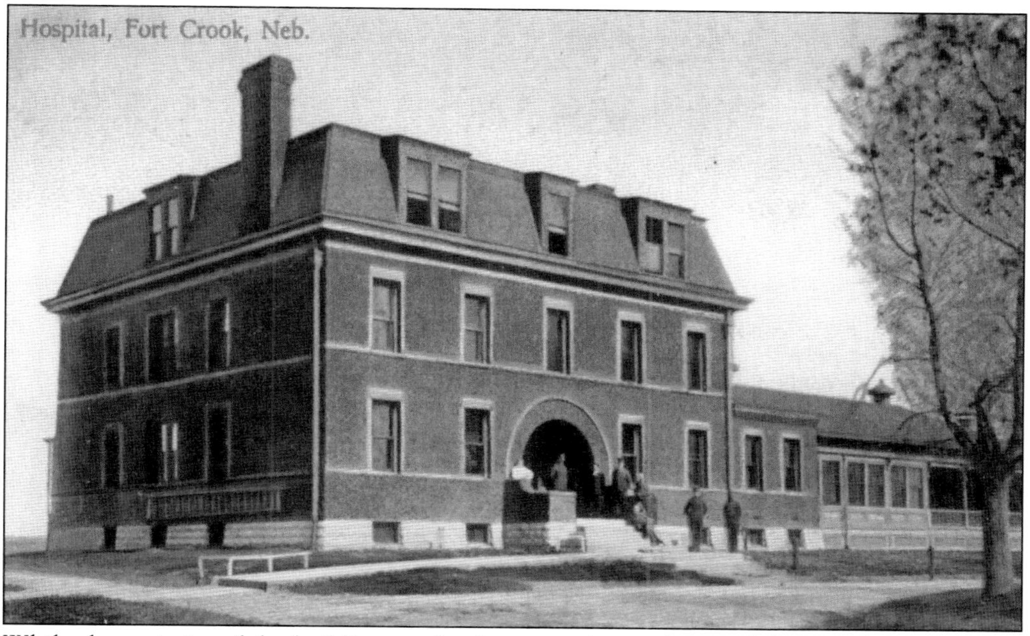

While the majority of the buildings at the fort were clustered around the parade grounds, the hospital was built some distance away. This isolation was probably a precaution against the spread of contagious diseases. The 1908 tornado did extensive damage to the hospital, tearing off the roof. Fortunately, no one was hurt. In 1941, the hospital was torn down to make room for the bomber plant.

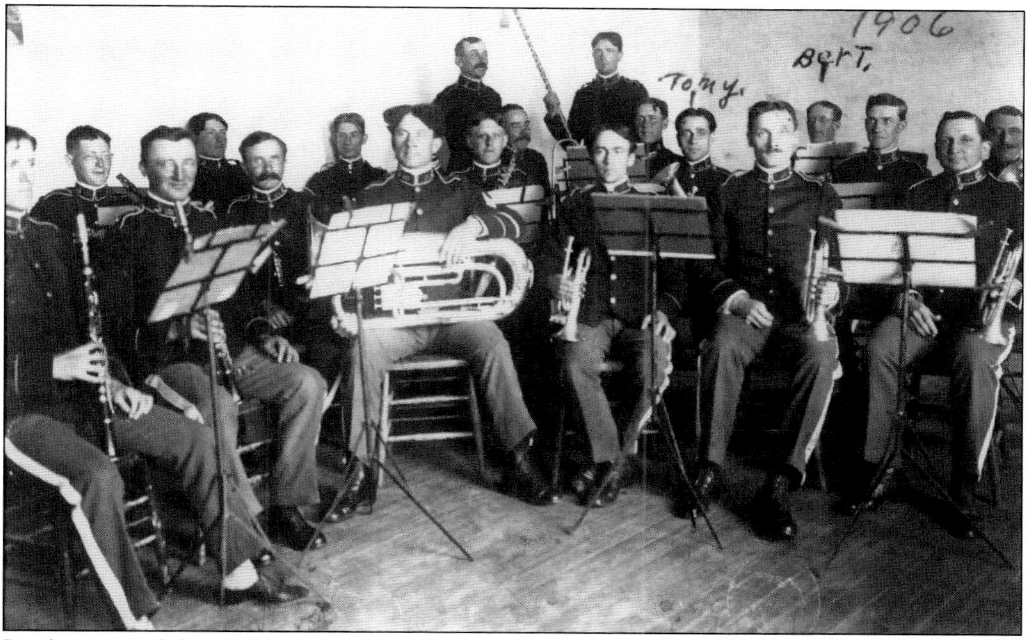

By the start of the 20th century, the US Army had begun the move to modernity, including uniforms, weapons, and tactics. Traditional US military bands, however, would still be commonplace for some time. In 1906, despite marching the entire 180 miles to Fort Riley, Kansas, for maneuvers, the 30th Infantry band was frequently able to hold rehearsals in its own band quarters at Fort Crook.

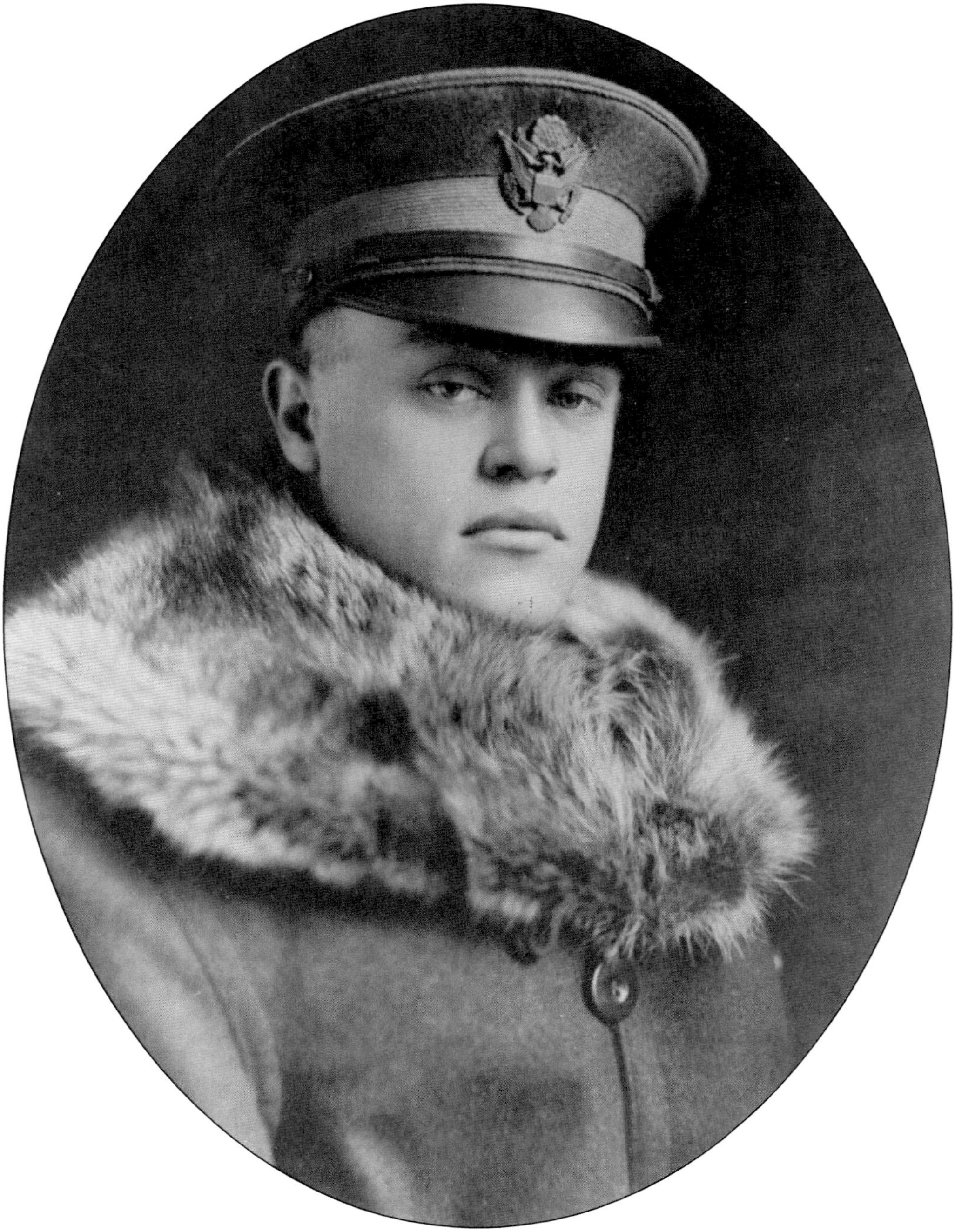

First Lt. Jarvis Jennes Offutt was born in Omaha, Nebraska, on October 26, 1894. A Yale graduate, Jarvis was one of a select 300 early flyers to be sent from the United States to Canada for aviation training by the Royal Canadian Flying Corps. During World War I, he was attached to the British Royal Air Force as a ferry pilot. One of his responsibilities was to deliver aircraft from English factories to bases in France. Offutt died on August 13, 1918, from injuries received while flying at Valheureux, France. In essence, his death would serve as a catalyst to further Fort Crook to serving as an aviation hub. The Fort Crook landing field was renamed Offutt Field in his honor on May 10, 1924. In 1948, Offutt Field became Offutt Air Force Base.

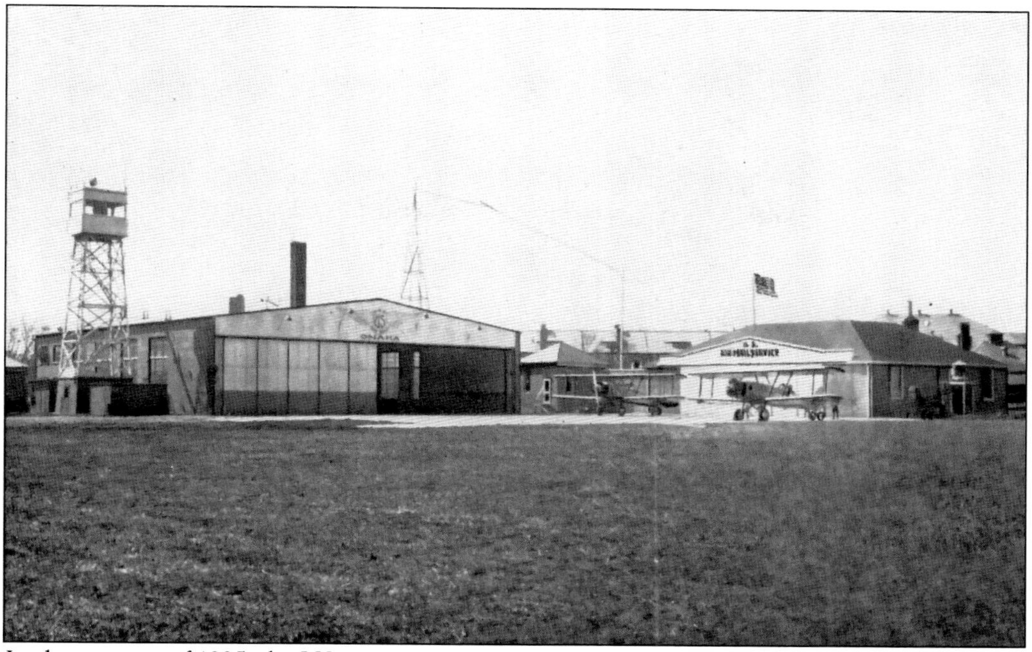

In the summer of 1925, the US Post Office completed a 10-plane hangar. Airmail service for Omaha and much of the surrounding area was flown in and out of Fort Crook for the next five years until service was transferred to Omaha Municipal Airport in 1930.

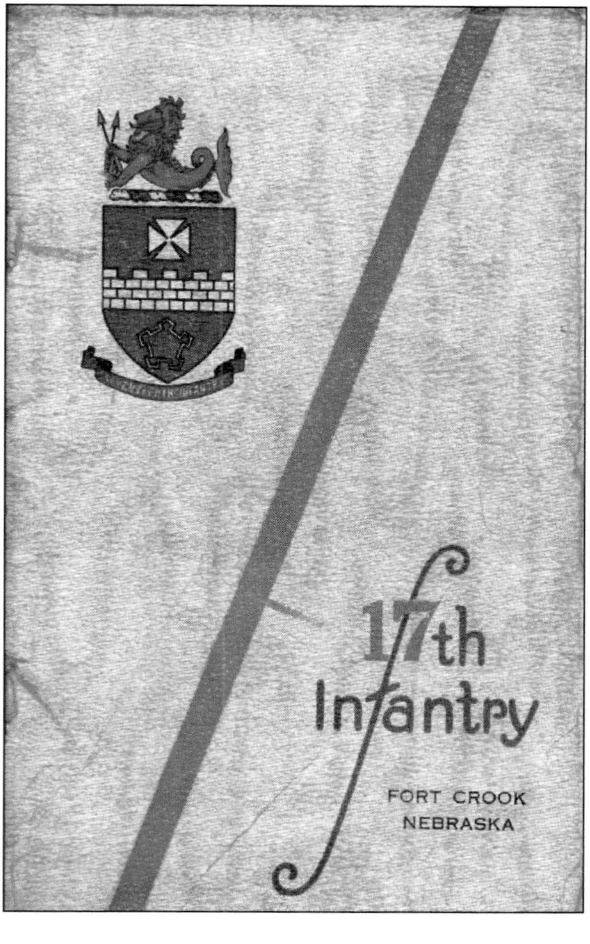

The interwar years at Fort Crook were particularly lean, but with the help of the Civilian Conservation Corps personnel, the base was able to make ends meet, even adding a theater and formal garden. Despite the Great Depression, the 17th Infantry took time off on May 4 and 5 in 1931 to celebrate Organization Day. This program lists the events, including a barbeque, movies, and a dance.

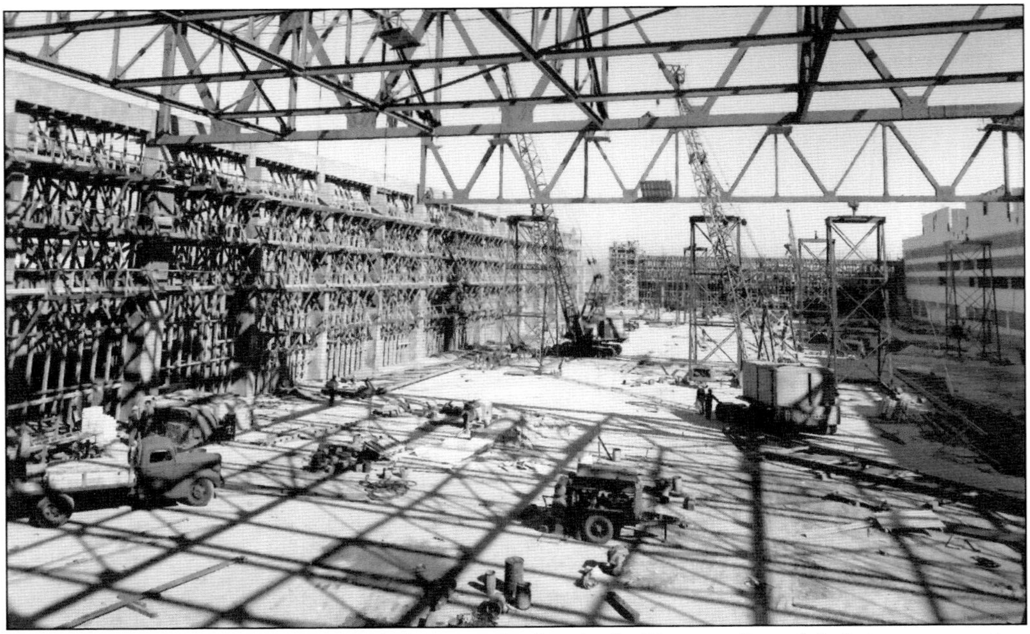

In December 1940, England stood alone in the battle for Europe. Brutal fighting was raging in China. With the world in flames, America was not sitting by idly—it was preparing for the inevitable. The construction of Building D, a bomber-building facility to be operated by the Glenn L. Martin Company, was to be in Bellevue's backyard, changing the role of Fort Crook forever.

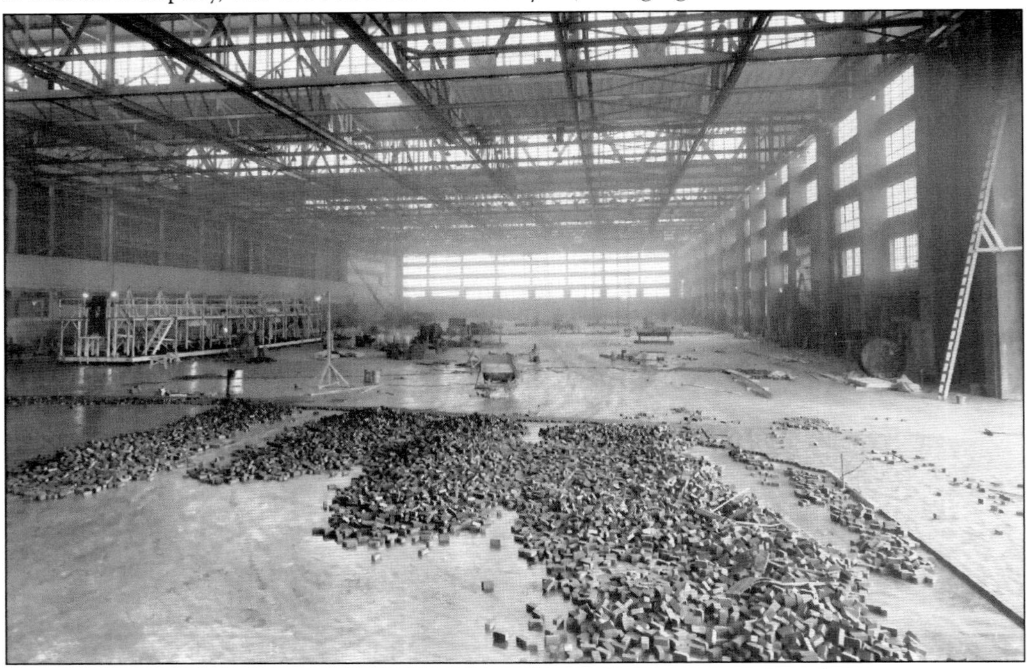

The undertaking to construct Building D, also known as the Martin Bomber Plant, was enormous. Building D required 250 miles of electrical wiring, 47,000 cubic yards of concrete, 10 million square feet of paint, and 10 miles worth of fluorescent lighting. With 1.2 million square feet of floor space, 25 full football fields could fit inside. The floor seen here was comprised of wood blocks rather than concrete to decrease the chance of an accidental detonation.

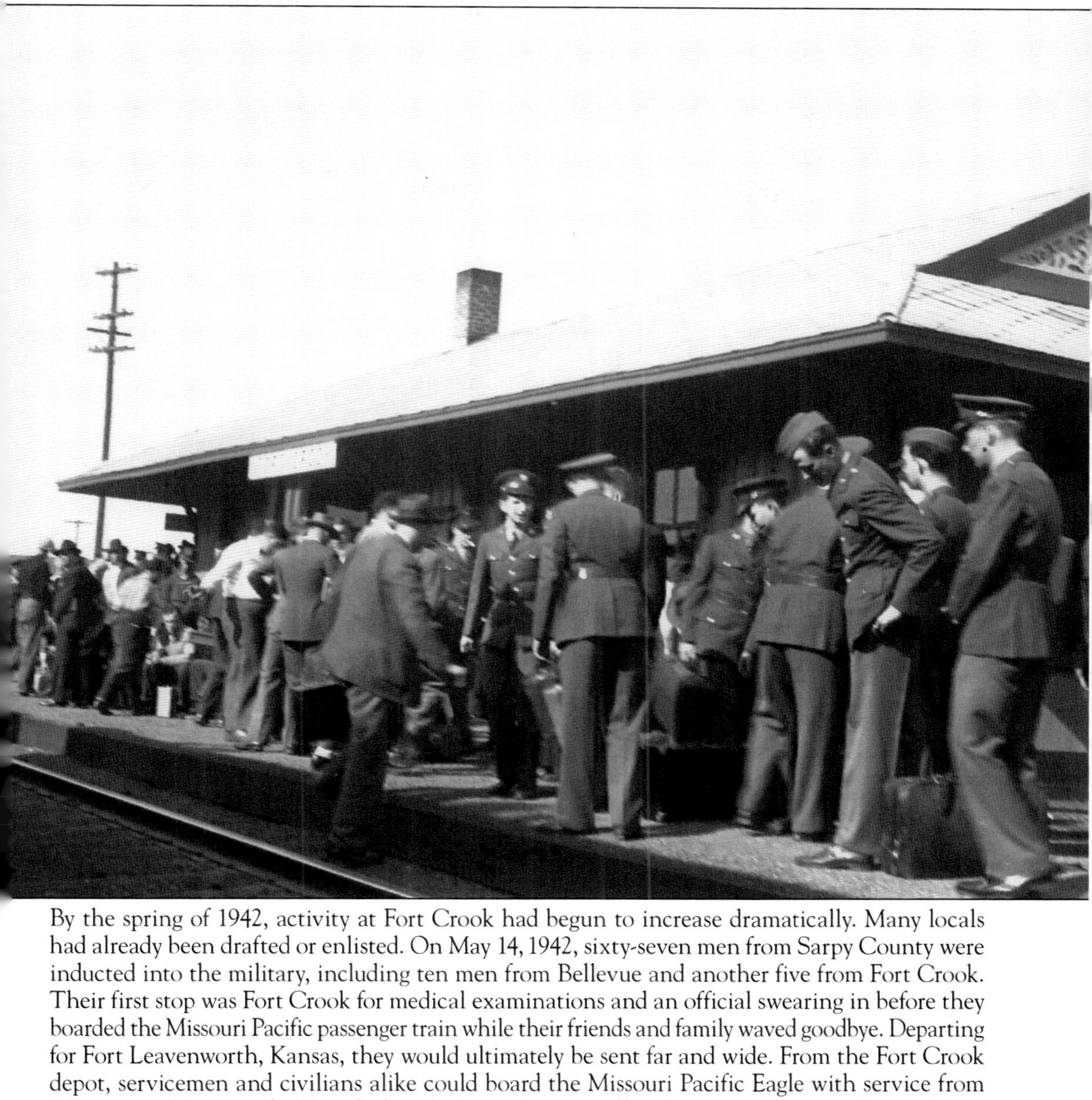

By the spring of 1942, activity at Fort Crook had begun to increase dramatically. Many locals had already been drafted or enlisted. On May 14, 1942, sixty-seven men from Sarpy County were inducted into the military, including ten men from Bellevue and another five from Fort Crook. Their first stop was Fort Crook for medical examinations and an official swearing in before they boarded the Missouri Pacific passenger train while their friends and family waved goodbye. Departing for Fort Leavenworth, Kansas, they would ultimately be sent far and wide. From the Fort Crook depot, servicemen and civilians alike could board the Missouri Pacific Eagle with service from St. Louis to Minneapolis. Even before the United States officially entered the war, the Eagle was stopping twice a day in Fort Crook, once at 8:58 a.m. and again at 5:35 p.m. By 1958, the depot was one of only a handful of buildings still remaining in the town of Fort Crook.

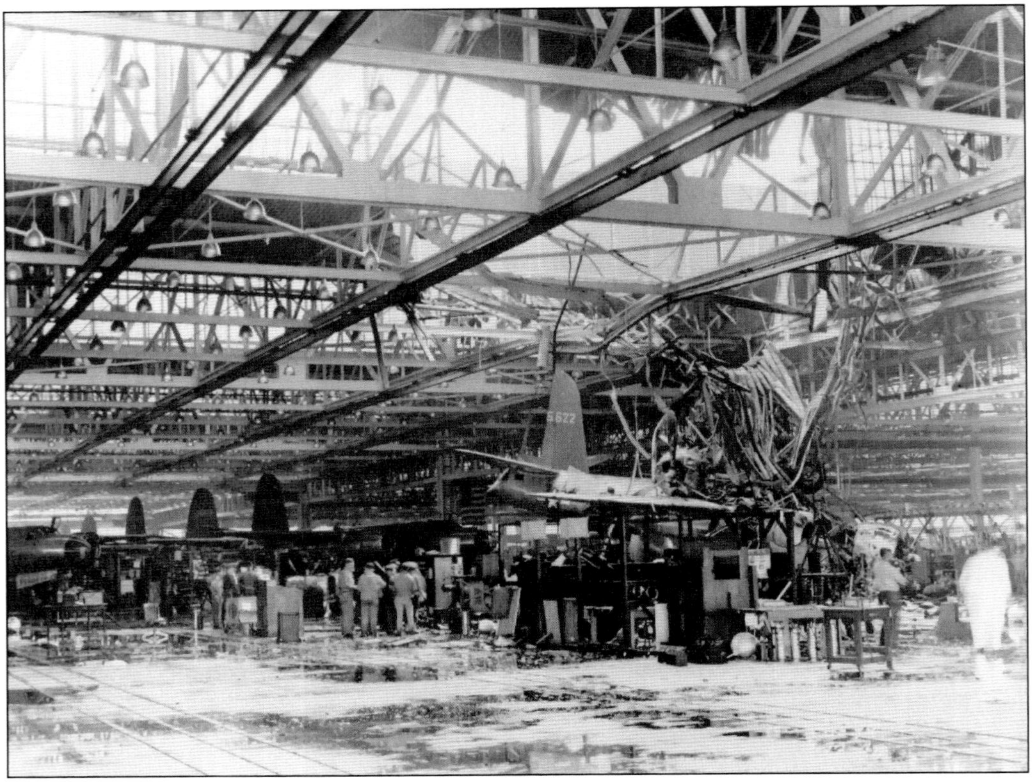

Despite its size and the efforts of Building D, the only serious accident took place on September 22, 1943, when a B-25 Mitchell created a 75-foot-long gash in the roof as it crashed into the structure, killing three of the four crewmen. The situation could have been much worse if not for the fact that many of the employees were on their lunch break.

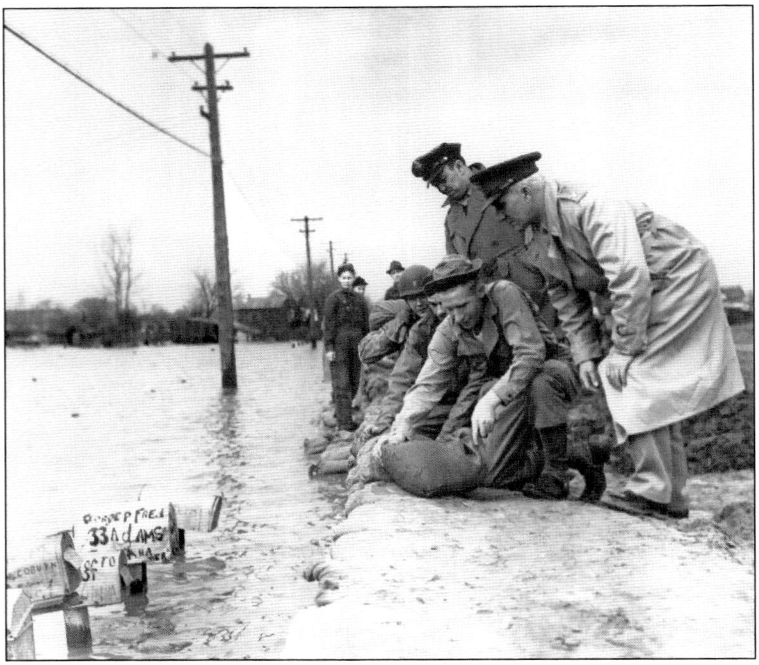

The army did what it could to help stem the tide during the April 1943 flood. When the brutal winter weather melted away with the arrival of spring, it could mean disaster for any riverfront property. Towns all along the Missouri River had fallen victim to flooding several times in the past, but the 1943 flood required evacuations and, even then, still caused significant damage.

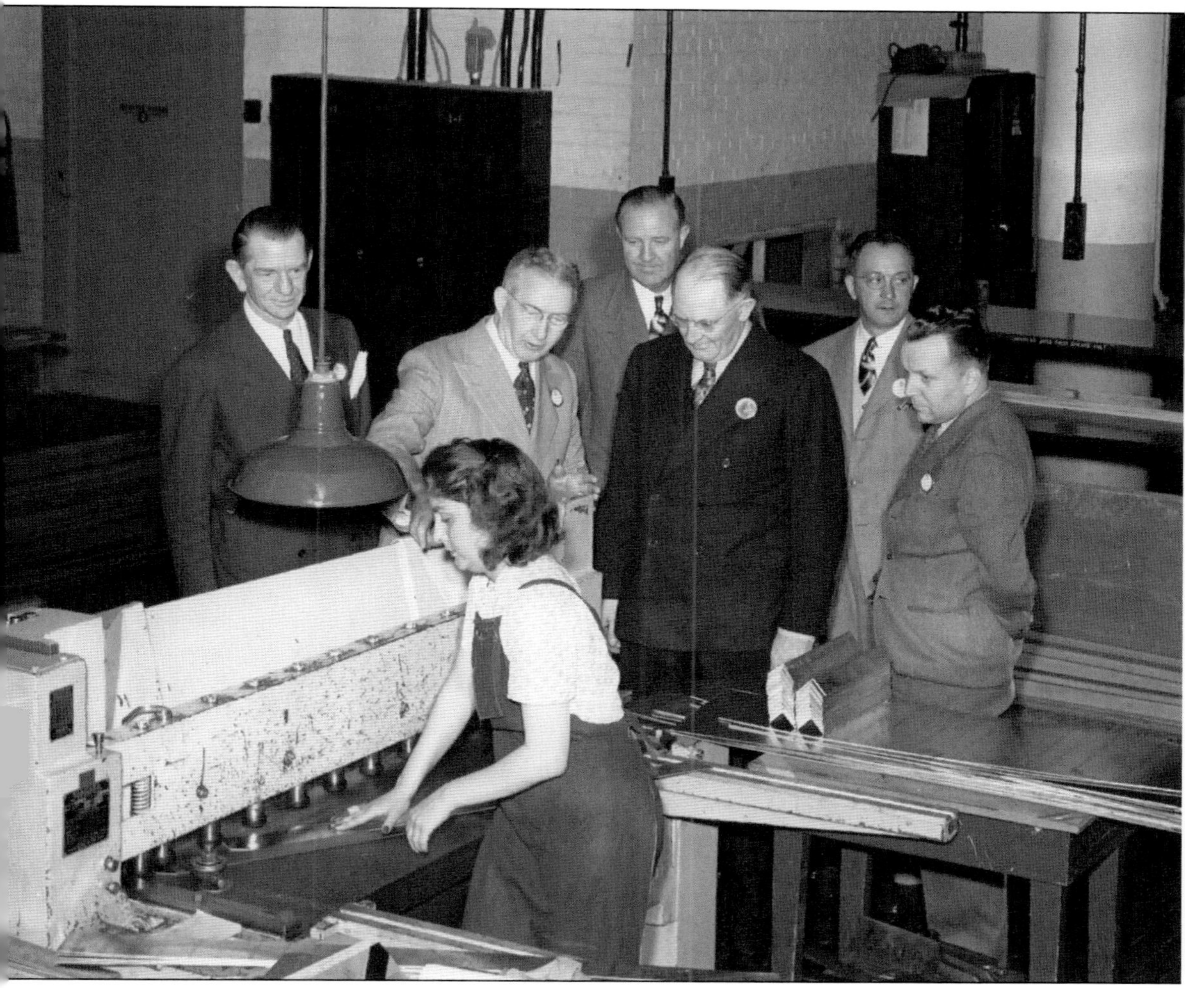

A major effort to the war, the Martin Bomber Plant churned out scores of B-26 Marauder and later B-29 Superfortress bombers, including both the *Enola Gay* and *Bockscar*, the B-29s that dropped the atomic bombs over Japan. Glenn L. Martin (second from left), the company's namesake, and his entourage commonly inspected production to ensure quality and morale. With much of the male population off to war, area women, many from Bellevue, made up a large portion of the workforce. Here, a real life "Rosie" works the dangerous job of pressing sheet metal, a sure way to smash one's painted nails (and fingers) if not for her proficient skill.

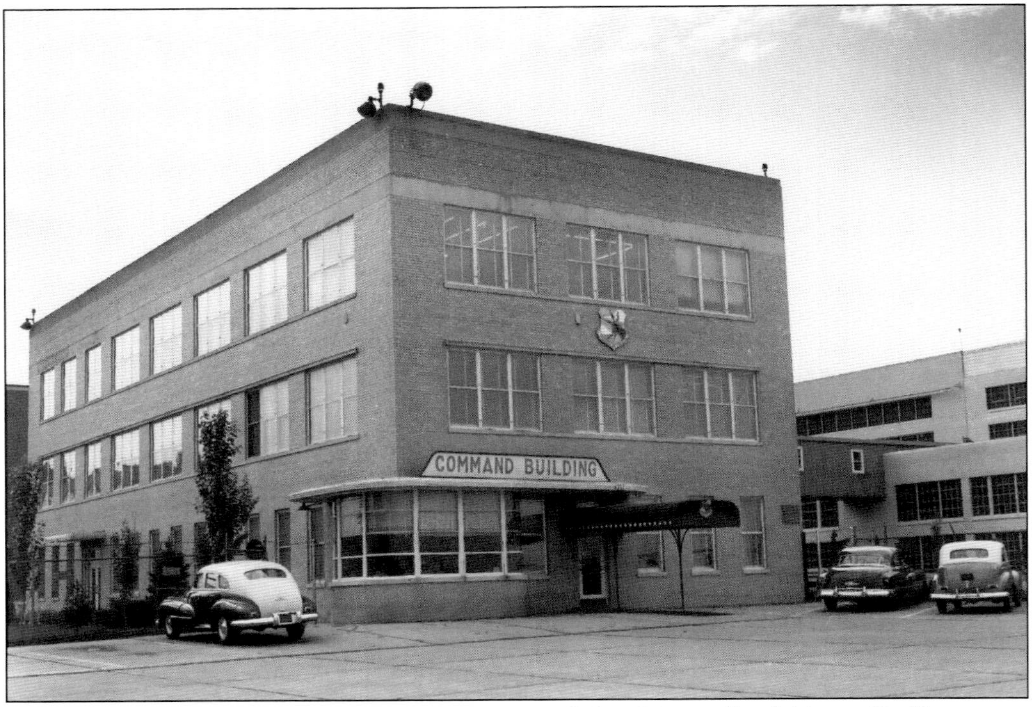

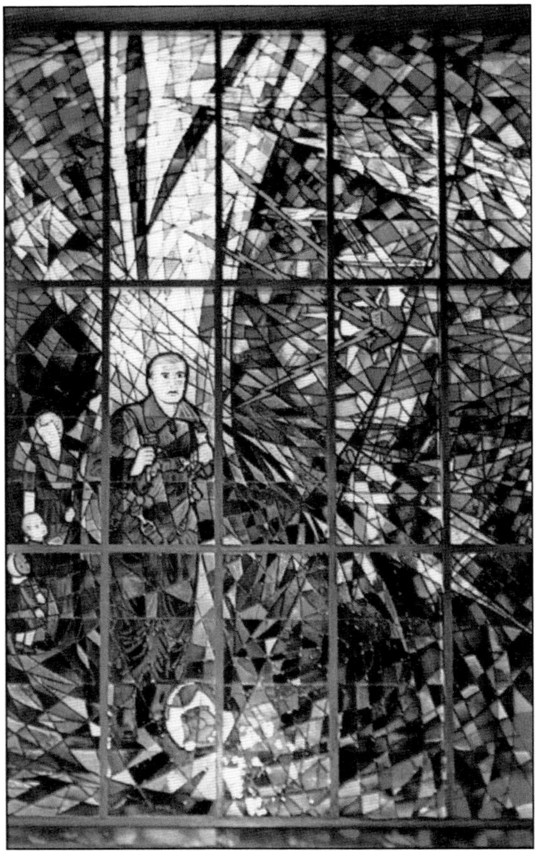

Behind the walls of this small office building sat the initial headquarters of Strategic Air Command at Offutt. From 1948 until 1956, Building A served as the nerve center for America's strategic nuclear arsenal. Once General LeMay took over command of SAC, he quickly determined that a bigger building was required. Today, Building A is still utilized as the base's law center.

The unique stained glass of the base chapel at Offutt depicts an airman with his family and the emblem of Strategic Air Command. The windows were purchased at a cost of $17,000 with funds raised from donations. Of the eight different firms that submitted sketches, it was determined that Wallis-Wiley Studio of California would have the honor of producing the memorial window.

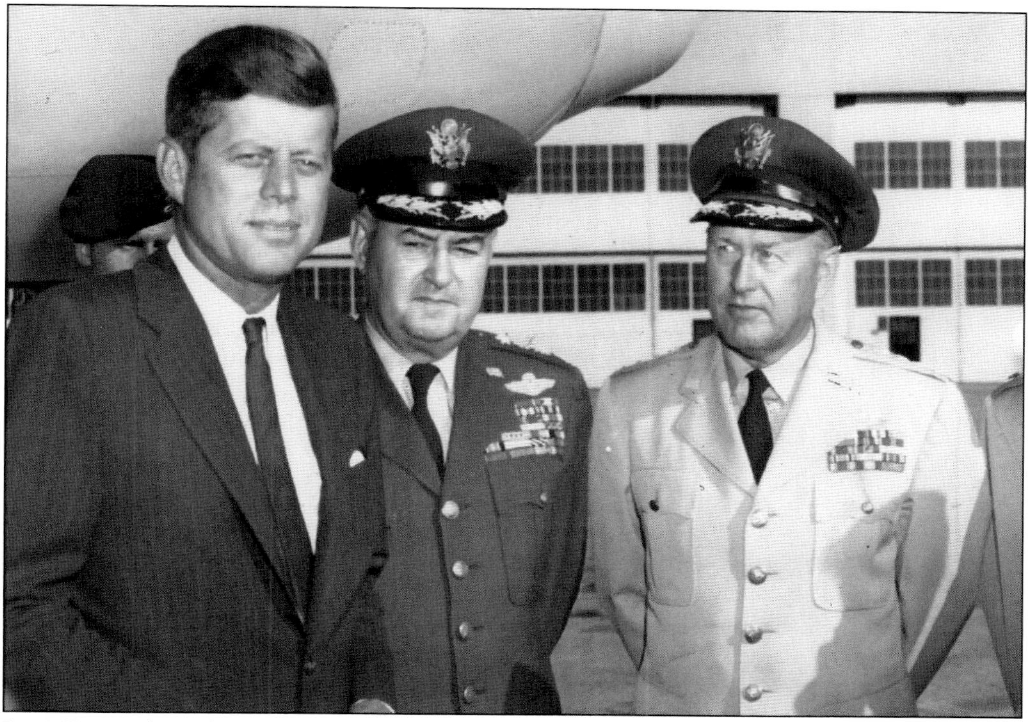

In 1960, presidential candidate John F. Kennedy visited Offutt to tour SAC Headquarters. Pictured with him are chief of staff of the Air Force Gen. Curtis LeMay (center) and Gen. Thomas Power, commander in chief of SAC. Partially visible behind Kennedy is a member of the SAC Elite Guard, an exclusive unit to SAC. Kennedy would again visit in December 1962, just a few short months after the Cuban Missile Crisis.

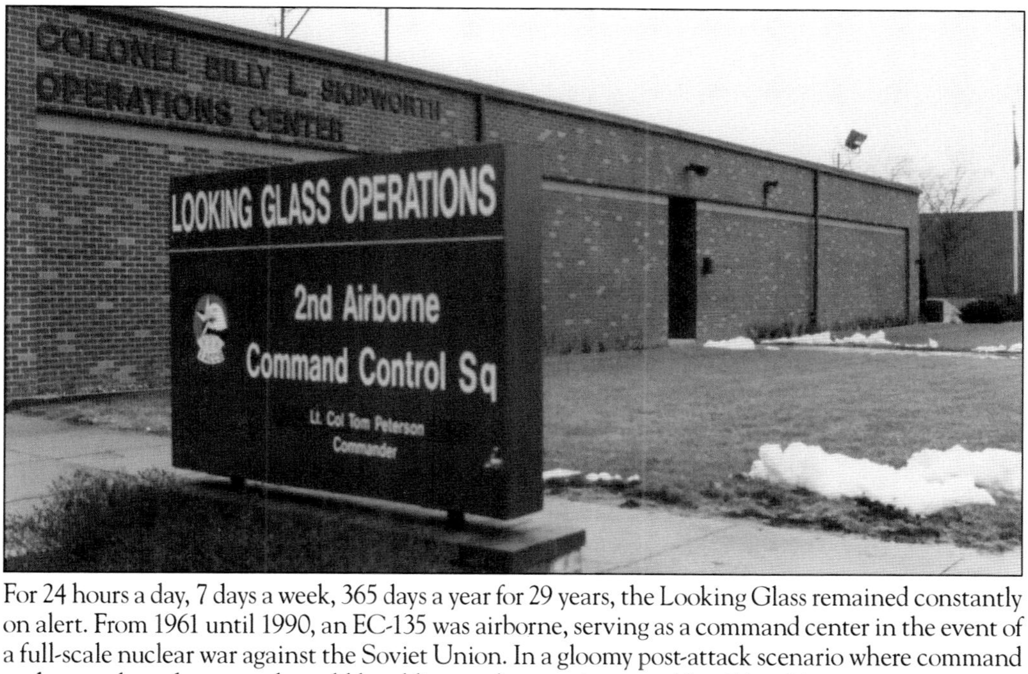

For 24 hours a day, 7 days a week, 365 days a year for 29 years, the Looking Glass remained constantly on alert. From 1961 until 1990, an EC-135 was airborne, serving as a command center in the event of a full-scale nuclear war against the Soviet Union. In a gloomy post-attack scenario where command and control on the ground would be obliterated, operations would still be able to continue.

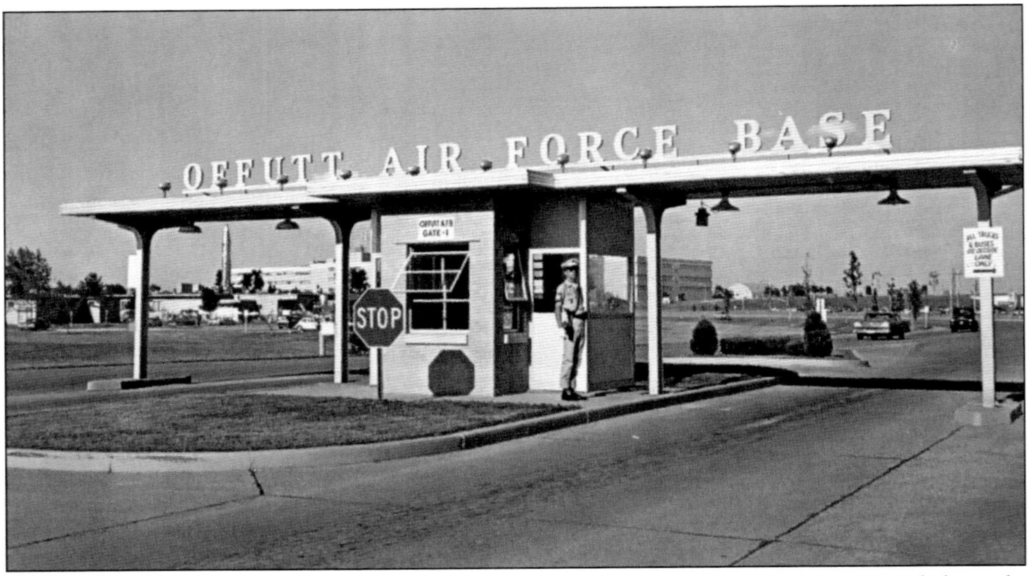

The Offutt Air Force Base main gate is where generals and airmen alike have passed through. A single, visible security officer and a stop sign stand watch over the front gate. At the time, the threat of nuclear annihilation took precedence for most Americans over the possibility of an unauthorized attempt to gain access onto a military installation.

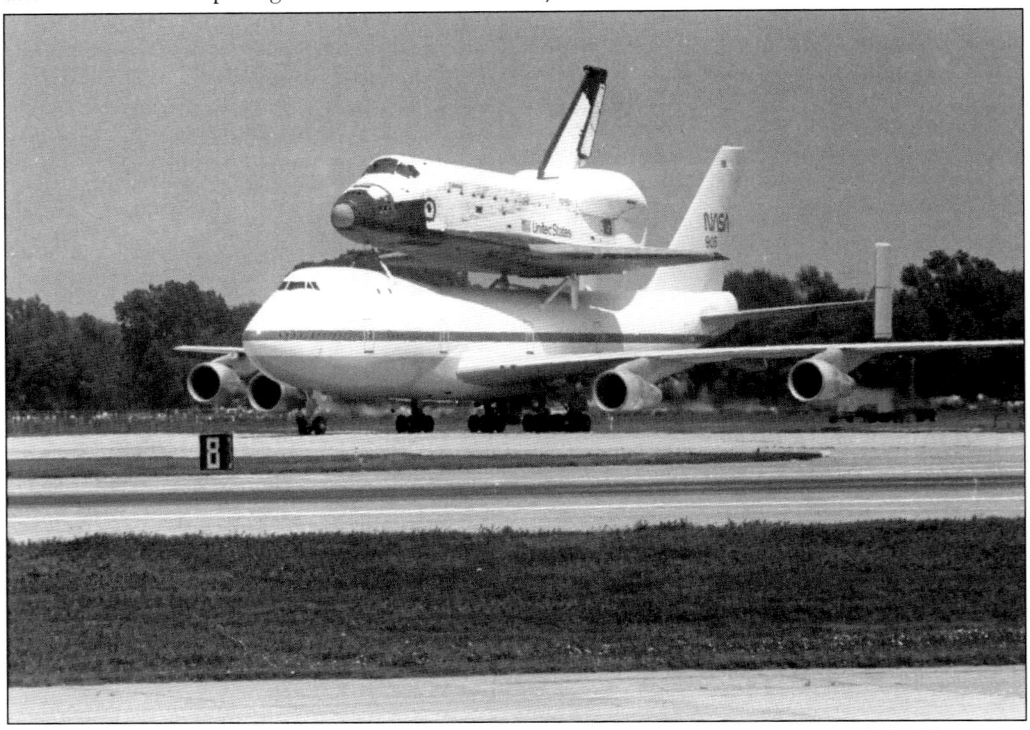

In July 2007, the space shuttle *Atlantis* arrived at Offutt, affixed to a NASA 747. The craft, following a mission to the International Space Station, was being returned from California to the Kennedy Space Center in Florida when it was forced to make a previously unexpected visit to Nebraska in order to wait out bad weather. The event marked the second time Offutt was visited by a space shuttle.

Eight

The Boom

As the 20th century becomes an ever-more distant memory, the future of Bellevue-Offutt awaits. Just as there was 150 years ago, there is great potential on the horizon. The last half of the last century of this community's history has been extraordinary. This chapter specifically chronicles the progressive nature of the years from 1950 and beyond. Census records show that while the population in 1940 was 1,184, it grew to 3,858 in 1950. By 1970, it was over 20,000. Today, it is over 50,000.

This success is due to the critical efforts of not just mayors and city council members, but also average citizens, the people of Bellevue who make up this community. Whether they realize it or not, they have served as a bridge from generations past to generations future. Some may not see the value in retelling stories of spending a Friday night at Southroads Mall or watching a girls' fast pitch softball game at the Cat Osterman Experience, but in time, this will also become part of Bellevue's historical narrative.

During this time, there has been both boom and bust, but through it all, prospects have remained enduringly hopeful. What the future holds is uncertain. What the past has held needs to continue to be preserved, as Bellevue continues to grow in scope, size, and importance well into the 21st century. One thing is for certain—when the first wagons of settlers crossed the Missouri River and made Bellevue home over 150 years ago, they would have never envisioned what the city has become today. What will it be 150 years from now?

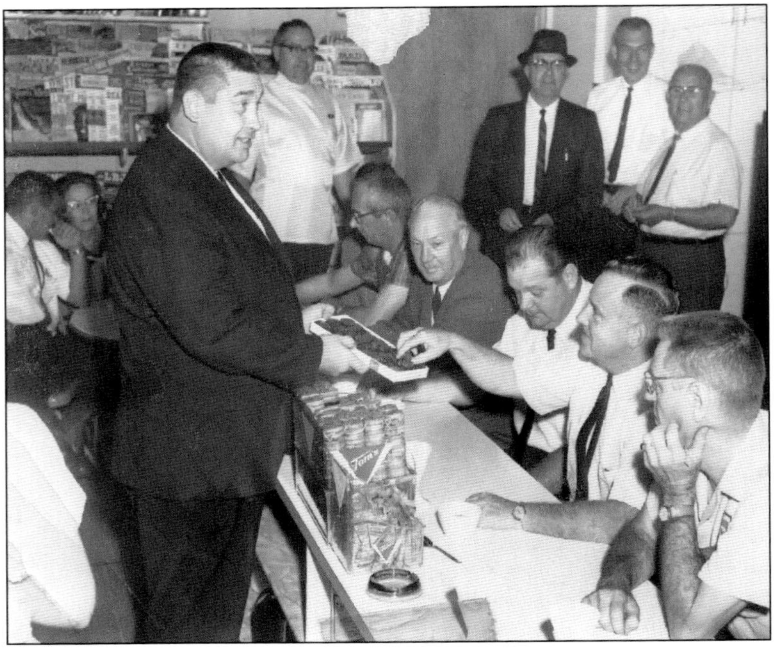

Chamber of Commerce manager Harold Smock offers chocolates to Mayor Haworth in honor of Be Kind to City Fathers week in 1964. Local businessmen including Hoyt Freeman, Hugh Campbell, and John Johnson of Johnson's Pharmacy look on. The weeklong event led into Father's Day.

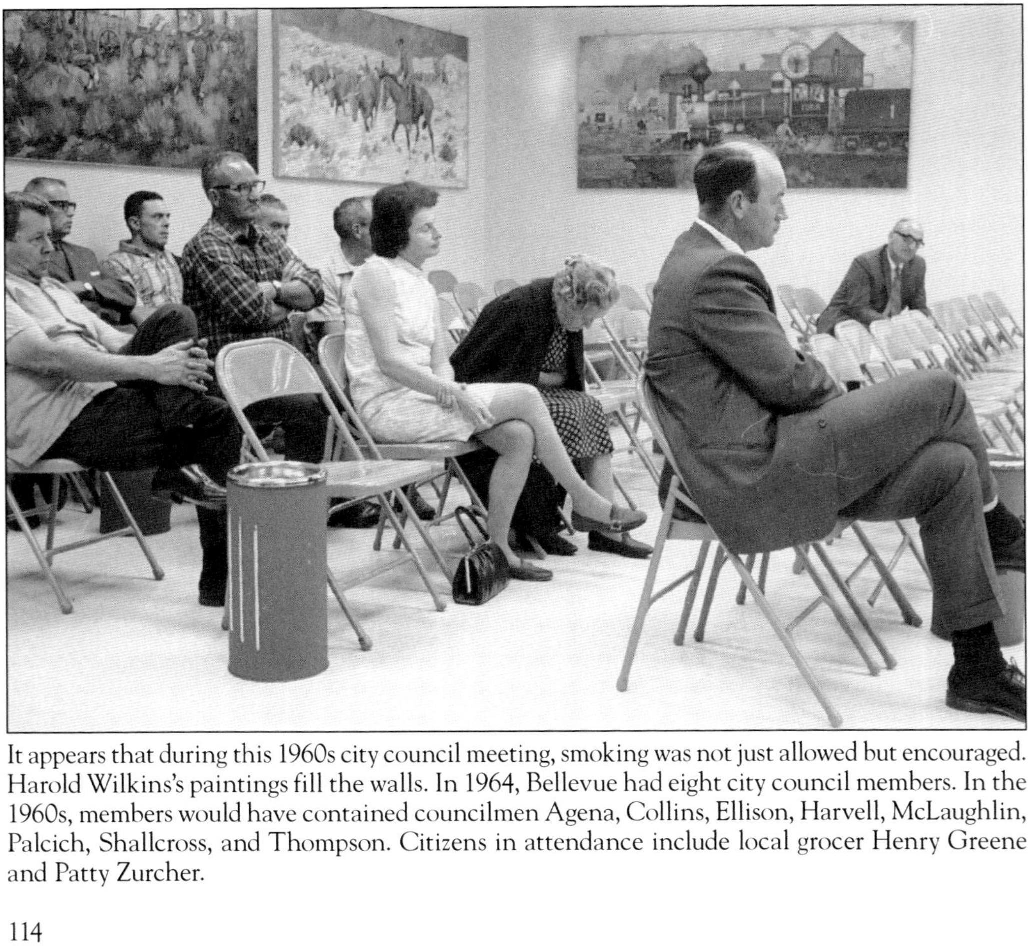

It appears that during this 1960s city council meeting, smoking was not just allowed but encouraged. Harold Wilkins's paintings fill the walls. In 1964, Bellevue had eight city council members. In the 1960s, members would have contained councilmen Agena, Collins, Ellison, Harvell, McLaughlin, Palcich, Shallcross, and Thompson. Citizens in attendance include local grocer Henry Greene and Patty Zurcher.

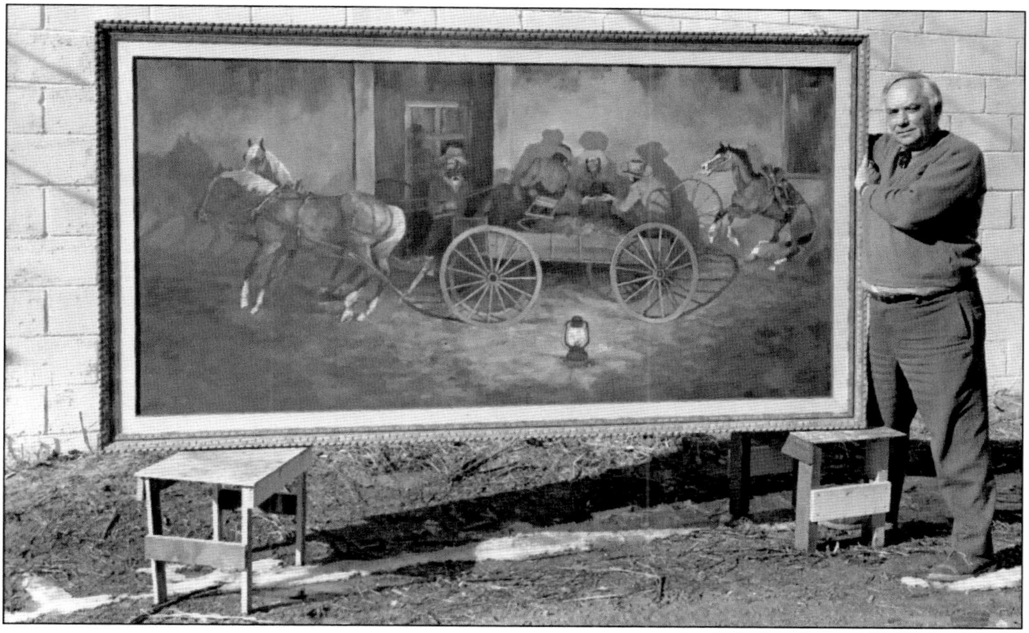

Bellevue artist Harold Wilkins, 1912–2003, was not originally from Bellevue but certainly left an impression. Like many who came to the area through Offutt, he decided to stay after his 28 years of service in the Air Force. In his Bellevue studio, Wilkins usually painted works of art with an American West theme incorporating wagons or men on horseback. A number of his other works reflected historic Bellevue and depicted Peter Sarpy and Lucien Fontenelle or buildings such as the early trading posts or the First Presbyterian Church. His works were a common site and can still be found in both private and public collections.

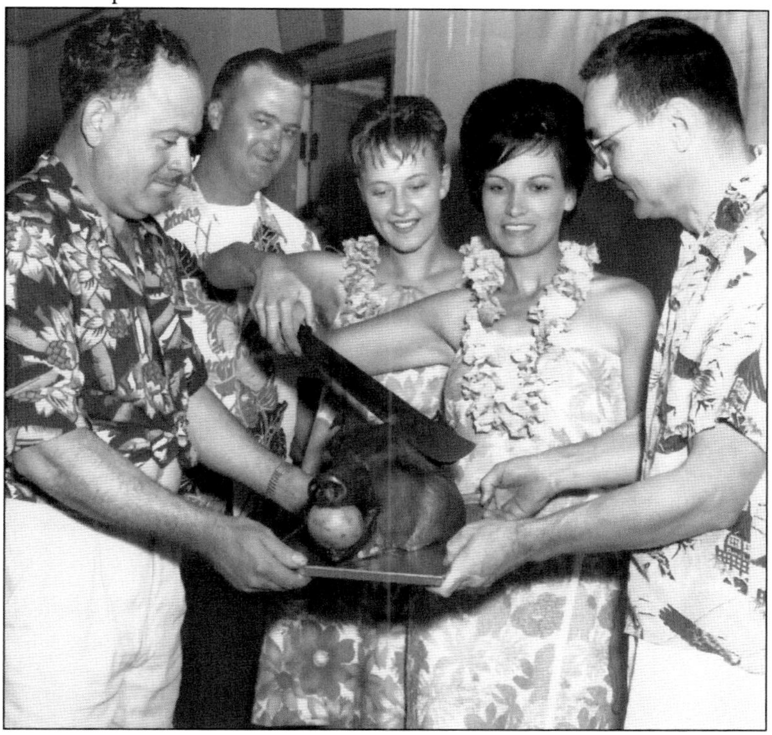

A roasted pig's head serves as a centerpiece for the fire department's Hawaiian night. From left to right are fire chief Lou Georges, Rich White, Rita Harder, Marge White, and Paul Ruffner. The Hawaiian luau was the kick-off party for the ticket sale for their annual dance in August 1964.

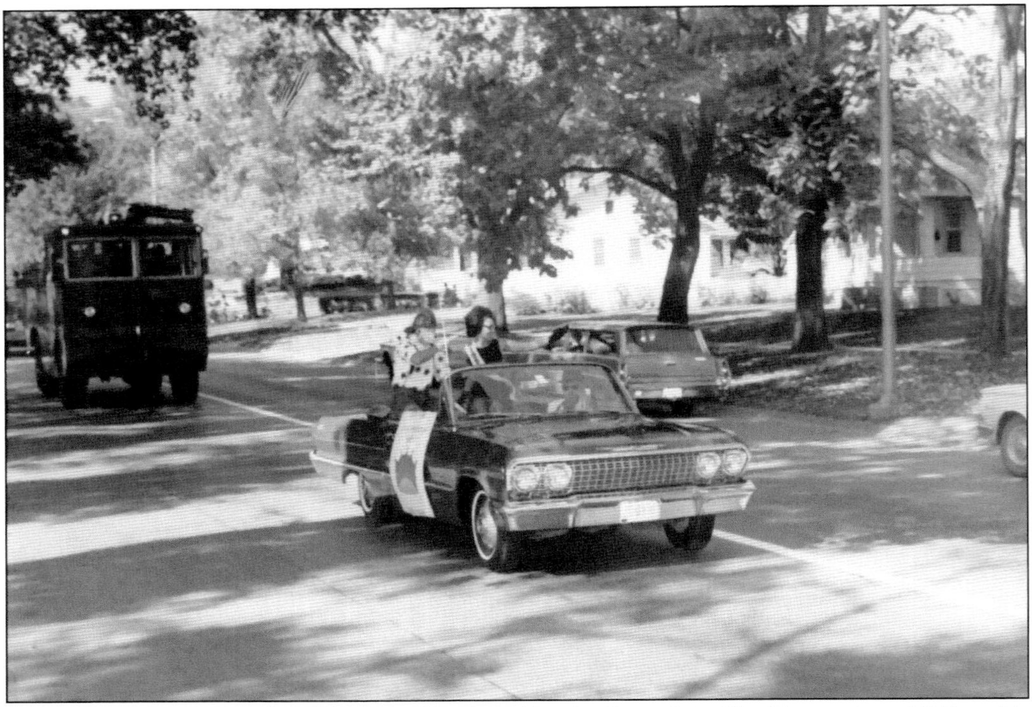

Sparky the Fire Dog, as played by David Ford, and Linda Cross, Miss Fire Prevention of Offutt Air Force Base, take part in the Fire Prevention Parade to kick off National Fire Prevention Week on October 2, 1965. Firefighters from Bellevue and Offutt have enjoyed a camaraderie, occasionally joining to share resources.

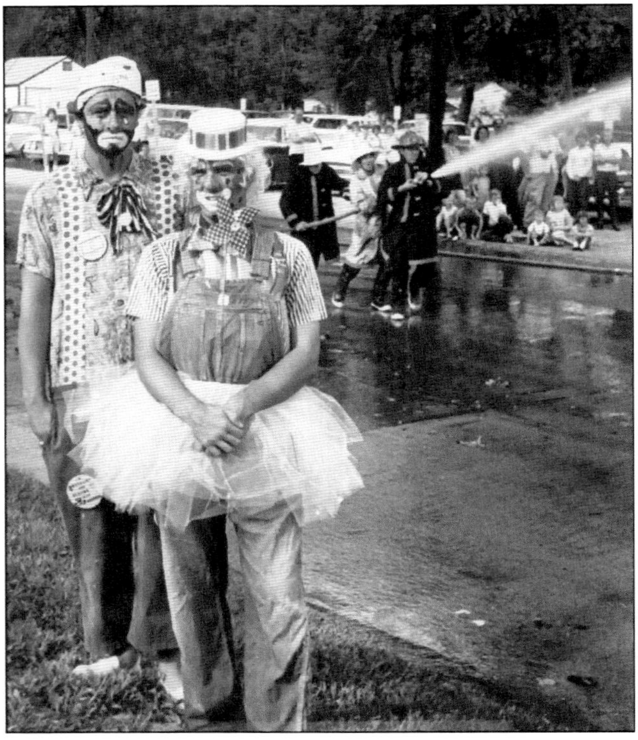

The clowns in this August 16, 1964 photograph, Larry Boykin (left) and Bill Wright of Bellevue, represent the junior chamber of commerce. In the background is the Bellevue water fight. Bellevue team no. 1 took first place, the Eastern Sarpy County firefighters won second, and Bellevue team no. 3 took third.

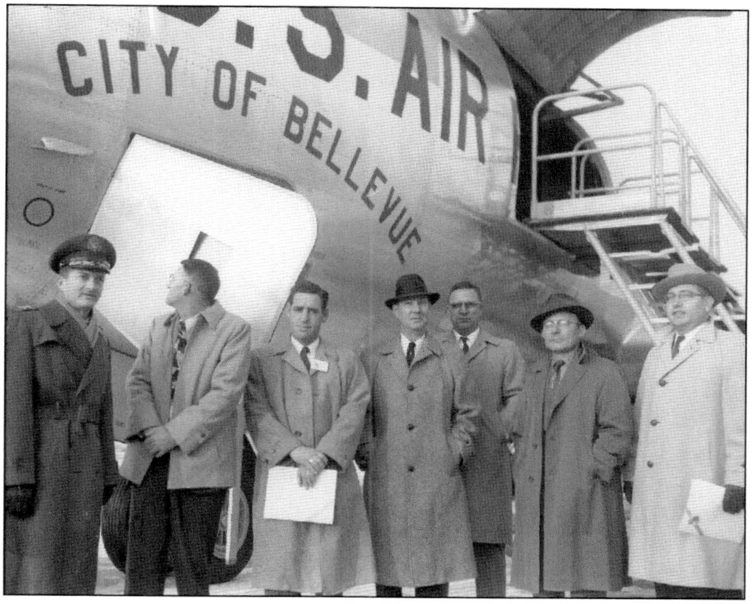

The *City of Bellevue* was a commissioned KC-135 Air Force plane, chartered to take Mayor Vern Woodle (second from left) and city council members, from left to right, Harlan Lewis, Hugh Cambell, unknown, Joe Morgan, and John Johnson, to Florida for a conference sponsored by the Air Force. Lewis and Morgan would each eventually go on to serve as mayor of Bellevue. (Courtesy Ron Woodle.)

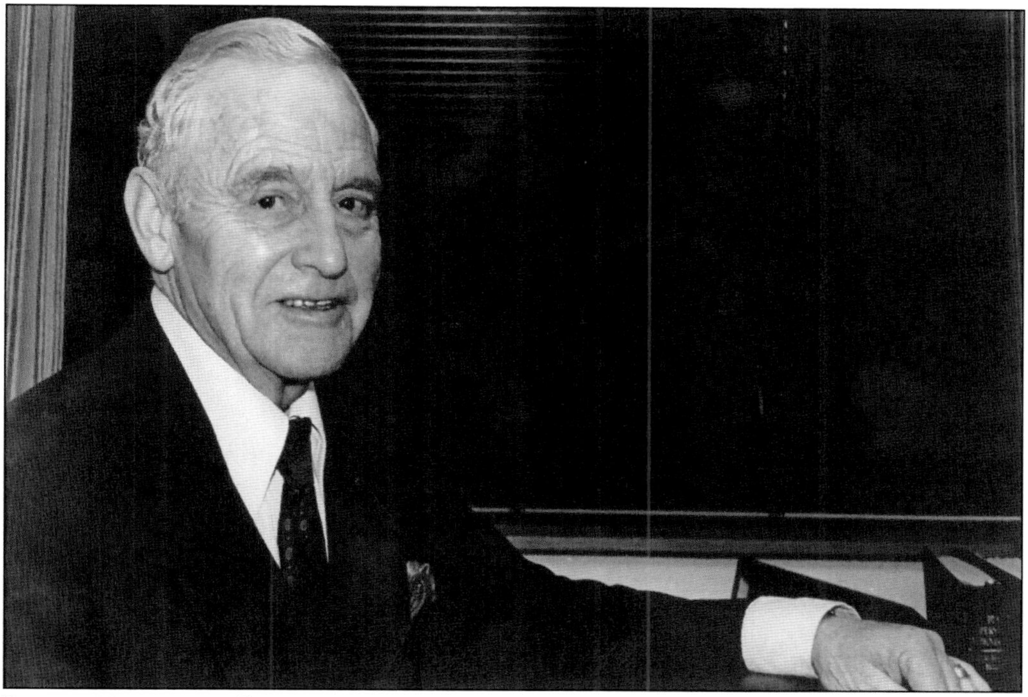

Born in Hoopeston, Illinois, in 1910, Robert Haworth relocated to Bellevue in 1948 when he was transferred to the Omaha area with his wife, Florence, and their family while working for the American Can Company. When he first came to Bellevue, it contained two paved roads. In 1962, he was elected mayor when it was a part-time, two-year position. He would serve as mayor for 21 years. (City of Bellevue.)

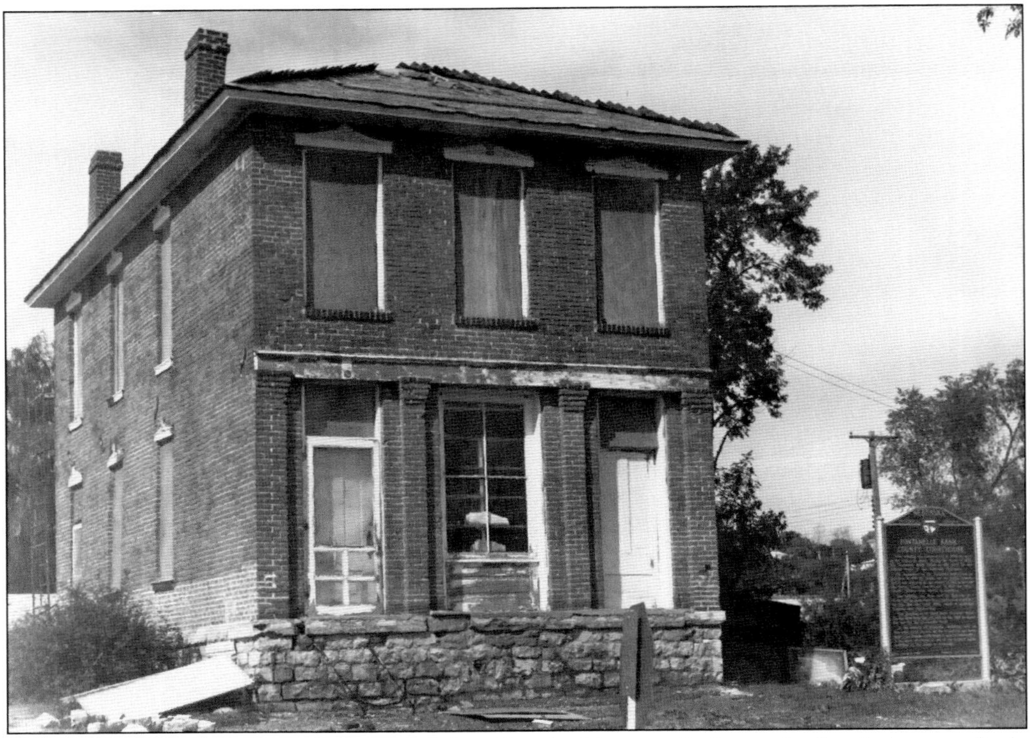

Sitting dormant, the old city hall, one of the oldest buildings in Bellevue, had sadly become little more than urban decay. The jets of progress propelled Bellevue, but in the process, the town had overlooked its past. The roof was dilapidated, windows were boarded up, and refuse collected around the perimeter. Rather than tear it down, concerned citizens, including Robert Haworth, recognized the historical value of the building. In 1972, with the aid of a grant for historic preservation, the first floor was remodeled to resemble how the building might have looked had it been the successful bank it was originally meant to be, complete with teller cages. Display cases chronicling the history of Bellevue were installed on the second floor. (City of Bellevue.)

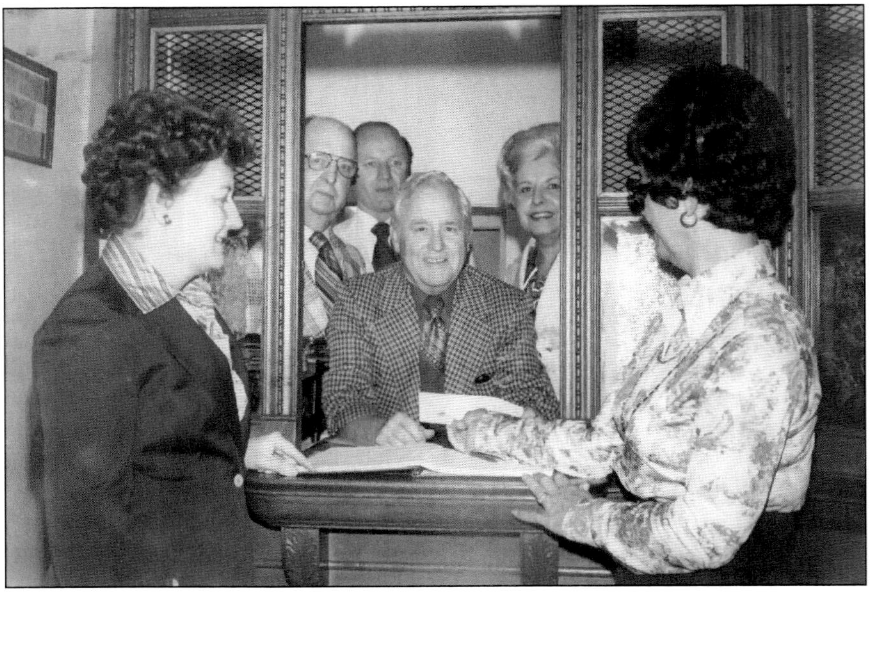

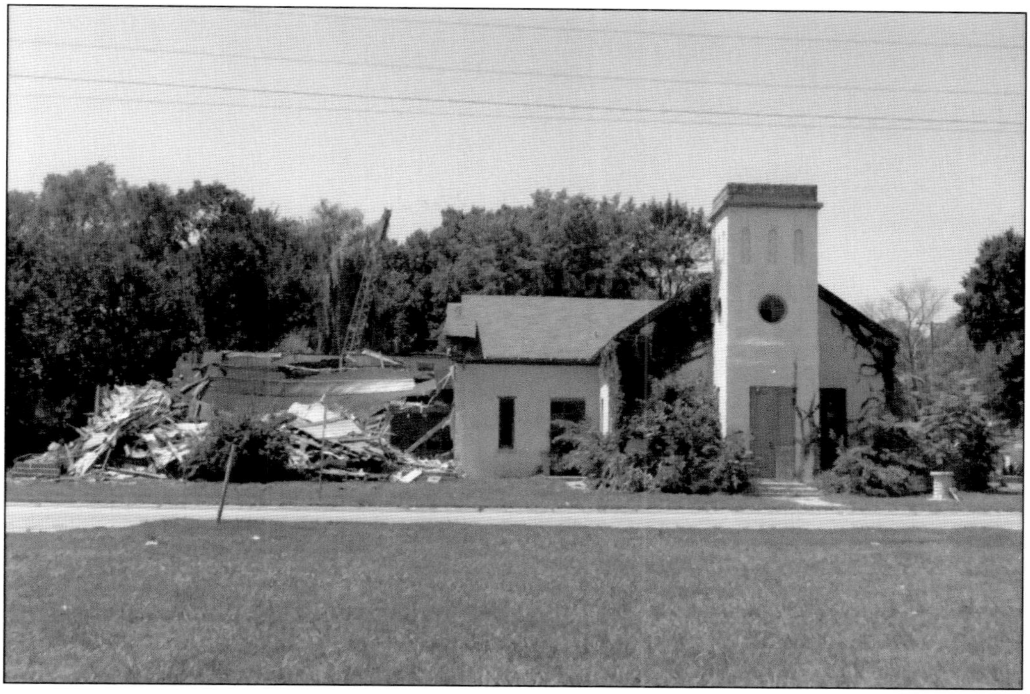

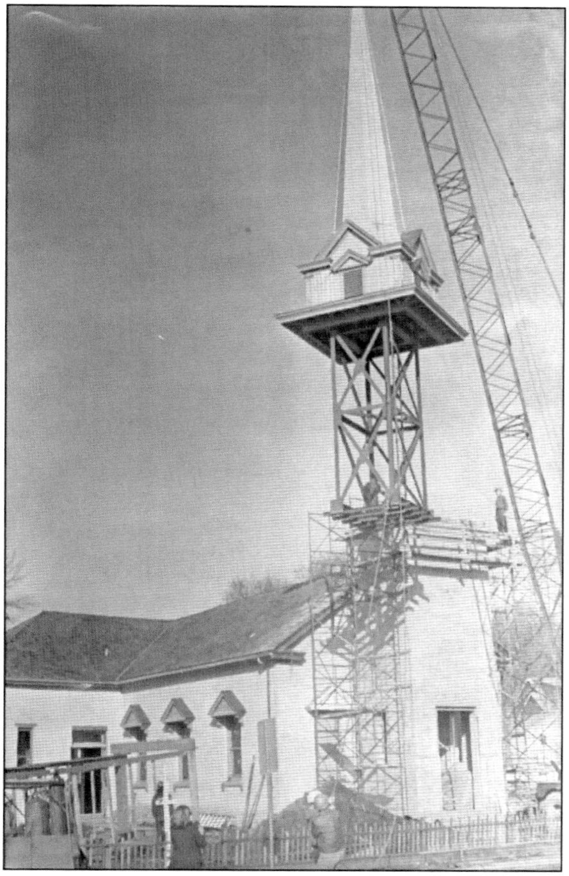

In addition to the revitalization of old city hall, the Presbyterian Church also underwent restoration efforts to restore the building to its original form during the mid 1970s. In poor shape and rotting, the south wing was demolished in August 1973. Not an original portion of the church, the south wing—before it was turned into a pile of rubble—provided extra space for the congregation to hold activities. Absent for 66 years following its forced removal during the 1908 tornado that struck Bellevue, the steeple was reinstalled in March 1974. The event was held with about 100 people in attendance. Over a two-hour period, the eight-ton steeple was raised 70 feet and secured in place.

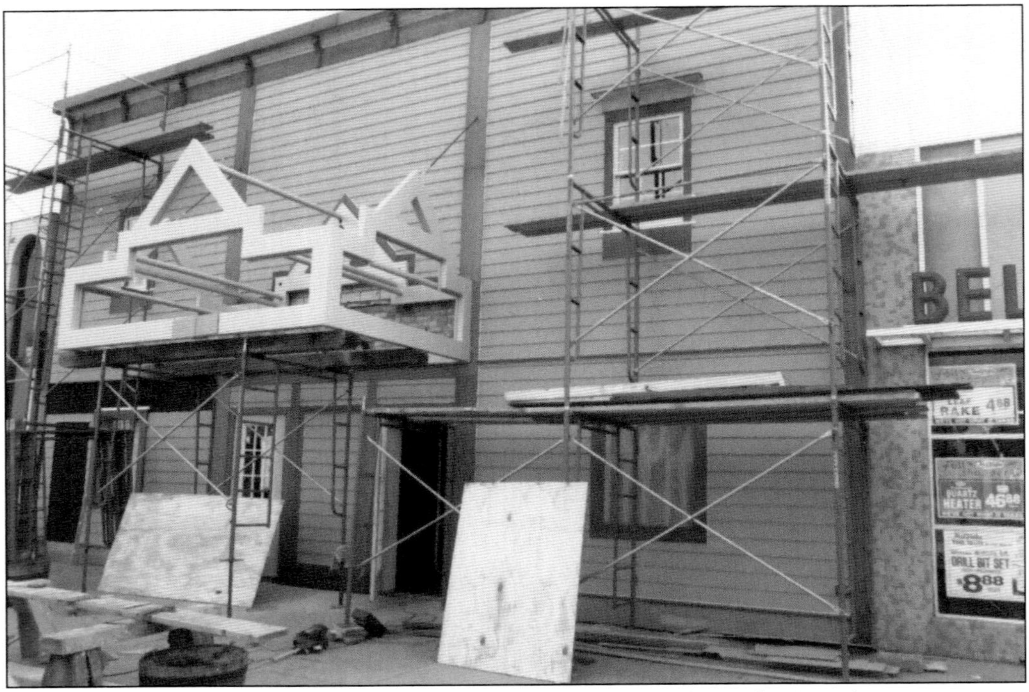

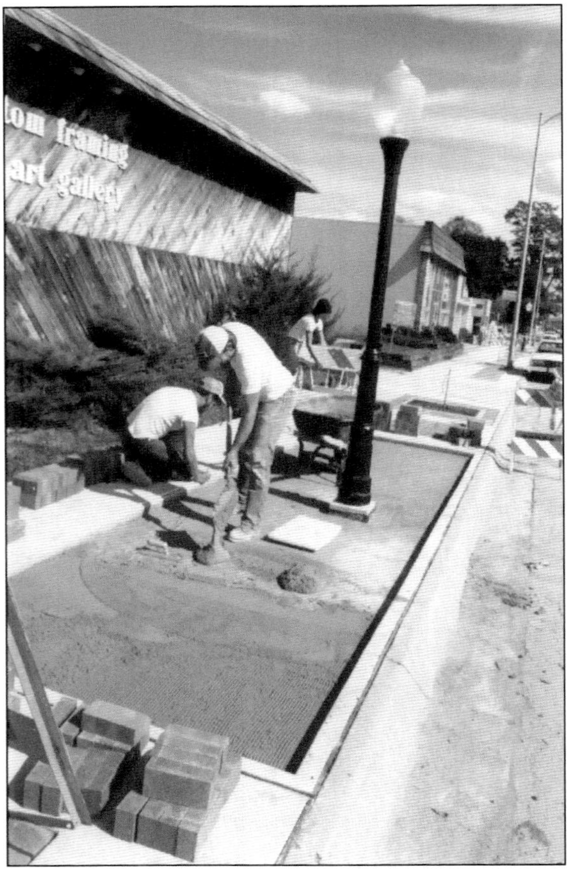

During the mid 1970s, there was a significant attempt to boost and enhance the commercial development of Bellevue's downtown. The city collaborated with the Chamber of Commerce and various area businesses to reconstruct the sidewalks and curbs, plant trees, and provide a facelift for several buildings, including the Bellevue Little Theater and Erwin's Jewelry Store. At the time, the Bellevue Chamber of Commerce, headed by Bob Offerjost, was located at 409 West Mission Avenue and was one of over 30 outlets in the downtown Bellevue area. Even with an estimated cost for sidewalk and curb repair alone at $70,000, local merchants, known as the Bellevue Development Corps, approved and supported the resolution almost wholeheartedly.

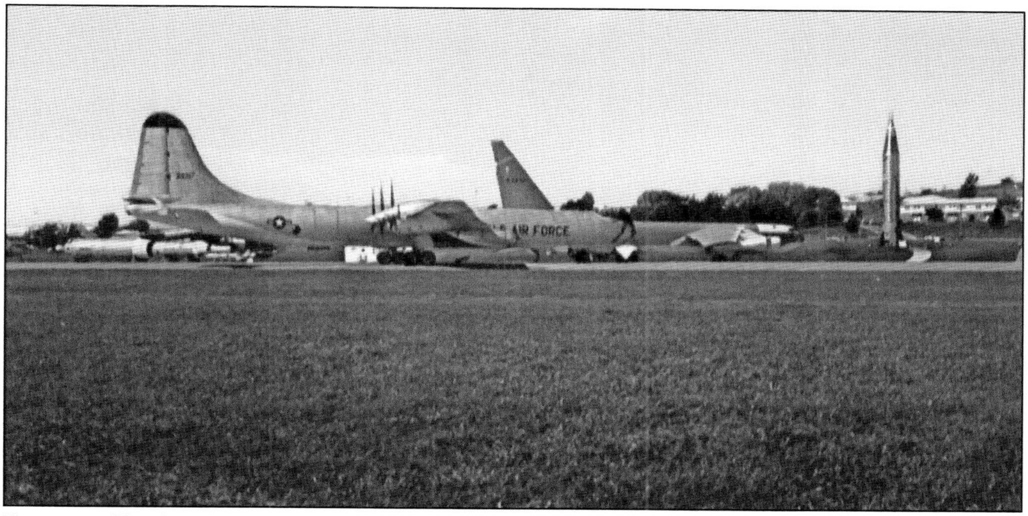

Envisioned by Gen. Curtis LeMay, the Strategic Aerospace Museum, later Strategic Air Command Museum, opened its doors in 1959. The museum, located on the edge of Offutt Air Force Base, obtained its first artifact, a B-36 Peacemaker, on April 22 of that year. Only one of four survivors, the plane, with its unique rear facing propellers, was featured in the 1955 Jimmy Stewart film *Strategic Air Command.*

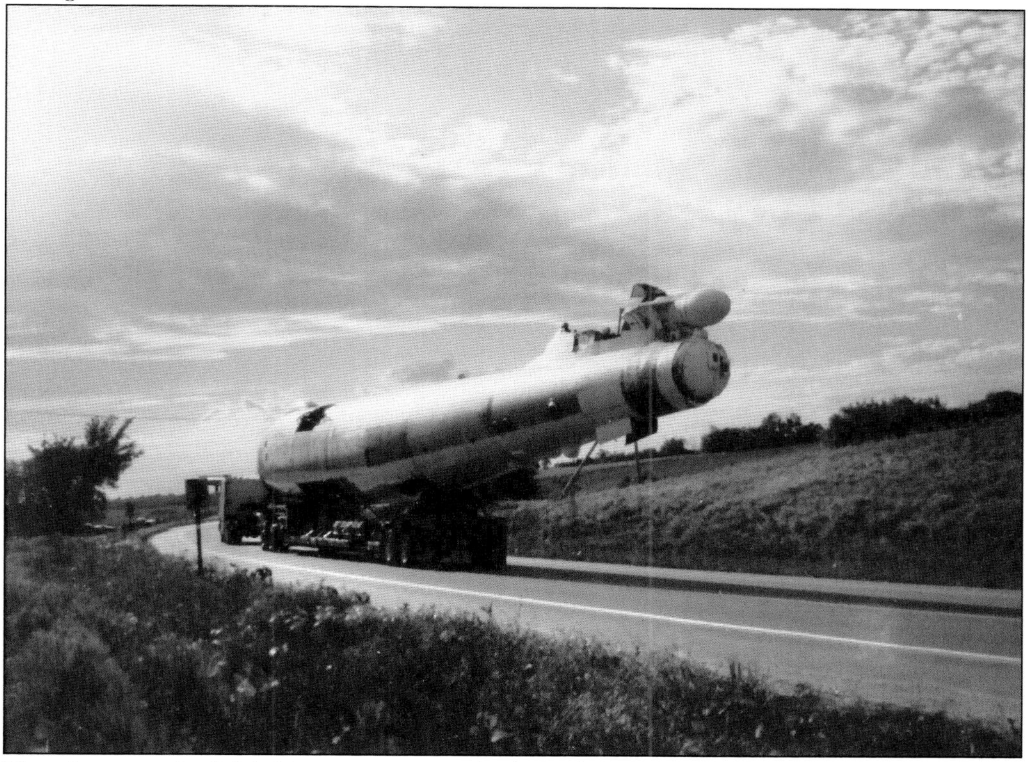

The planes at the SAC Museum sat outside through summer heat and winter cold. As the collection grew in size and importance, it was decided to relocate the museum from the Bellevue-Offutt community to nearby Ashland, Nebraska, where a $33 million campaign provided indoor accommodations. Loaded on flatbed trailers, the first plane to be transported the 36 miles to the new museum was the SR-71 Blackbird.

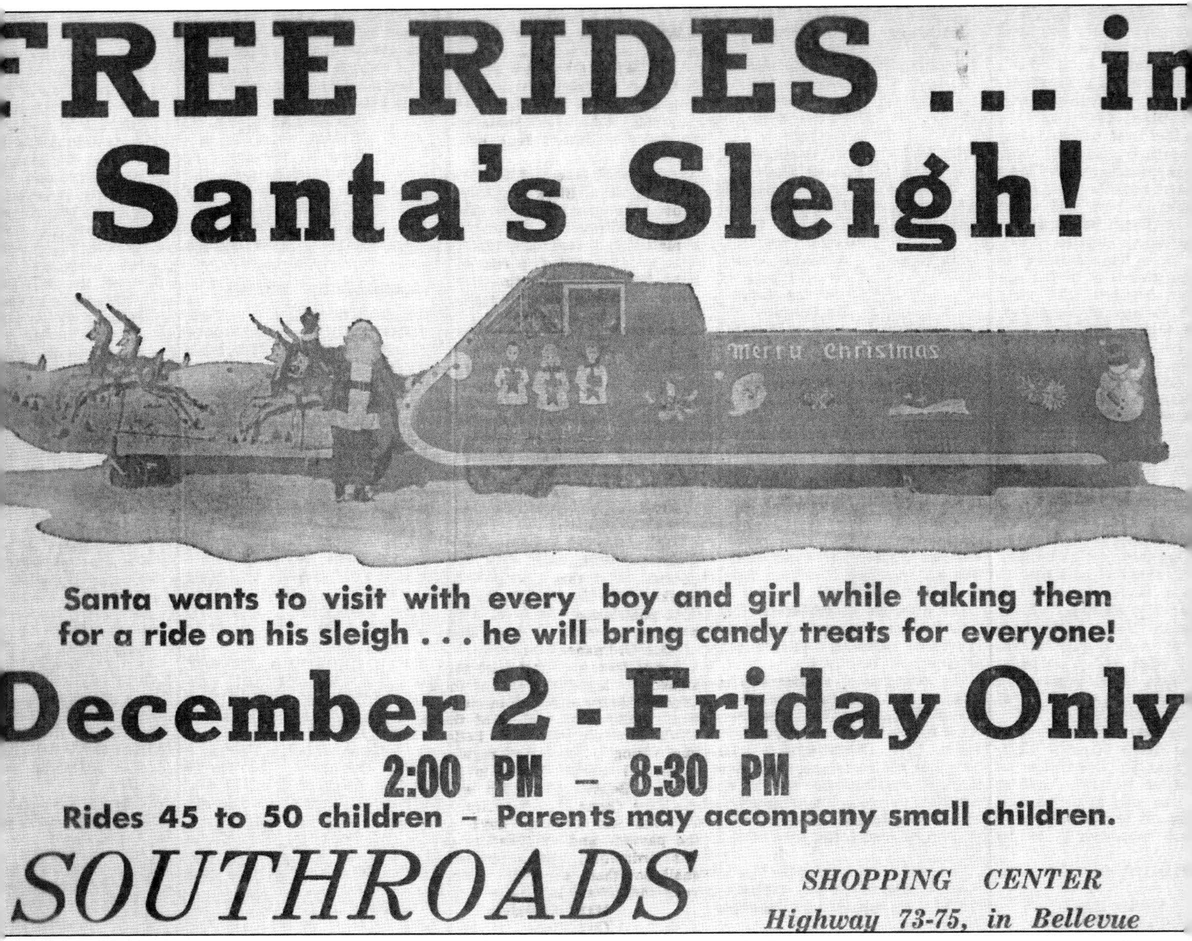

Free rides in Santa's sleigh were offered during the inaugural Christmas celebration at Southroads Mall in 1966. With 500,000 square feet of retail space, the mall had Brandeis and JCPenney as anchor stores, with other stores such as Woolworths, Kay Bee Toys, and even a four-screen movie theater. With the Sears located nearby, it created a nice shopping district and made for a busy and exciting place in Bellevue. The new mall did not just provide a place for local teens to patronize on a Friday night but plenty of new employment opportunities as well. Unfortunately, malls do not live forever. Once the Brandeis chain collapsed, the JCPenney departed not long after, leaving a dying mall. Today, it has been reborn serving as offices for TD Ameritrade and a handful of other technology companies under the moniker of Southroads Technology Center.

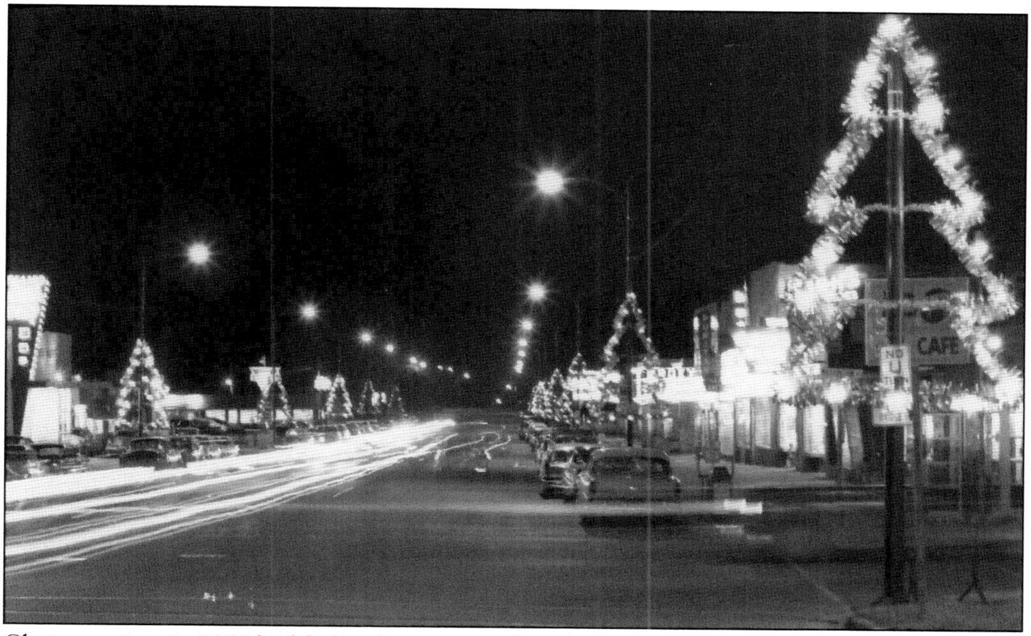

Christmastime in 1962 highlights the activity along Mission Street. Added decorations erected by the junior chamber of commerce spruced up the area, and despite it being December, snow had yet to cover the landscape. Even though the Roxy Theater had a brightly lit marquee, the big attraction was President Kennedy and Vice President Johnson's visit to Offutt.

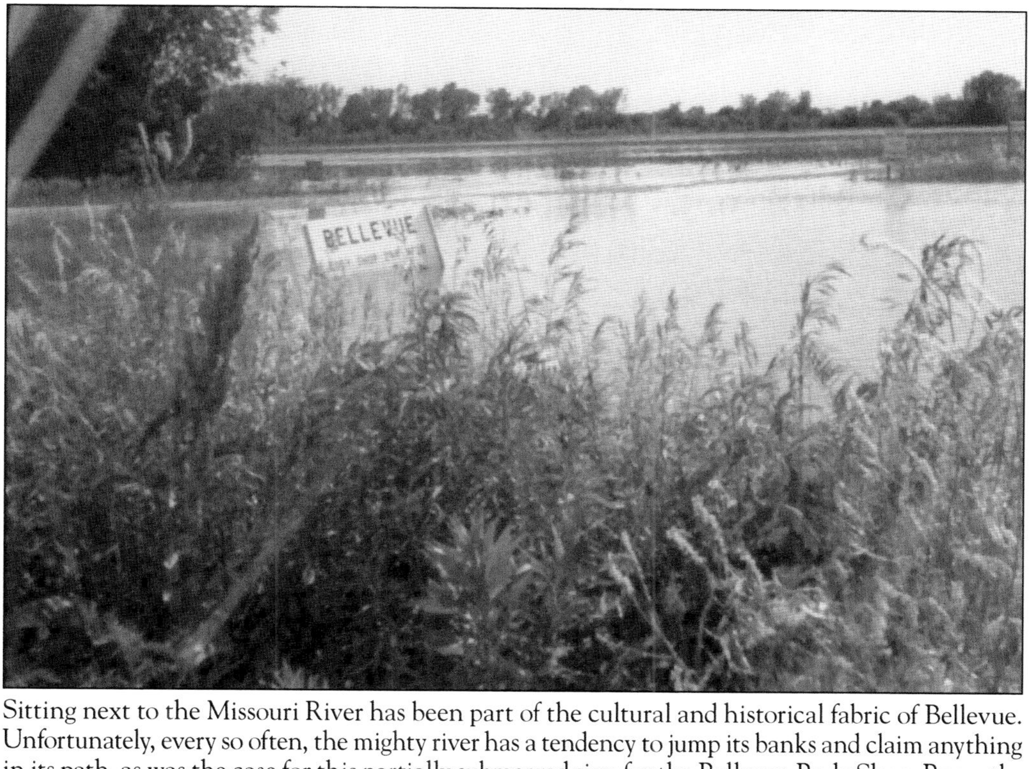

Sitting next to the Missouri River has been part of the cultural and historical fabric of Bellevue. Unfortunately, every so often, the mighty river has a tendency to jump its banks and claim anything in its path, as was the case for this partially submerged sign for the Bellevue Body Shop. Recently, Haworth Park has fallen victim to the river's floodwaters. (Courtesy Lloyd Dowding.)

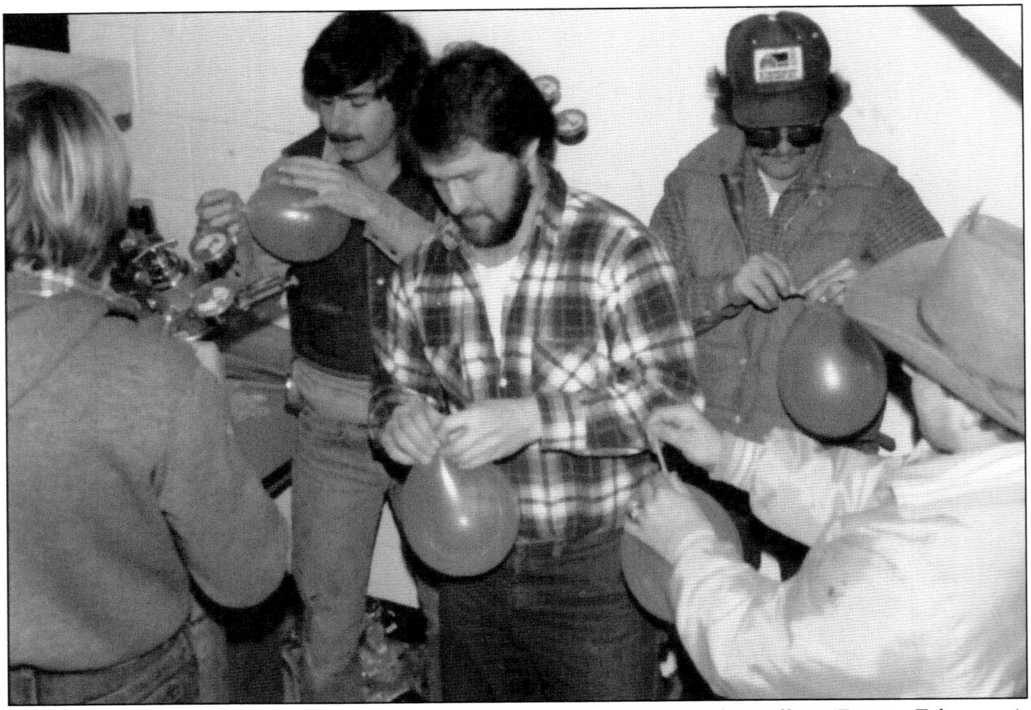

A large crowd gathers outside Bellevue City Hall to commemorate Paul Needham Day on February 1, 1982. Needham, a US Air Force logistics officer, had been held hostage for 444 days following the capture of the US embassy in Tehran during the Iranian Revolution. 14,000 balloons, one for each Bellevue-Offutt family, were released into the sky in honor of the hometown hero's return. The route to city hall had 444 yellow ribbons, one for each day, and 52 American flags, one for each hostage. Also present in Bellevue for the festivities was Capt. Charles Williamson, a pilot and Bellevue High School graduate involved in the ill-fated Operation Eagle Claw, an attempt led by special forces to rescue the hostages.

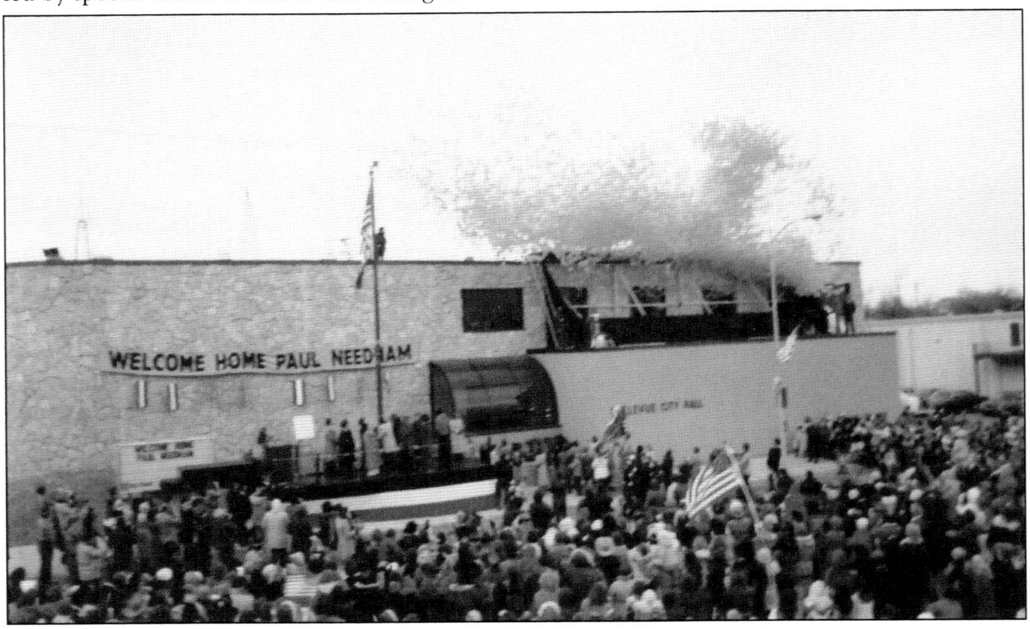

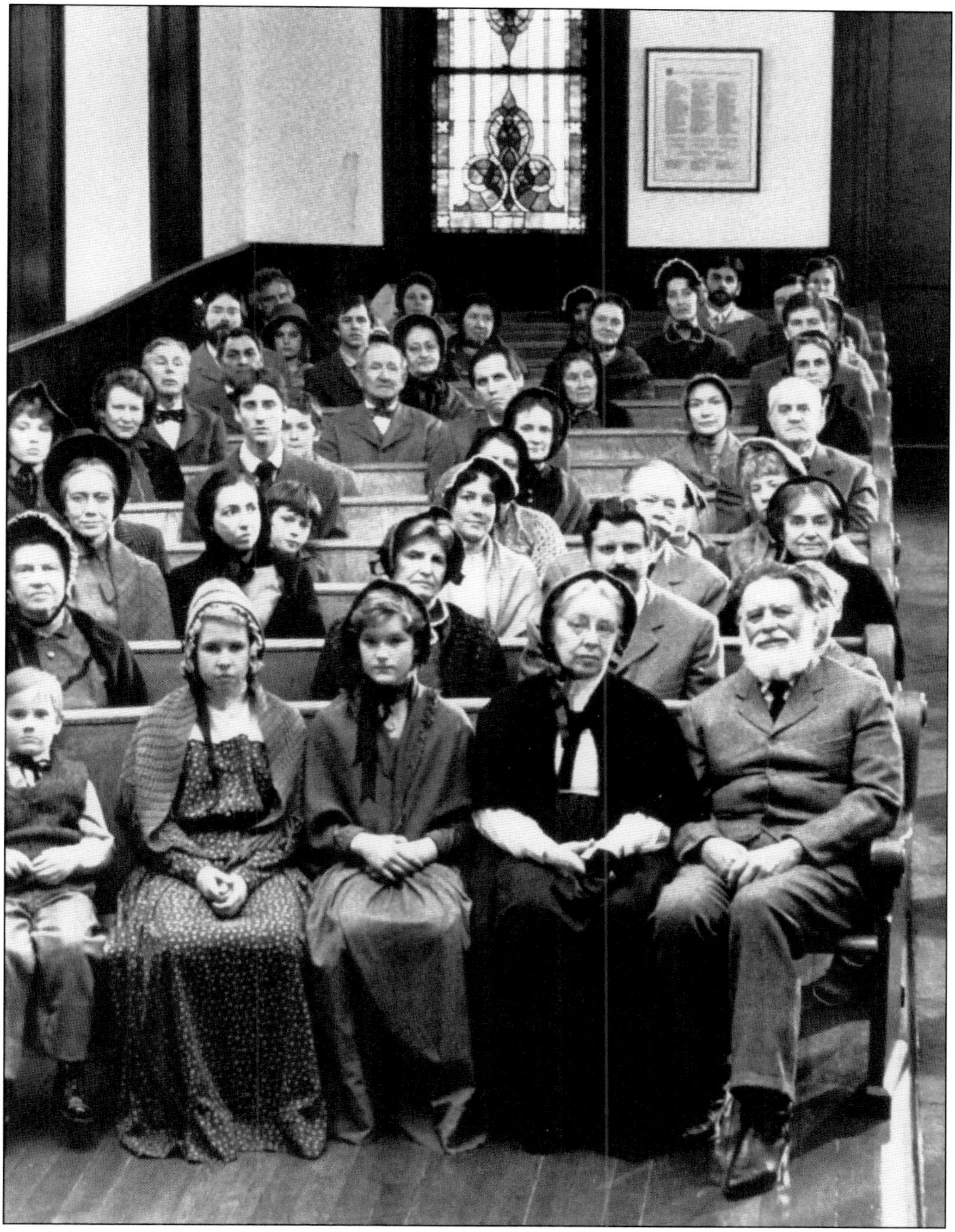

This photograph could be over 100 years old, except it's not. In late 1987, local Bellevue residents gathered at the First Presbyterian Church in provided replica costumes to serve as extras for the television film *The Trial of Standing Bear.* Standing Bear and the Ponca were forcibly removed from their lands. In the upheaval, they faced terrible conditions. Even worse, they were forbidden to bury their dead in their tribal homeland. In 1879, Standing Bear sued the government in the landmark case Standing Bear v. Crook and won. The judge ruled that an Indian was indeed a person and should be granted basic human rights. While local talent filled the pews, William Shatner served as narrator.

Bibliography

A Chronology of Offutt Air Force Base. Offutt Air Force Base, 1962.

Creigh, Dorothy Weyer. *Bellevue College 1880-1919*. Hastings: Hastings College, 1962.

Goss, Chaucer C. *Bellevue, Larimer & Saint Mary: Their History, Location, Description and Advantages*. Bellevue: John Q. Goss, 1859.

Iske, Clarence, Robert Rayfield, and Roy Cunningham. *A Brief History of the Anderson Grove Church*, 1993.

Iske, Gary. *Bellevue: A Pictorial History*. Marceline: Heritage House Publishing, 1991.

Morton, Sterling J. *Illustrated History of Nebraska*. Lincoln: Jacob North & Company, 1905.

Sarpy Centennial Committee. *View of a Century in Sarpy County*, 1967.

Shallcross, William. *Romance of a Village: Story of Bellevue*. Omaha: Roncka Bros, 1954.

Simmons, Jerold L. ed. *"La Bellevue Vue" Studies in the History of Bellevue, Nebraska*. Marceline: Walsworth Publishing Company, 1976.

ABOUT THE SARPY COUNTY MUSEUM

Located at 2402 Clay Street in Bellevue, the Sarpy County Museum is dedicated to collect, preserve, and interpret historical information and artifacts about Sarpy County. To help achieve this goal, a number of volunteers support the staff of one by assisting the executive director in a variety of tasks including but certainly not limited to serving as docents, working with collections, preparing displays, staffing the museum, and participating in museum programs.

The museum features permanent exhibitions, including an interactive scale model of Fort Crook in 1937 prior to its drastic transformation with the onset of World War II. Temporary exhibitions have included the ever-popular quilt show and *Barn Again!*, an exhibit offering an examination of the cultural and historical significance of barns and agricultural buildings, a sight that is fast fading within Sarpy County.

The Sarpy County Museum also houses a wide selection of invaluable archival resources including historical newspapers, maps, scrapbooks, photographs, court dockets, and additional primary documents that are crucial to understanding the history of Sarpy County. These resources are open and available to the public. In the coming era, these records will be digitized for improved preservation and accessibility.

Additionally, several historic properties, including Bellevue's historic Log Cabin, the CB&Q Depot, and the Moses Merrill Mission site, are affiliated with the museum. The cabin and depot have been preserved to nearly their original condition. All sites are available for tours.

Primary support to fund these endeavors comes from Sarpy County, as well as grants, fundraisers, memberships, and donations from readers like you. It is through these financial efforts that the museum can continue to save our history.

The Sarpy County Museum is on Facebook and Twitter and can also be contacted at 402-292-1880 or info@sarpycountymuseum.org. The museum is open Tuesday through Saturday from 10:00 a.m. to 4:00 p.m. We hope to see you soon!

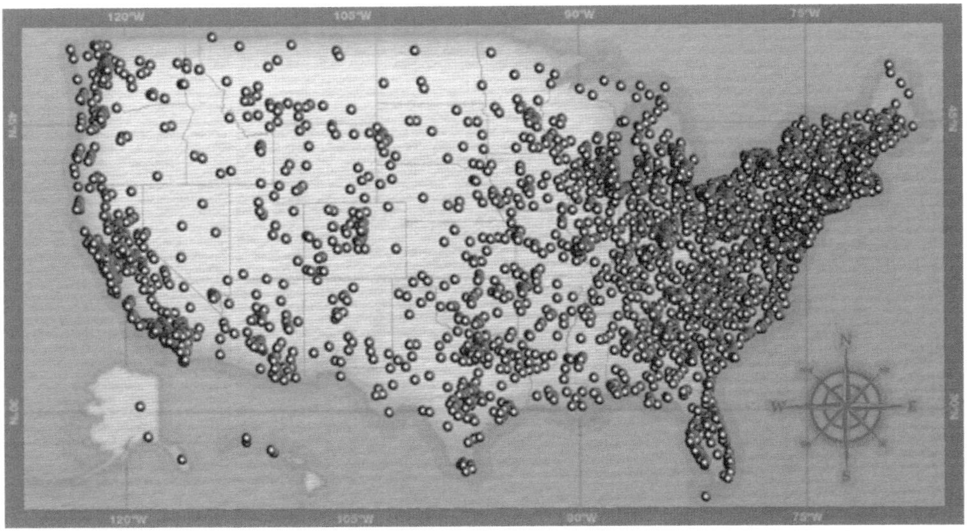